MORE PRAISE FOR *SHRINKAGE*

"*Shrinkage* rewards the reader with a courageous, honest journey that will be familiar to those struggling with or caring for someone with cancer. Bald Bryan shows us that because he never, never gives up, the darkest moments can yield great meaning and moments of clarity. This is a must read for anyone who feels alone dealing with serious illness. Oh hell, this is a must read for anyone with a pulse."

—DR. DREW PINSKY

"It's amazing what goes on in Bryan's head. I mean, besides the cancer. This is by far the funniest memoir by a radio personality fighting brain cancer that I have ever read. It's honestly brilliant."

—TESSA STRASSER

"I knew Bryan for over a year before someone told me he had a brain tumor. How was this possible? Isn't there some kind of sign you wear when you get that diagnosis? Yes, there is. Positivity and relentless kindness. Bryan's book gives the reader a glimpse into how to approach one of life's true nightmares with complete pragmatism and calm. This book is a must read. Bryan is to be rewarded for such incredible honesty coupled with brilliant prose. I am very, very proud to call him my friend."

—JAY MOHR

"An insightful memoir of Bryan, who maintains his sense of humor and positive outlook on life while battling brain cancer. An honest, smart read that further shows why Bryan is a lynchpin of the uber-successful Adam Carolla podcast."

—NATALIE COUGHLIN

"Bryan is truly the most underrated of comedic sidekicks and talents in radio and new media. His lightning fast responses in his verbal wit and his drops are hilarious and, at times, uncanny. What makes Bryan's book even more special is his life journey, which will inspire all who read it."

—MARIA MENOUNOS

"As a fan of the show, I loved the insight into a time I only had glimpses of via the podcast. Expected it to break my heart a bit, didn't expect all the funny." —JOHN CHO

"Bryan's story is heartwarming, funny as hell, and as inspirational as they come." —JERRY O'CONNELL

"Since none of us is getting out of this alive, we are all measured, in a way, by the prospect of that mortality. Bryan Bishop has faced his ultimate truth with wit, compassion, honesty, and art, providing the rest of us with what we need most—inspiration." —KEN BURNS

shrinkage

BRYAN BISHOP

shrinkage

manhood, marriage,
and the tumor
that tried to kill me

Foreword by Adam Carolla

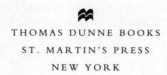

THOMAS DUNNE BOOKS
ST. MARTIN'S PRESS
NEW YORK

THOMAS DUNNE BOOKS.
An imprint of St. Martin's Press.

SHRINKAGE. Copyright © 2014 by Bryan Bishop. Foreword copyright © 2014 by Adam Carolla. All rights reserved. Printed in the United States of America. For information, address St. Martin's Press, 175 Fifth Avenue, New York, N.Y. 10010.

www.thomasdunnebooks.com
www.stmartins.com

Library of Congress Cataloging-in-Publication Data

Bishop, Bryan, 1978–
   Shrinkage : manhood, marriage, and the tumor that tried to kill me /
Bryan Bishop.
      pages cm
   ISBN 978-1-250-03984-2 (hardcover)
   ISBN 978-1-4668-3533-7 (e-book)
   1. Bishop, Bryan, 1978—Health.   2. Cancer—Patients—United States—
Biography.   3. Radio personalities—United States—Biography.   4. Television
personalities—United States—Biography.   I. Title.
   RC265.5.B57 2014
   362.19699'40092—dc23
                                                                    2013046494

St. Martin's Press books may be purchased for educational, business, or promotional use. For information on bulk purchases, please contact Macmillan Corporate and Premium Sales Department at 1-800-221-7945, extension 5442, or write specialmarkets @macmillan.com.

First Edition: May 2014

10 9 8 7 6 5 4 3 2 1

For Christie, my 50/50 partner

ILU

contents

Contents

Contents

foreword

I met Bryan in 2002 when he was a young phone screener for *Love-line*. At the time, he had a few more hairs and a lot more pounds, but he always had confidence. Bryan is smart and knows it. And wants you to know it. As you read this book, you'll see just how sharp and clever he is.

That's why, when I got the job taking over for Howard Stern on the West Coast in 2006, I brought Bryan with me to screen calls. I could not imagine anyone else being equal to that monumental task. You have to pick up the phone, talk to the person, type their question, *and* put them on hold. There are very few people who can pull off that Herculean task.

Bryan, despite spelling his name with a Y, later became part of our on-air family because of his uncanny ability to memorize thousands of sound drops and the corresponding codes on the computer (sorry for all that tech jargon; I forgot you may not all be as computer savvy as I am).

When the radio station flipped formats to a computer playing Rhianna songs, I took him to work with me on my CBS sitcom pilot, "Ace in the Hole," as a "floor PA" or something like that. Essentially a runner for the studio taping days. I knew that if the show got picked up he'd easily make his way up the ladder and I wanted to get him in on the ground floor.

The night before he was due to start working I got a call. It was a black chick who wanted to know if I was satisfied with my cable provider. I was. Then I got another call. It was Bryan and he did not have good news. Dizziness and other symptoms he'd been feeling as the radio show was collapsing were the result of brain tumor. The irony of the guy with the biggest brain on the staff—the guy who has the encyclopedic mind, the guy who goes on game shows—having it attacked by a tumor was sadly lost on no one.

I hung up with him and immediately called Dr. Drew. Drew simply said, "Death sentence." God bless that bedside manner. The last person Drew diagnosed with a death sentence was my wife's best friend, Jennifer, who was dead within six months at age thirty-three.

This is where Bryan's journey begins and my foreword ends. I've got some stuff on TiVo I need to get to. I won't say much more, I don't want to step on any of the stories you're about to read. But I will answer one question I'm sure all of you have at this point. No, the CBS pilot didn't get picked up. I blame it on the fact that we didn't have Bryan handling whatever the hell it was that he was supposed to be handling.

—Adam Carolla

shrinkage

Prologue

If you're reading this, it means I'm already dead.

Just kidding. I'm not dead.[1] I've just always wanted to say that. It's one of three things I've always wanted to say with 100 percent sincerity but never had the right opportunity. The other two:

"I suppose you're all wondering why I've summoned you here tonight" and . . .

"Can your casino please provide me with a security escort so I can safely transport my winnings back to my helicopter?"

Of those three phrases, you can clearly see why I chose the first one to start off this book. Although, it's *technically* not the first time I've used that line. Or maybe it is. You be the judge.

When I was first diagnosed with brain cancer at age thirty, my fiancée (Christie) and I decided to make out a last will and testament. In a sad reflection of my (im)maturity, I cared far less for what was *in* my will than how it started out. I insisted that it start with the line "If you're reading this, it means I'm already dead."

This was comedy of the highest order to me. To Christie, not so much. But this gallows humor would, I believed, help me get through whatever challenges cancer was going to throw at me. So please bear that in mind as you read this book. If a joke seems morbid or twisted or in some other way irreverent, just remind yourself,

---

[1] Spoiler alert.

"This is the guy who thought it would be funny to start his last will and testament with 'If you're reading this, it means I'm already dead.'"

Please, enjoy.

I.

Breaking Bald

or, A Not-So-Mini Biography

"I suppose you're all wondering why I've summoned you here tonight."

I wanted to start this chapter off with an appropriate quote. Let's see . . .

"I was born a poor black child." —*Navin Johnson*

Close, but that one isn't quite right.

"The details of my life are quite inconsequential." —*Dr. Evil*

That's more like it. But here we go anyway with the obligatory "biography/early-life chapter." I'll try not to make it too painful.

My parents (Mike and Nancy) were married on October 15, 1977, in the San Francisco Bay Area. It was apparently a hip seventies wedding; their first dance was to Chicago's "Colour My World," and the groomsmen wore ruffled tuxedos. After the reception, the newlyweds were whisked away in a 1932 Packard. They were from large Catholic families. My dad was twenty-three and the youngest child of four. My mom was just twenty years old and the middle child of five. They had met at a grocery store near San Francisco called QFI. Not in the produce aisle like in some romantic comedy[2]; they both worked there. I was told that QFI stood for Quality Foods International and was at one point the third-largest grocery-store chain in the San Francisco Bay Area. I would argue that by confining yourself to one

---

[2] In the trailer, their eyes meet as they both reach for the last piece of okra, and the voice-over says, "This summer . . . there's love on aisle seven!"

geographic region, you forfeit the right to call yourselves *international*, but I admire their bravado.

Less than three months after the wedding, my mom found out she was pregnant with me. This would be a shock for any twenty-year-old newlywed, but it was especially shocking for my mom, who had a copper IUD inserted in her at the time. For those of you who weren't sexually active women in the 1970s, a copper IUD (intrauterine device) was a form of birth control that a doctor would implant inside a woman's hoo-ha (the technical term for her reproductive organs). Worldwide, it's the most commonly used type of reversible birth control, meaning a doctor can remove it from a woman's body at any time. The failure rate for these devices is low, especially in the first year—as low as 0.1 percent. Yet my mom's IUD failed, resulting in a bald, bouncing baby boy. I know what you're thinking, and I agree: This can only mean that I am the Chosen One.

This is what happens when your birth control fails. God, I'd kill for that head of hair today.
(Bishop Family)

I was born on September 13, 1978, in San Mateo, California, about fifteen minutes south of San Francisco. Like most babies, I was born bald, and I actually had a nice, full head of hair until I was about thirteen years old, when it began falling out. So you could say I had a run of about twelve good years with hair.

Three years after me my brother, Adam, was born, in 1982. So by the time my parents were in their midtwenties, they had been married for four years and had two young sons. I spent the first nine years of my life in San Bruno, California, also about fifteen minutes south of San Francisco. Growing up in San Bruno was like growing up in Manchester, England, with slightly better food. It was constantly cold and foggy. In every picture of me taken outside from birth to age nine, I'm wearing a coat or a sweater (or both). There are pictures of me at the *beach* with a heavy jacket on. Fortunately, there aren't a lot of pictures of me outside; I was known as "the indoor kid" and Adam was known as "the outdoor kid." Ironically, this has stayed true all the way to our current professions: I crack wise on a podcast (indoors) and Adam is a project manager for one of the largest landscaping companies in the Bay Area (outdoors).[3]

The happy family. Check out my sweet boots. *(Bishop Family)*

We weren't poor—or if we were, I didn't know it. But we definitely weren't rich. My parents hadn't gone to college. In fact, at that point, nobody in my family had; I came from a blue-collar family. My dad's dad (my grandpa Frank) was a garbageman in San Bruno. My mom's dad (my grandpa Robert Lorenzini, or, as he was known to everyone,

---

[3] By *landscaping*, I don't mean they arrange rocks and cacti in your neighbor's front yard. They built and maintain Stanford's athletic fields, for example.

Babe) was a fire captain in South San Francisco. But from their working-class upbringing my parents had learned resourcefulness. For example, my mom learned how to decorate cakes when she had me. So when it came time for special-request birthday cakes, she was able to make them herself. One year I had a Big Bird cake, complete with yellow coconut shavings. Another year, I had a sweet Transformers cake, upon which my mom had "drawn" a Decepticons insignia.[4] Were they equal to the quality of something you might see on *Ace of Cakes*? No, but they were close, and for a fraction of the cost. And I never knew the difference. All I knew was that I had a totally awesome Transformers birthday cake, and all the other kids were jealous.[5]

A compilation of some of my mom's homemade birthday cakes. *(Bishop Family)*

This resourcefulness wasn't just reserved for cakes. My childhood birthday parties featured "games" that were usually along the lines of

---

[4] The year was 2007, and I was twenty-nine years old.
[5] They were even more jealous when I polished off my fifth piece of cake. I was a fat kid.

pin the tail on the donkey, beanbag toss, or sack races. All home-made, of course. Perhaps the best example of my parents' resource-fulness when it came to party games was a relay race where two teams of kids took turns running across the yard to a pile of my parents' old clothes, and the first team to throw the clothes on over their own clothes and then tear them off again were the winners. Not exactly heady stuff, but you know what? We had a blast! Kids don't care how much you spend on their birthday parties. *Adults* care how much you spend on your kids' birthday parties. My parents probably spent $35 total on tiny beanbags, a piece of plywood, and some paint for my birthday. Compare that to a few hundred bucks for an afternoon bounce-house rental, which kids are going to get tired of after about half an hour, and pony rides, which are probably going to give your kid encephalitis. Add in the inevitable lawsuit when the pony wrangler gets drunk and accidentally "drops" his overalls, and it's just not worth it.

Here we are at my fifth birthday, playing the clothesline game. Everyone got a bag of clothes, and whoever hung all of theirs on the clothesline first won. Later, I realized that we were just doing my parents' laundry for them. *(Bishop Family)*

Vacations were resourceful, too. Many summer and winter vacations were spent at my grandparents' house in Lake Tahoe, California. My dad's parents had retired and moved to a cabin in the
mountain town, about four hours east of San Francisco. It was a great
place to vacation as a child. It was warm in the summer and it would
snow in the winter. My grandma Marie was . . . well, some might
describe her (diplomatically) as challenging. I'll say she was eccen-
tric. She loved card games (really, anything that involved an element
of gambling), yet she hated playing with children. Once in a while,
she would get roped into playing a big family game of Go Fish or
something, and one of us kids would do something a kid does, like
spill a soda or play out of turn, and she would explode, "THIS IS
WHY I DON'T PLAY WITH KIDS!" She was part Syrian, and I
picked up some Arabic curse words from her as an impressionable
child.[6] She wasn't exactly a health nut: Her favorite foods, as I recall,
were chicken skin, pizza (with extra salt liberally sprinkled on top),
coffee, frozen Milky Way bars, 7UP, and peanut-butter-and-butter
sandwiches. Actually, that last one was a lunch special that she would
make for me (I was overweight). She barely tolerated some of my cous-
ins, yet she loved the hell out of me. I was never exactly sure why;
maybe it was because as the youngest child, my dad was *her* baby,
therefore I was her baby's baby? Regardless, I could do no wrong in her
eyes.

One of her habits would most mold me into the person I am today.
My grandma had a movie collection that put most video stores to
shame. But she never bought a movie. These were the resourceful
Bishops, remember. She owned two VCRs and would make a duplicate
of every single movie she ever rented. You know those FBI warnings
that pop up before every movie you rent? My mom would tell me
they were aimed at my grandma. She had shelves and shelves of video
tapes, purchased in bulk from Costco, each with about three copied
movies on it. She cataloged every movie on an index card, complete

---

[6] Years later, I would delight a Lebanese college buddy of mine by telling him to "eat shit" in Arabic.

with (and I'm not joking or exaggerating) a description of the movie, a list of the actors, and *a star rating.*

But illegally pirating rentals was only part of her OCD/hoarding-disease combo. Every week, on the day *TV Guide* was released, she would drive to the grocery store and buy a hot-off-the-presses copy. More than once, I witnessed a poor manager using a box cutter to cut open a box of *TV Guides* while she stood there berating him. "Why aren't these on the rack?! They're supposed to be on sale today!" Then she would go home and—with a highlighter—go through every movie playing on every channel and set up her recording schedule for the week. On many occasions, if someone wandered too close to the VCR while she was recording a movie, she'd yell, "Don't touch anything! I'm recording!" If you were lucky, she'd be in the kitchen, getting herself a frozen candy bar and a 7UP. In which case you got "yelled at" by a yellow Post-it note that she affixed to her VCR: "DON'T TOUCH—RECORDING!"

I was in movie heaven. This is probably how I became an indoor kid. Here I was in the glorious Sierra Nevada mountain range. I could fish or ski or snowboard or go for a hike. But, no, what did I do? I watched movies with my grandmother.

So I got my love of movies, my love of fattening foods, and my love of gambling from my dad's mom. But I got my love of trivia from my mom's parents. I'll explain.

My parents had me and my brother when they were relatively young, meaning that by the time we were nine and twelve, for example, they were barely in their

My grandpa Babe, just before he retired from the fire department. *(Bishop Family)*

9

thirties. They wanted to go on vacations and have fun without two young children in tow. So they'd often leave me with one set of grandparents and leave Adam with the other. One time, when I was about twelve, they left me with my mom's parents, Babe and Betty, for about five days. Babe Lorenzini, as I said earlier, was a retired fire captain in South San Francisco. They would give me a card for my birthday or Christmas with money inside—ten or twenty bucks, something age appropriate. From as far back as I can recall, whenever my grandfather gave me any gift money, he would write inside the card, *Remember, education = money!* It was a simple and smart piece of advice.

Well, during the few days that I stayed with them, Grandpa Babe decided to reinforce this advice that education really did equal money. Being that they were grandparents, one of their favorite afternoon activities was watching *Jeopardy!* Only this time, we would watch it together. My grandpa said I could play along with the contestants on TV, and for every question I got right, he'd give me a quarter. Then, for every question I got right in Double Jeopardy! he'd give me fifty cents. And if I got the Final Jeopardy! question right, he'd give me a dollar.

My grandpa hadn't accounted for a couple of things. First, I was a smart kid. I had been selected for a school program called GATE, which stood for Gifted and Talented Education. Mostly we played computer games and solved riddles, but I got to miss an afternoon of class once a week, so I was thrilled. Second, I was an unusually well-read kid. Remember, I was the indoor kid. I doubt my brother would have done as well at answering *Jeopardy!* questions. He was busy with other things, such as "having friends" and "being good at sports" and "not getting beat up by bullies." You know, stupid stuff that I didn't have time for. Finally, my grandpa failed to take into account that *Jeopardy!* aired twice a day, every day. So we were set for ten viewings of the show while I was staying with them.

I don't remember exactly how much money I won off my grandpa during that stay, but I know it was in excess of $40. Which is kind of astounding, if you consider it was mostly accumulated in twenty-five- and fifty-cent increments. I remember being overwhelmed by my winnings. Forty dollars is a lot of money to a twelve-year-old kid of relatively humble beginnings, especially in 1990.

Sadly, this is easily one of the two or three greatest highlights of my life from this period.[7] I was in middle school, which is a tough enough time for anyone, but consider the following: I was overweight. I had glasses. Thick ones. I was smart/nerdy and I liked things that nobody else cared about, least of all the cool kids. Such things as Oakland A's baseball[8] and WWF wrestling[9]. I was losing my hair, which made me sort of a genetic freak. I was barely average at sports, which meant I wasn't making a ton of friends on the baseball diamond. And I had just moved to town a couple of years earlier, which meant that while everyone else had friendships that went all the way back to preschool, I hardly knew anyone.

Really, I had no friends. People think this is an exaggeration, so I'll be totally honest with you: During the excruciating years between ages nine and fourteen, I had two friends: Joe Knipp and Kenny Bourquin. Joe was a friend from Little League and Kenny was a social misfit like me, who loved *Saturday Night Live* and *Get Smart*. Again, we were thirteen. It always amuses me when I run into someone from my middle school and I introduce them to my wife. She'll say, "How do you guys know each other?" And the person will answer, "Oh, we were friends in middle school." Social decorum dictates that I smile and nod and act pleasant, but inside, I'm saying,

---

[7] My other two greatest highlights from that time in my life? Hitting a grand slam in the first inning of my Little League championship game and the Oakland A's winning the 1989 World Series. We then lost the championship game in the last inning, and the A's dynasty turned out to be fueled entirely by steroids. The lesson: Never get excited about anything.

[8] We lived in Giants country, and every other kid I knew was a Giants fan. I'm much more of a Giants fan nowadays, but I was an A's fan at the time because that was the first Little League team I was on, and your first Little League team always ends up being your first favorite team when you're a kid.

[9] I could easily have given a doctoral dissertation on the WWF when I was eleven years old. That's how much I cared about it. In fact, here are the top five things I loved as an eleven-year-old that nobody else cared about: (5) Baseball cards; (4) Jose Canseco; (3) WWF wrestling; (2) *Saturday Night Live*; (1) journalism. Hard to see why I had no friends, huh?

"Really? We were friends? Because I don't remember getting invited to your birthday parties. Or talking to you. Ever."

Luckily, I sort of hit my stride, socially speaking, in high school. It all started with a summer film program for high school students held at Northwestern University in Evanston, Illinois. It was the summer before my senior year of high school. I had learned about a summer journalism program at Northwestern, held by the National High School Institute (NHSI). This was kind of like applying to college: I had to submit my transcript, my SAT scores, letters of recommendation, the whole nine yards. I was rejected by the journalism program (no doubt due to my terrible grades—more on that in a minute), but I got a letter a week or so later that basically said, "I know we rejected you from our journalism program, but would you consider attending our Creative Media Writing program instead?" I looked into it, and *creative media writing* meant "screenwriting." I had never considered screenwriting before but (a) I loved writing, (b) I loved movies, (c) I didn't have a bunch of close friends, and (d) the friends I did have were all serious baseball players, which meant they'd be busy all summer playing in their respective summer leagues. So, faced with the choice of a summer spent writing with like-minded students at a prestigious university versus sharing a bedroom with my thirteen-year-old brother, I eagerly accepted their offer.

Starting in 1987, my brother and I were roommates. When Adam was 5 and I was 8, my family moved into a two-bedroom, one-and-a-half bathroom house in San Carlos, California. Think about that: four people, two bedrooms, one shower. Adam and I would share a bedroom for the next ten years, all the way through middle school and high school (for me). They say "familiarity breeds contempt." Let's just say I was *very* familiar with my brother for those years. For the record, teenage boys should *not* share a bedroom. What probably seemed like an adorable experiment when we were 8 and 5 ("They'll *love* getting to play together all day, every day!") became a powder keg of raging testosterone by the time we were sixteen and thirteen. Just a poorly conceived plan from the start.

So you can see how I was chomping at the bit to get out of the house. That it was a scholastic endeavor meant my parents were behind it 100 percent. It was one of the few times I had shown any enthusiasm about something related to my education. I had saved up enough money from my after-school grocery-bagging job to pay the summer tuition,[10] so off to Illinois I went. It was a magical summer. I learned a ton about movies and writing, but the summer was more important for me socially. Whereas I had previously been shunned or mocked for my nerdier tendencies—my enthusiastic love of movies or trivia or wrestling or sports—now I was in an environment where such knowledge was celebrated. That's a small piece of advice I have for any parent whose teenager is going through a tough time. Find something that the teen loves—sports, for example—and find a place where the teen can be celebrated for it. If your teen isn't a great athlete, but he loves sports anyway, send the kid to sports-announcing camp (they actually have those) and watch him or her blossom. If they're bookish and into science, send them to science camp or space camp. That summer, I grew my love of movies, expanded my style of writing, and made some great friends—I even met my good buddy JD, who would eventually be the best man in my wedding. I returned to school for my senior year and became a confident, outgoing, and almost-popular person.

That (mostly) carried over into college. Somehow, by the skin of my teeth, I got accepted into USC. My grades were abysmal, but I had a relatively high SAT score, a couple of glowing letters of recommendation, and I put together a portfolio of my published writing samples, as if to say, "See, I wasn't goofing off and playing video games the whole time I wasn't doing my homework; I was actually bettering myself!" It must have worked because I was somehow allowed to enroll in the fall of 1996. In my four years at USC, I changed majors once (from print journalism to creative writing), had three semicelebrities for

---

[10] Some teenagers save up their money for a car. I saved mine essentially to go to summer school. Still confused as to why I had no friends?

The gentlemen of Pi Kappa Phi. There I am, front and center, back when I was just known as "Balding Bryan." I think this picture was taken at an event on a boat. There is also one other "celebrity" in this picture. Bonus points if you can spot him. *(Author's collection)*

professors,[11] and even founded a fraternity. When I enrolled in college, I had no idea what a fraternity even was. I went through rush my first semester as a freshman, but didn't exactly fall in love with any of the houses on USC's Fraternity Row. Once the semester got rolling and I hadn't joined a fraternity, I kind of felt left out. So me and my buddy JD—the same guy I had met the summer before at North-western (he had enrolled at USC at the same time as me)—decided to join a house the next semester. Before we could, though, a couple of recruiters came from the national offices of Pi Kappa Phi. They said they were founding a chapter at USC and needed some strong leaders to start the chapter. They should have been honest and said

---

[11] I had a film class taught by film critic Leonard Maltin, a creative writing class taught by author T. C. Boyle (probably the best class I ever took), and a screenwriting class taught by Ron Fried-man, the writer of both *Transformers: The Movie* and *G.I. Joe: The Movie*. Guess which of those three had me the most starstruck?

they needed some suckers, but we didn't find that out until later. I figured, here was a chance to do something really interesting and unusual—rather than just join a house, we'd establish our chapter and mold it in our image, carefully selecting members who reflected the ideals that we set forth in our charter.

Basically, we were idiots. Founding a fraternity chapter is an insane amount of work. If you're a college freshman just interested in having fun and drinking beer for four years, pick a good fraternity and join up. Not that my experience wasn't enjoyable; it was, I believe, exponentially more rewarding for me than if I had simply joined another, established house. But I wasn't like most people. I wasn't interested in just drinking beer for four years.[12] In my time as a founding father of Pi Kappa Phi's Delta Rho chapter, we earned our charter, bought a house in the middle of the Row, and raised a ton of money for charity along the way. I served as the chapter's historian (alumni-relations chair, essentially) and rush chairman. My senior year, the other members voted me Brother of the Year. What I'm about to say may sound corny (because it *is* corny), but it's the greatest honor of my life, before or since. My brothers—many of whom I'd recruited as rush chairman—of the chapter I helped found essentially said, "Of all the people doing all they can for this house this year, you did the best."

I may not have had many friends before my senior year in high school, but at least I was a good student. Oh, wait, strike that. I was a *horrible* student. Just terrible. Despite being deemed "gifted" at age ten and placed in a special program for like-minded fifth-graders, my grades started to slip. Actually, they "slipped" the same way Tom Cruise's character slipped off the roof of a building at the end of *Vanilla Sky*. Twice in middle school, I achieved a grade point average below 2.0. I once failed PE in the sixth grade. Not because I couldn't do any of the exercises, but because every day I forgot my green gym shorts that we were required to wear. If you forgot any part of your PE uniform, you got docked a point. Well, I got docked a point every single day that semester.

---

[12] I mean, I definitely did that, too. Make no mistake.

That same semester, I took a yearly standardized test that was mandated by the school district. It measured you aptitude-wise and was partly designed to identify kids with special needs who were performing beneath their grade level. In every area related to English—reading comprehension, language, etc.—I tested at a 12+. That meant I was reading and writing at above a twelfth-grade level as a sixth-grader. It was the highest score the test could report. So when I brought home a report card with a 1.67 GPA and an F in PE, my parents were understandably confused and angry.

The cracks in the armor had started to show years earlier, but nobody had recognized them. In my first few years of school, I got straight A's in all subjects. But in the behavioral section—the portion where they give you an O (outstanding), an S (satisfactory) or an N (needs improvement)—I got a lot of N's. The comments, from year to year, were along the lines of "Bryan is very hyper in class" and "Bryan needs to do a better job of controlling his outbursts." I remember dozens and dozens of occasions when a teacher would scold me for yelling an answer out of turn. My only vivid memory of second grade is from the very first day. I was the new kid in class—I had changed schools again that year[13]—and when the teacher asked the class a question, I blurted out the answer. She gently reminded me, "Now, Bryan, I know you're new here, but in this class, we raise our hands." You'd think my public shaming would have corrected my behavior, but nope. At the end of the semester, my report card had that familiar refrain: "Bryan is disruptive in class." In fact, here's a sampling of actual comments made by my teachers on my elementary-school report cards:

"Likes attention! Speaks out of turn" . . . "VERY verbal. He needs to control his self-discipline in a group situation" . . . "A bit mature mouth ('No way, Jose'—teenage jargon)" . . . "Excitable. Can get carried away" . . . "Needs to be more patient" . . . "Chooses to act out and not

---

[13] I changed schools every year from kindergarten to fourth grade, which only exacerbated my problems in the classroom.

only disturb his classmates but has not been able to finish his own work" . . . "Many daily assignments have not been completed on time" . . . "Behavior has deteriorated in class. Principal will be phoning to set up a conference" . . . "Needs to watch his self-control at times, as he gets very involved and forgets that he is to work reasonably quiet" . . . "Needs to apply more consistent daily self-control effort" . . . "Often not on task in class" . . . "Excessive socializing in class" . . . "Study skills need improvement" . . . "Inconsistent quality of work."

And of course a whole bunch of N's in Demonstrates Self-Control, Demonstrates Self-Discipline, Conduct, and Listens Attentively.

So by the time I got to middle school, things had spiraled out of control. Despite testing at a college level for reading and language skills, and despite being placed in a program for gifted students just a year or so earlier, my academics were falling apart. I would forget assignments all the time, and when I would remember them, I'd forget to do them until the last minute. On many occasions, teachers would announce to the class (as the final bell rang), "Don't forget, your final projects are due tomorrow," and I'd think, "Oh, crap, I don't even know what she's talking about." My parents have home-video footage of me hurriedly applying dried macaroni to the roof of a model Spanish mission at the kitchen table. "What is that, Bryan?" my mom asked from behind the camera.

"It's my report on a Spanish mission," I said.

"It is? When is it due?"

"Tomorrow."

"Hm, first I've heard of it," she muttered passive-aggressively.

It wasn't just assignments I'd forget. I lost my glasses on an almost monthly basis in middle school. Sometimes I'd find them—in my locker or in a jacket pocket—sometimes I wouldn't. There's home-video footage of this, too. My mom taped me sitting in front of the TV—as close as I could get—squinting to see because of my severe nearsightedness.

"Bryan, where are your glasses?" she asked. My parents asked me this all the time. It was like the chorus to the world's worst song.

I looked at the camera. "Um, they're in my locker," I lied. Of course I had lost them again.

"Oh, I see," my mom said, clearly not buying it. My forgetfulness was apparently placing a financial strain on my family. One day, my grandpa, Frank, (of all people) took me aside and said, "It'd be really helpful if you could find your glasses. It's really putting a burden on your mom and dad." That's how you know we weren't rich, by the way. A $90 pair of glasses was about to financially break a family of four.

"Okay, Grandpa, I will," I said. And I 100 percent meant it. I wanted nothing more than to remember such things as, oh, I don't know, doing assignments and not losing my glasses every two months. But I was completely incapable of doing so. My absentmindedness wasn't limited to big school projects, either. I rarely did homework. Again, not because I couldn't or because I didn't want to, I would just . . . space out, I guess. My poor parents would tear their hair out trying to figure out why I was doing so poorly in school. They had me put on a program where I physically handed each of my teachers a chart every day with my homework assignments on it. It was supposed to remind me to actually *do* the homework. Instead, I just stopped bringing the form to my teachers. My parents would incredulously ask, "Why?" It's a good thing they never took me to a psychotherapist. He would probably have thought I was trying to kill them with my indifference.

My problems continued into high school. I attended Junipero Serra High School, an all-boys Catholic School in San Mateo, California. One day, in Mr. Sullivan's sophomore honors English class, he gave the class an extracredit assignment. We had to write an essay on some topic—it was toward the end of the semester and I had already mentally checked out. I had somehow tested my way into the class— that is, I achieved a high enough score on my placement tests the summer before that they had put me in the advanced class—but had performed so poorly that semester that my demotion back to regular English the next year was all but inevitable. So when Mr. Sullivan handed out the essay assignment to everyone, I stuffed it into my backpack and thought, "Eh, I'll get around to it later tonight." Then, I pulled out a piece of paper and started to doodle. Forty-five minutes later, Mr. Sullivan announced, "Five minutes left." I thought to myself, "What the hell is he talking about? And why isn't anybody talking?" I looked around and saw the entire class with their pencils in their hands, writing furiously. To my horror, I realized that the extracredit assignment wasn't a take-home assignment—it was an *in-class* assignment. I panicked, realizing that everyone else in class had spent the last forty-five minutes writing their extracredit essays. In that instance, what was I going to do? I feebly wrote a few sentences, then the bell mercifully rang. Everyone dropped his paper off on Mr. Sullivan's desk. I wrote a final sentence or two, then meekly dropped my paper onto his desk. He instantly saw that I had only written a paragraph, whereas all the others had used the front and back of their papers.

"Nice effort," he said to me sarcastically. For a moment, I wanted to protest, but what was I going to say? "Sorry, I wasn't paying attention when you explained the assignment"? I was damned if I did, damned if I didn't. I said nothing and walked out of class with my tail between my legs.

Mr. Sullivan wasn't the only teacher I ran afoul of during high school. I probably pissed off more teachers than I didn't. My junior-year history teacher, Mr. Bertetta, was a cool guy. He'd graduated from my high school in the sixties, and he always wanted to tell us about going to see the Doors or the Rolling Stones in college. I should have been enraptured—all

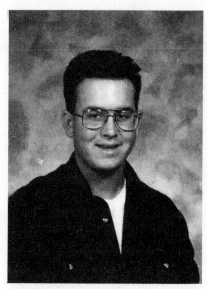

"The worst student"?! Come on! Look at that face! (Actually, stop looking. Let's just pretend this picture never happened.) *(Bishop Family)*

I listened to in high school was classic rock—but instead, I would uncontrollably blurt out whatever came to mind, just to annoy him. One day, after I'd particularly disrupted class, I came home from school to find my very pissed-off mom waiting for me by the answering machine. She pressed play and revealed a very angry message from Mr. Bertetta. It included the sentence "Your son is the worst student I've had the misfortune of teaching in twenty years." Part of me wants that on my tombstone. My mom, not so much.

2.

Making ADHD Pay

or, How I Turned a Disorder into a Career

It wasn't until a decade later that I realized what had been going on for all those years. For two years in my twenties, I worked for Channel One News, an in-school news network for teens. This cross between MTV News and CNN was an incredible incubator of young news talent; it notably helped launch the careers of a young Anderson Cooper, Maria Menounos, Lisa Ling, Serena Altschul, and Bryan Bishop. Actually, I wasn't allowed anywhere near the cameras. I was a writer for their Web site. Every morning, we would all gather in the conference room and watch that day's episode, so we saw what the kids saw. One day, the show did a story on ADHD (attention deficit/hyperactivity disorder) in teens. I barely looked up as the story started—I didn't know much about ADHD and I wasn't all that interested. But as I heard the doctor being interviewed, a few things he said started to grab my attention. He said that kids with ADHD aren't dumb or slow—in fact, they're often of higher intelligence and are (or should be) in advanced classes. He also said kids with ADHD were forgetful, often misplacing essential supplies such as textbooks and backpacks. They have trouble remembering to turn in homework assignments, despite repeated reminders. They daydream, have trouble listening when spoken to, and struggle with directions. And—this is the one that made me sit up in my chair—they're often dismissed as just being "hyper."

In that instant, more than a decade of academic misery finally snapped into focus. The whole time, when everyone thought I was hyper or forgetful or that I just didn't care, I was actually suffering from crippling Attention Deficit /Hyperactivity Disorder. Suddenly, it all made sense. The shouting out in class. The lost glasses. The unheard instructions. The forgotten homework assignments. The high test scores. The blown extracredit. It all added up. After the staff meeting, I went straight to my desk and did a little extra research on my own. I came across this checklist from the National Institutes of Health on ADHD symptoms in children. I was shocked at how accurately it described me as a young person:

- *Fails to give close attention to details or makes careless mistakes in schoolwork*—Yep.
- *Does not follow through on instructions and fails to finish schoolwork, chores, or duties in the workplace*—Bingo.
- *Does not seem to listen when spoken to directly*—What's that you say?
- *Has difficulty organizing tasks and activities*—You bet.
- *Avoids or dislikes tasks that require sustained mental effort (such as schoolwork)*—Bingo again.
- *Often loses toys, assignments, pencils, books, or tools needed for tasks or activities*—100 percent.
- *Is easily distracted*—I'm sorry, what'd you say?
- *Is often forgetful in daily activities*—That's a lot of bingos.
- *Has difficulty playing quietly*—Yep.
- *Is often "on the go," acts as if "driven by a motor," talks excessively*—To this day, in fact.
- *Blurts out answers before questions have been completed*—All the time.
- *Has difficulty awaiting turn*—Absolutely. My God, read my teachers' comments above!
- *Interrupts or intrudes on others (butts into conversations or games)*—Yes, yes, a thousand times, yes!

I was convinced. My parents, on the other hand, were not. When I presented them with this newfound evidence of my childhood disability, I treated it like a revelation. "Look! Remember all those negative comments on my report cards? Finally, we have an explanation as to what the hell was wrong with me all those years! Rejoice!"

My mom furrowed her brow and frowned. "Hm. I don't know about that."

"But listen to all these symptoms!" I pleaded. I basically described my childhood for them in about thirty seconds. "It all adds up!" I declared triumphantly.

My mom thought about it for two seconds—literally, she was silent for two seconds—then said, "No, it was more passive-aggressive."[14]

Passive-aggressive! As though I *chose* to put myself through a nightmarish adolescence. That's like a person who's born gay saying, "I wasn't *born* this way, I *chose* to make the first eighteen years of my life a living hell. Why, you ask? Who knows! I guess I'm just passive-aggressive that way!"

Luckily, in my adulthood, I figured out ways to turn most of these negative traits into positive ones, and I've ended up with a career that takes advantage of a lot of my ADHD "symptoms." My job, essentially, is to interrupt Adam (or the show) with a comical aside; literally, I blurt out my contributions, be it verbally or through my sound effects. Of course, I do my best to time it so I'm not interrupting him midsentence (some might say I fail in this regard). Because the show is live and totally improvised, there's no script to follow, no lines to forget, and no cues to miss. Mentally, we're on the go the whole time, constantly changing directions and making it up as we go along. All the equipment I need—my sound-effects machine, my computer, my mixing board, and my microphone—stays in the studio, so there's nothing I can lose or forget to bring to work.

Being the sidekick on *The Adam Carolla Show* is the perfect job for

---

[14] This was my *mother*, by the way. The person who is supposed to support and believe in you unconditionally. "I'm going to flap my arms and fly to the moon, Mom." "Sounds good, Son! Pack a sweater, it gets cold up there in the substratosphere!" My boss, Adam Carolla, has this notion that my mom spoiled me with too much love and support as a child. Somebody read this chapter to him and ask if he still believes that.

me. It plays to my strengths while mitigating my weaknesses. But I haven't always been so lucky. Before I started my career in entertainment, I had a series of part-time and barely full-time jobs to try to make ends meet. My first job ever was bagging groceries at a local supermarket for two years. I followed that illustrious career choice with stints as a bartender, a writer for a Web site that never launched, a summer-camp counselor, a high school junior varsity football coach, and a secret shopper for Jack in the Box fast-food restaurants. I was fat (228 pounds) and unhappy. I needed a career change. I decided to focus on doing something—*anything*—related to the entertainment world. But I had to start at the bottom.

Call Screener, 106.7 KROQ-FM (Los Angeles)

I answered an ad on EntertainmentCareers.net for a part-time call screener at KROQ, a legendary alternative radio station in Los Angeles. This was early 2001, so the only thing they were an "alternative" to was pleasant-sounding music. The station was playing *lots* of Limp Bizkit and Linkin Park. I think the only reason I got the job was that I showed up to the interview in a coat and tie. KROQ appealed to a stoner/surfer demographic, so the fact that I could string two sentences together probably separated me from the rest of the applicant pool. Also, the fact that I knew words "demographic" and "applicant pool." It was a cool job; far and away the most exciting job I'd had up to then. The pay was terrible—just above minimum wage. One year, the minimum wage in California got raised to an amount that was more than what I was making, so the station had to start paying us a few cents more just to meet it. But I got free concert tickets, occasionally got to meet a celebrity who was hanging out in the halls, and got to tell my friends that I was working at the "world-famous" KROQ, where Carson Daly, Jimmy Kimmel, and Adam Carolla had gotten their start. MTV's *Total Request Live* and Comedy Central's *The Man Show* were very popular back then, so my working at the same radio station they had all started out at meant I was tangentially tied to their success. (Give me a break. A few months earlier I was tasting Jumbo Jacks for a living. I was desperate for anything resembling success.)

As a call screener, my job was to take requests from listeners for four hours, which felt to me cruel and dishonest, because KROQ, like all corporately owned radio stations, didn't really play listener requests. The playlist was generated by the music director and given to the DJs well ahead of time, sometimes by hours. I know this for a fact because my job often included taking the list of songs and ads from the music director's office and handing it to the DJ. Yet, like idiots, our job was to take requests from the clueless public. "Yeah, you bet, I'll try to get that on for you" was my refrain. If someone happened to request a song that was already scheduled to play that hour, we were supposed to tell the DJ so they could say, "So-and-so requested this one," on the air. So it seemed as if we were playing the listeners' requests when we really never did. It was a ridiculous masquerade, but it fooled a lot of teenage fans of the station's, so . . . mission accomplished?

Call Screener, *Loveline*

After about a year at the station, the producer of the syndicated show *Loveline* approached me in the halls one day and asked if I'd like to start screening calls for *Loveline*. I jumped at the chance. *Loveline* was hosted by Dr. Drew and Adam Carolla and had been a hit TV show already on MTV. I listened to the radio version all throughout high school. Plus, now with *The Man Show*, Adam Carolla was quickly becoming one of my comedic heroes. It also paid a whopping $12 an hour, versus the $6.75 per hour I was making at KROQ for a regular midday shift. I thought I was being promoted after a year of exemplary call-screening performance, but I later realized that the one thing people hated to do in radio was work.[15] They

---

[15] During my time at *Loveline*, the producer came into work maybe three or four times a week, on average. *Maybe*. And that was on a particularly ambitious week. She sent her associate producer, Lauren, in her place. That was another great thing about working at *Loveline*: the boss (in this case, the producer) often wasn't there. The show was so successful that it was essentially on autopilot.

needed a new call screener for *Loveline*. They were going to put an ad online, then read through a hundred résumés and conduct a dozen interviews? Hell no. They walked down to the screening room and picked out the chubby kid who wore a polo shirt to work every day.

In case you didn't believe me, here I am: chubby kid in a polo shirt. *(Author's collection)*

Working for *Loveline* was awesome. Not only were celebrities on the show almost every night, but *the show was hosted by two celebrities!* Keep in mind that I was still a wide-eyed (and wide-assed) twenty-three-year-old, so meeting actors and musicians was a much bigger deal to me back then. Plus I got to meet Anderson, the show's engineer. I considered him to be the best sound-effects wizard in radio. In my opinion, he was every bit as important to the show comically as Adam was. When we first met and started working together, Anderson hated me. You've probably surmised by now that I am a fairly upbeat, optimistic person. Anderson is . . . not. He used to pull his sweatshirt hood over his headphones to avoid having to talk to me. He mistook my can-do attitude for ass-kissing. Whereas I was a real "go-getter," he was more of a "Go get it yourself, you son of a bitch, and screw you for asking me." Eventually we became friends, but not before he nick-named me "KAB"—for "Kiss-Ass Bryan"—or "Kabbie" for short.

Writer, Channel One News

After five years of barely making enough money at part-time call-screening jobs to pay my rent, I finally decided to take a full-time corporate gig, complete with an office, a parking space with my name on it, and life insurance. Ironically, it was the last time I'd have any of those things. I was hired by Channel One News to be a writer for their Web site. It was the best job I'd ever had. I had a great boss, fun coworkers, and we produced some great work, although I remember the first couple of stories I turned in to my editor, Beth, were terrible. I tried to convince her that *I was* a good writer, I just hadn't written seriously in a few years. Luckily she stuck with me, gave me some chances, and made me a much better writer in the process. We even won a Webby Award while I was there for Best Youth Site, beating (among others) Noggin, Scholastic.com, and the Girl Scouts.

I was in my midtwenties. I had a steady and creative office job with full benefits doing what I loved (writing). I had finally dropped the fifty extra pounds I'd been carrying for years. I had quit or been fired from all my previous part-time gigs and was now settling into corporate life when one day in late 2005, while sitting at my desk, I got a surprising phone call, from a guy named Mike Maddocks. I had met Mike once while working for a day on one of Adam Carolla's TV pilots about a year earlier. I hadn't heard from him since, so I had pretty much forgotten about ever having met him. He explained that he was working on Adam's newly launched Comedy Central talk show *Too Late with Adam Carolla*, and that they needed some production help. In my mind, I immediately thought of how I would politely say no to Mike: "Thanks, but to be honest, I really have no desire to take an-other part-time job . . . or worse, a full-time job that'll be over in two months and leave me unemployed." Before I could put my thoughts into words, Mike explained they needed a segment producer for their viewer-phone-calls portion of the show, and Adam had specifically asked them to look into hiring me for the spot. I didn't realize it at the time, but Adam had been impressed by my go-getter attitude when I was just a lowly call screener on *Loveline*. My tenure at *Loveline* had ended ignominiously a few months earlier,[16] so I was understandably surprised that he had recommended me for the segment-producer job.

I asked what the salary was. "Two thousand dollars a week," Mike said. "We're in production through the end of November." I nearly swallowed my tongue. Not only was $2,000 a week the equivalent of a six-figure salary (over a full year, of course), but if I took the job and it only lasted until the end of November, I would make more money in those three months than I had made up to that point in the year at Channel One.[17] I told Mike I needed a little bit of time to consider his offer. He said he needed someone to start work on Monday. It was Thursday afternoon.

I stepped out of the office building to gather my thoughts. It was a great but scary opportunity: great pay, short-term, no job security. I called my parents for advice, and they basically said, "Go for it." I finally settled on this thought: Here was a (literally) once-in-a-lifetime opportunity; a window, if you will. And that window would only be open for a short time. And once it was closed, it was painted shut. Chances were slim that I'd take the job and someday say to myself, "Man, I wish I hadn't taken a chance on that TV show." But the chance of my regretting it if I'd passed it up? Probably pretty high.

I called Mike that night and told him I'd take the job. Then the ominous reality of telling Beth about my decision crept in. Normally people gave two weeks' notice when they leave a job. I was going to give Beth two hours' notice. The next day at work, Friday, I was a bundle of

---

[16] I was fired for making some jokes on (what was intended to be) a humorous blog from behind the scenes at *Loveline*. It's not as if I published their cell phone numbers or said, "This show sucks and the hosts are assholes."

[17] My salary at Channel One? Thirty-five thousand dollars a year. At that rate, I would have paid off my student loans sometime around my 133rd birthday.

nerves. Beth was not only a great boss, but she was a good friend. She had stuck her neck out and taken a chance on a (very) unproven young writer less than two years earlier, and now I was going to basically tell her, "Happy Friday, I won't be coming in to work on Monday."

And that's how I told her: I went into her office, closed her door, and began, "So, I won't be coming in to work on Monday . . ." She was a little disappointed, but mostly she was happy for me. Even a little bit proud. Looking back, I think she knew there wasn't a ton of room for growth for me there at Channel One. She congratulated me on my new job. I told her that I'd worked out a deal with my new boss (Mike). My second week on the job was actually a "dark" week for the show, meaning they wouldn't be producing any shows that week. It had been planned into the schedule from the beginning, but the timing was fortuitous. I told Beth that I had told Mike that I'd need to go back to Channel One for a couple of days that week to help with whatever transition they needed. Beth was thrilled, I was happy, and Mike was satisfied. In just a matter of hours, I had decided to take the biggest leap of my professional life.

Segment Producer, *Too Late with Adam Carolla* (Comedy Central, 11:30 P.M.)

Too Late was a talk show hosted by Adam Carolla on Comedy Central in late 2005. Adam actually had two shows on the air at that point: *The Adam Carolla Project* was running on TLC during the same time period. The TLC show, while underpromoted, was a good show. When people asked what I was doing during that time, I told them I was working on Adam's new TV show. They'd say something like "Oh, I love that show where he renovates the house!" To which I'd reply, "No, you're thinking of his good show. I work for the other one."

The "other one" was a late-night talk show on which Adam interviewed guests and performed comedy bits in front of a confused audience. The show was poorly conceived. One of the problems was the aforementioned audience. A lot of Adam's humor is intelligent, topical, and filled with semi-obscure pop-culture references. Because we taped the show in the afternoon, the audience wasn't exactly filled with employed, educated comedy enthusiasts. They were largely unemployed/unemployable seat-fillers or European tourists who had been duped by guys with clipboards asking, "Do you want to see a TV show taping?" They thought they were going to see an episode of *Everybody Loves Raymond* or *The King of Queens*, but instead they got Adam Carolla talking to callers and interviewing Kevin Nealon. It didn't take long for the producers to jettison the live studio audience. It also didn't take long for Comedy Central to jettison the show.

Coincidentally, right around this time Adam was announced as Howard Stern's replacement for CBS Radio's West Coast markets. Stern was leaving terrestrial radio for satellite radio. At the time, Stern was the biggest name in morning radio; his show was heard in dozens of markets across the country, and when he departed for satellite radio, the thinking was that the job was too big for any single replacement host. So CBS Radio's western markets were awarded to a proven in-house talent: Adam Carolla, currently the cohost of *Loveline*. Knowing that I was about to be out of a job (it was already November, and the show was scheduled to go on hiatus soon, with no promise of being renewed), I waited around after the show one night to talk to Adam about possibly going to work on his new radio show, which was to be launched just after the New Year. He said that he wasn't sure which positions—if any—were still open, but to talk to him the next day and he'd have some more information for me about possible employment.

The next day, I again waited around to talk to Adam after the show. He told me there was good news and bad news: The bad news was that they had pretty much filled all the spots on the show. The "good" news was that they still needed a call screener. I was devastated. A move back to call screener would represent a major step back in my career. Actually, it would be several steps back. I will go out on a limb and say nobody in the history of entertainment has gone from TV segment producer to radio call screener for his or her next job. It'd be like the secretary of defense telling the president, "For my next job, I'd really like to be an intern in the Illinois State Senate. Can you make that happen for me?" And not only was the pay terrible—$12 an hour—but it was again a part-time job. No benefits. No sick days. No vacation time. I would be back to my pre–Channel One days if I took the job. If I didn't take the job, I had two choices: look for another writing job in the corporate world, or look for another segment-producer job on a different TV show. The segment-producer path looked the most promising; some people worked for years in television to become

My "jock card" (aka publicity shot) from the first week at the show. It's still unclear why this photo was chosen out of the dozens we took that day. Maybe they wanted people to think I was a Las Vegas magician. *(KLSX)*

a segment producer, and I had been handed the job without even asking. It was like drawing the Chance card in Monopoly that allowed you to go straight to Go and collect $200.

But something told me not to. I was not only a huge Adam Carolla fan, but a huge Howard Stern fan, also. For much of my high school life, it was Howard in the morning and *Loveline* at night. Now, I was faced with the opportunity to be a (admittedly small) part of radio history: Adam Carolla takes over for the (self-appointed) "King of All Media," Howard Stern. And I had a chance to be there, on the front lines, for the whole thing. Thanks to my low overhead, I had some cash saved up from my stint on the TV show. I thought to myself, "I'll take the call-screener job, do it for as long as I can afford it, then, when I run out of money, I'll just take a real, full-time job somewhere."

Worst-case scenario, I'd be looking for a new job in five months, but I'd have some great stories about a historic period in radio. I took the job.

Call Screener, *The Adam Carolla Show* (CBS Radio, Mornings, Syndicated)

The Adam Carolla Show debuted on Tuesday morning, January 3, 2006, at 6:00 a.m. Pacific time. The original lineup included Adam Carolla as host, Rachel Perry as news girl, Dave Dameshek as the sports guy, "Big Tad" Newcomb as the show's fat flunky, Mike Lynch as the show's sound-effects guy, Angie Fitzsimmons as the associate producer, and Jimmy Brusca as the show's producer. If that seems like a lot of information, don't bother trying to remember any of it, because within a year, the only person from that list who would still be employed in the same position was Adam.

For the first five months of the show, I dutifully screened the calls. Occasionally, I was included in an on-air comedy bit,[18] which I did an insane amount of preparation for. During March, for example, we created "Limerick Wars," in which we would choose a person from the staff and write insulting poems about him or her. You probably know what a limerick is. It's a type of Irish poem with a singsongy cadence that starts out with something like "There once was a man from Nantucket . . ." As I said, I did an inordinate amount of preparation for these occasional on-air bits, and the result was something insulting like this, about Adam himself:

> *Adam likes to have his ass kissed*
> *When Tad forgets his water, he gets pissed*
> *His hair's made of brillow*
> *His giant teeth are yellow*
> *Man, I hope I don't get fired for this.*

---

[18] A *comedy bit* is a routine or game or some comedic "thing" that usually gets repeated. Think "Jay-walking" on the *Tonight Show* or Letterman's "Top Ten List."

Or this one, about our producer, Jimmy Brusca:

> *Brusca's a guy we can't stand*
> *His bitching's getting out of hand*
> *He eats like a pig*
> *His jokes, we don't dig*
> *Thank God he's about to be canned.*

Unfortunately, I had no control over how often I got to be on the air. The only influence I had was doing the best possible job I could do when I *was* given the rare on-air chance. It was sort of like being a pinch hitter versus being an everyday player in baseball. If you're an everyday player—an established star in the big leagues—you can afford to go 0 for 4 once in a while. If you're a pinch hitter, you need to make the most out of your trips to the plate. I was still a pinch hitter when it came to being on the microphone, so I was in "make every comedy bit count" mode.

The one thing I *could* control was pitching bits. We were a new show, so outside of a couple of regular comedic tropes we'd trot out each week or so, the show was always on the lookout for new things to do. Adam was particularly welcoming of new ideas; after each show, the entire staff would gather in the studio for a postshow wrap-up meeting, and everyone was encouraged to pitch new ideas for bits. This was where I shined. Everyone pitched ideas, more or less, and Adam, being the comedic genius that he is, would usually point out some flaw in the idea that no one had thought of. My batting average for pitching on-air bits was actually pretty high. Not only did I get a bunch of ideas on the air in those first few months, but a few of my bits—"What Can't Adam Complain About?," "The Bitch Bag," and "Totally Topical TiVo Trivia"[19] —went on to be long-running staples of the show, some of which we still do today.

---

[19] These bits were all originally my ideas. However, credit where it's due: These bits wouldn't have been anywhere nearly as effective as they were had it not been for Mike Lynch's improving upon my original idea in each case. So thanks, buddy.

My success with pitching bits—combined with my ability to at least tread water on the air—meant that when the rarest of rare chances for some extended mic time came around, I was ready to step up to the plate and take my swings.[20] Our on-air sound-effects guy, Mike Lynch, had a destination wedding scheduled for early May in 2006. The wedding was in Ireland, with a weeklong honeymoon to immediately follow. He had planned it all months before ever landing the job with the show, so it couldn't be moved or changed. Faced with being without Mike Lynch for two weeks, Adam made the call to have me fill in as the on-air sound-effects guy.

I was thrilled. For two weeks, I got to emulate my favorite sound-effects guys—Fred Norris from the *Howard Stern Show* and Anderson from *Loveline*. I can't imagine I was particularly *good* during those two weeks, but it was fun, and my friends and family got to hear me on the mic a handful of times. I decided I could die happy, at least in a radio sense. I had screened calls for a few months, made no money, blown through my savings, witnessed radio history firsthand, and even got to be Adam's sidekick for two weeks. Not a bad story to tell my grandkids someday. One day toward the end of my two-week run as the fill-in sound-effects guy, I was sitting and waiting for the postshow meeting to begin. It was just me, Adam, and our producer in the studio. I looked at the empty call-screener booth through the window on the other side of the room and said to them, "It's going to be weird going back to that call-screener booth." I meant it almost offhandedly, with a shrug, as in "What're you gonna do?"

To my shock, Adam replied, "Yeah, we gotta figure out what we're gonna tell Lynch."

"I don't know," our producer answered, shaking his head.

As the rest of the staff trickled in for the meeting, Adam and our producer kept talking about what they were "gonna tell Lynch." I almost wondered out loud, "What do you have to tell him?" Then it finally dawned on me—"*Holy shit, they're thinking about making me the*

---

[20] That's three baseball metaphors in as many paragraphs, if you're counting.

sound-effects guy." As their conversation progressed, I thought, *"Holy shit, they* are *making me the sound-effects guy."* Then, like a kid who realizes that Santa Claus, the Easter bunny, and the tooth fairy are all make-believe, at the same moment my thoughts came so fast they piled on each other like a train that jumped the tracks. *"There's no way they just decided this now. They must have decided this in the last couple of days. They must have had conversations about this when I wasn't around. What do I do? Lynch is going to kill me. The guy leaves for his wedding and I take his job! What kind of an asshole does that?"*

What I didn't know was that Lynch was actually doing two full-time jobs prior to his wedding: He was the show's only writer in addition to being the on-air sound-effects guy. Mike is a gifted writer, and Adam wanted him doing that job full-time. He wanted Lynch to be writing during the show, contributing on-the-spot jokes and timely material, as well as "managing" and developing bits. Dave, our sports guy, joked that I was like Lou Gehrig, stealing poor Wally Pipp's job, but I liken it more to when Tim Duncan joined David Robinson's San Antonio Spurs. Robinson was already a great player, but his game was augmented by the arrival of Duncan, who was a great player in his own right. Despite playing similar positions, the pair went on to win two NBA championships.

It took a while, but by 2008 the show had found its groove. You'd have to ask fans of the show which incarnation they preferred, but for my money the 2008 lineup of Adam, me, and Teresa Strasser was the pinnacle of the radio-show days. To continue the Spurs analogy, we were like the great championship San Antonio teams of that decade: Adam was Tim Duncan, the comedy Hall of Famer, one of the best to ever play the game at his position. The offense ran through him. He got the most shots and scored the most points. He rebounded our bricks and slammed them home. Teresa was like Tony Parker. She was a pass-first point guard, always looking to pass the comedy ball and set up a teammate. She and Adam ran a textbook pick-and-roll. I was like Robert Horry (or Manu Ginóbili, if you want to make a receding-hairline comparison): picking my spots and draining the occasional three-pointer. Had management simply left us alone, I truly believe we would have evolved into a top-rated morning show.

Unfortunately, we never got much of a chance. CBS Radio "flipped" the format of our station in February 2009, meaning they laid off the entire staff and changed the programming completely. Instead of providing twenty-four-hour-a-day talk, the station would play Top 40 pop music. This happens more often than you think; has there ever been a station you listened to and enjoyed that was suddenly one day playing Mexican ranchera music? Probably. In our case, the struggling economy was the straw that broke the camel's back. CBS Radio looked at our station and saw that they were essentially paying morning-show-size salaries to everyone who was on the air, round-the-clock (except me, of course). They decided that they could get the same ratings out of a nearly DJ-less pop station for a fraction of the cost. From a strictly dollars-and-cents perspective, the move made sense. CBS Radio would get slightly better ratings for pennies on the dollar. Still, it was a tough pill to swallow. But my layoff was made easier by one thing: I was engaged to Christie, the love of my life.

3.

Falling in Love

or, "Will You Stop Talking Please?
I'm Trying to Kiss You"

The story of how Christie and I met is . . . convoluted. Whenever anyone asks, "How did you guys meet?," we both kind of look at each other and silently have this conversation with our eyes: "Do we tell them the *whole* story? Or do we make it simple and just say, 'At a wedding'?" Since this is a book and I have a word count to oblige, you get the whole story.

We met at a wedding. Sort of. It was late March 2007. Our mutual friends Adam and Claire were getting married in Claire's hometown of Scottsdale, Arizona. Scottsdale is a tremendous town if you're a young person in your twenties. It's part of the Phoenix/Tempe area and is home to thousands of hot coeds. I don't mean *hot* as in "attractive" (although many are); I mean *hot* as in "Dear lord, it's 127 degrees, I'm going to wear as little as possible today!" They're literally too hot to wear a normal amount of clothes.

Being that it was a destination wedding, the couple hosted a rehearsal dinner for all out-of-town guests the night before the wedding, in the back room of a big Mexican restaurant. It was complete with a taco bar and free margaritas. I knew about twenty people, and they all knew about twenty people, so I was meeting friends of friends all night.

At one point, I was talking to my friend Elizabeth, and she introduced me to a girl she had been talking to, Christie. "Bryan works for *The Adam Carolla Show*," said Elizabeth.

"Oh! I know someone who works on that show!" Christie said excitedly.

"Really?" I asked. "Because there's only like eight of us, and half the guys are named Mike."[21]

"No, it's definitely not someone named Mike."

"Is it Dave Dameshek?" I asked, referring to our old cohost.

"No."

"Is it Danny Bonaduce?" I asked, referring to our current cohost. Christie laughed. "No, it's not Danny."

"Then is it Adam himself? Because otherwise I'm out of names."

"No. Damn it." She turned to her friend Lyndsey, who was standing nearby. "Lyndsey! Who do I know at *The Adam Carolla Show?*"

Lyndsey looked at her, then at me. "Bryan," she said. "Bryan is the one you know."

Flashback time! A year and a half earlier, I was in a relationship with a girl named Jamie who lived part-time in Scottsdale.[22] Jamie and I were both big USC football fans, so when USC was scheduled to play Arizona State in Tempe that year, it was a no-brainer to make a weekend out of it and go to the game together.

On September 28 of that year, Lyndsey (a friend of mine whom I had just seen at Elizabeth's wedding, coincidentally) sent me this e-mail about her high school friend Christie:

> *It was good seeing you and Jamie at the wedding. I wanted to ask you for Jamie's email or phone number in Phoenix. I talked with her at the wedding about my good friend Christie, who lives there and knows no one and is not very happy. Jamie said she'd love to take her out. If that's cool, let me know when you get a chance.*

---

[21] It's true. We had Mike Lynch, Mike Dawson, Mike August, and Mike Cioffi at the time. It didn't take us long to start calling everyone by his last name.

[22] Unless you're in the military and stationed overseas, long-distance relationships are a loser move. Take it from me. Although, if it's any consolation, she was living in Los Angeles when we met. Who am I kidding, it's no consolation.

Jamie and I said sure, the more the merrier. I emailed Lyndsey's friend Christie the next day:

> *Lyndsey mentioned that you just moved to the Scottsdale area. My girlfriend is from there, and we'll be in town this weekend for the USC/ASU game. Do you want to meet us for drinks Fri or Sat night? We'll be hanging out with a few of our local friends either in Tempe or Scottsdale. Send me your phone number and we'll call you when we're in town!*

Christie told us that she was a big USC football fan, too, so Jamie and I invited her to tailgate with us and to attend the team pep rally the night before the game. What I didn't know was that Christie had just broken up with her long-term boyfriend (who, Christie still suspects, may have killed her dog). She had moved to Scottsdale for a job, and now that she and her boyfriend had broken up, she knew nobody outside of work. She had even bought two tickets to the game, thinking that she would go with her boyfriend. Once they broke up, her attitude was "Screw you, I'm going to the game by myself."

Jamie and I (and Jamie's parents) met up with Christie at the official USC pep rally at the Marriott in downtown Scottsdale on Friday night. Here's what I remember about that night: It was hot. That's all. I don't remember meeting Christie (let alone speaking to her). I don't remember the pep rally.

Apparently we all made plans to tailgate together the next day. (I don't remember this either.) It was a day game, so the tailgating started early. Fortunately for Arizona State students,[23] the tailgating technically never stops. Again, I remember very little about any interactions with Christie; my thought at the time was "Here's a friend of a friend I'll never see again. Best-case scenario, Jamie has a new friend in Scottsdale." Indeed, Christie spent most of the time talking

---

[23] If you're a "student," shouldn't you technically be "studying" something at least part of the time? What then do we call ASU students? Enrollees? Partners? Revelers? Pukers?

to Jamie and her parents. She would later describe her impression of me as "a nice enough guy, seemed like a good boyfriend, a little quiet and aloof."

Christie even came over to Jamie's parents' house for dinner that night—another fact that I had completely forgotten by the time we met again. Apparently Christie and Jamie spent hours in the kitchen together making dinner. We must have discussed that I was about to start working on the new *Adam Carolla Show*, which was going to debut in January. I have zero recollection of this. Seriously, when I concentrate hard and try to think of that night, it's as if I were Tyler Durden at the end of *Fight Club*; there's someone missing from every scene.

Sadly, I remember everything about the actual game that day (quite vividly): USC came in undefeated and ranked number one in the country; Arizona State jumped out to a three-touchdown lead at halftime; Matt Leinart hurt his knee but returned to the game; USC had something like 200 yards rushing in the second half and came back to win the game. By the way, and this is not a lie, I had to look up zero information on this game that happened in 2005. I'm curious to see what my editors dig up when they fact-check this chapter.[24]

So when the weekend was over, Christie went back to her life in Scottsdale and Jamie and I went back to our lives in Los Angeles. Christie and I never spoke again, and we both promptly forgot about each other. Within a year, Jamie and I would break up.[25]

Back to the rehearsal dinner in Scottsdale. Christie and I had a good laugh over our *both* having forgotten about each other. We each wanted to give the other shit about forgetting, but we were equally culpable. Christie was living back in LA now (where she was from) and was still single. We made small talk, caught up a little, and then

---

[24] The copy editor wanted to change "three-touchdown" lead to a "21–3" lead. I argued (successfully) that 21–3 *is* a three-touchdown lead, as it would take three touchdowns to regain the lead.

[25] She dumped me and moved to France. That's how you know an ex-girlfriend wanted out of the relationship: She moves as far away from you as possible post-breakup. At one point in 2006, I had three ex-girlfriends, and they lived in Kansas, New Jersey, and France. Apparently dating me was like living near Chernobyl. Once the meltdown happens, the survivors need to get the hell away from the blast zone.

Christie (*second from the left*) with some friends just before the wedding, looking quite good in her turquoise dress. (*Author's collection*)

(and this is a badass move if you can pull it off, fellas) I said to her, "Well, I'd love to stay and talk, but I have a date." A *date*! In Scottsdale! The weekend of a friend's wedding! During the rehearsal dinner! It wasn't much of a date, just a friend of a friend whom I'd met once who lived in Scottsdale. We went to a bar, had a few drinks, and said goodnight. Blah.[26]

The wedding was the next evening. At the reception, I found Christie and we talked the entire time. Easy, natural conversation. She was whip-smart and looked *very* good in her turquoise dress. When the wedding began, we discovered that we had been assigned to sit at the same table. Our friends Adam and Claire claim they did this on purpose because they *knew* we'd hit it off. I believed them until Christie

---

[26] The girl spent half the evening pointing out guys in the bar whom she had slept with. She may have been trying to signal to me "Hey, I'm easy!" but it was creepy. Plus the guys all looked like the gangsters from the movie *Eastern Promises*.

and I planned our own wedding. In retrospect, we realized that we had been seated at the dreaded "orphan table," the table where you stick the wedding invitees who don't belong to an obvious group (work friends, school friends) or who won't fit at their group's table. It's sort of an Island of Misfit Toys table. It can either go superwell or superawkwardly. Luckily for Christie and me, it went superwell. So well that I don't even remember who else was at our table. *That's* how smitten I was with Christie.[27]

We danced and we laughed at how many weird coincidences had brought us together that evening: the weekend in Scottsdale that neither of us remembered. The fact that her high school friend (Lyndsey) had married one of *my* college roommates (Rich). And that we were *both* at Lyndsey and Rich's wedding—with other dates, of course (me with Jamie, Christie with the boyfriend who may or may not have killed her dog). And now, here we were, in Scottsdale (again), of all places.[28] Months later, we would discover a picture of both of us on the dance floor at Lyndsey and Rich's wedding—dancing with our own dates.

Halfway through the wedding, we stole off to the adjacent golf course[29] to have a romantic moment together. It was a beautiful spring night in Arizona. The sun had just set, and Christie looked beautiful. I positioned myself to lean in for our first kiss. There was just one problem: Christie wouldn't stop talking.

If loose lips sink ships, Christie could have sunk the entire Spanish Armada. She loves to talk. Sometimes, when we're talking, she'll pause and say, "Let's talk!" And alcohol is like fuel to her verbal fire. So while I'm getting ready to plant a kiss on her, Christie's going on and on about work, and Scottsdale, and wedding food, and God knows what else. Finally, I interrupted her.

---

[27] I like to claim that when you get my attention, you get 100 percent of my attention. Christie will claim that I never notice things. Can't it be both?

[28] This convoluted situation has led to a number of people taking credit for setting up our relationship. Adam, Claire, Rich, and Lyndsey (among others) have all claimed credit. Let me settle this once and for all: You're all wrong. *God* set us up. Obviously.

[29] Wherever you are in Scottsdale, you're adjacent to a golf course.

"Will you stop talking, please?" I said with a smile. "I'm trying to kiss you."

We kissed. My eyes were closed, but I'm guessing it was picturesque. We returned to the wedding and danced the night away. Later, we headed back to my hotel room, but Christie kept her virtue. We kissed a little more and I eagerly offered to take her on a "real date" once we both got back home to Los Angeles.

The pressure was both off *and* on for our first official date back home in Los Angeles. Off because we'd already shared our first kiss (high five!); on because I figured as a native Angeleno,[30] she'd seen and done everything in the city. She assured me that, no, she hadn't seen and done everything in LA, partly because she'd been living out of state for the past six years and partly because LA is so big.

Quick note to everyone living outside Southern California: Los Angeles is *huge*. I once saw a map online that showed that seven major US cities can comfortably fit within LA's city limits: San Francisco, Boston, Minneapolis, Pittsburgh, Milwaukee, St. Louis, and Cleveland . . . *plus* the Island of Manhattan. With room to spare!

So I got to planning. Luckily, planning is something I do well. I wanted to do something involving wine tasting, since we had initially bonded over our shared love of wine. Plus it would show that I was a good listener. (Christie would argue that this is the *last* time I showed I was a good listener, but fortunately, this isn't her book.) I also wanted to pick a place for dinner that was upscale (but not *too* upscale) while also casual (but not *too* casual). Think white napkins but no tablecloth. And if I could throw in something that utilized my E-level celebrity, that'd be nice, too.

Well, it turns out that no one thing incorporates all of those elements. So I did what any eager guy would do who's trying to get into a hot girl's pants—err, trying to show a lady a good time: I planned

---

[30] That's what they call people in Los Angeles: Angelenos. I think it sounds dumb, but what's a better alternative? Los Angelites? Los Angelans? Plus, the term for the residents of an area sounds dumb to anyone not from there. I'm from San Francisco, so San Franciscans sounds perfectly normal to me, but Floridians and Minnesotans probably think it sounds stupid.

three separate events for our first date. We'd start off by doing a wine tasting at a small local wineshop. We'd follow that up with dinner at a little French restaurant in a part of town that had recently undergone a bit of a rebirth (thereby ensuring that she had never been to this part of LA). Finally, I called in a favor and had us put on the guest list at a comedy club.

Fellas, a few tips as it relates to planning dates. First, the wine tasting: Pretty much every decent wine store has tastings. They're usually on the same day of the week (Saturday afternoon, in this case), they're mostly above-average wines, they're almost always cheap (this one was $10 a person, I think), they usually involve charcuterie[31] or some kind of finger food, you can get tipsy (or more important, your date can get tipsy), it's a social atmosphere, and everyone generally has a good time.

Second, the restaurant: Pick a restaurant that's on the newer side. Your date will appreciate how on top of restaurant trends you are, and if the service or the food sucks, you can just say, "They must be still ironing out the kinks. Give it a month and this place will be a well-oiled machine." Not only are you absolved of all responsibility for a bad meal, but now she can say she's already been to the hottest new restaurant in town before anyone else!

Finally, the comedy club: I will never, ever understand why people go to a movie on a date instead of a comedy club. And this is coming from a guy who loves movies so much that I host a podcast about movies![32] There's no interaction in a movie theater. You sit there silently until the movie ends, when one of you is contractually obligated to ask the second-worst question you can ask in a movie theater: "So what'd you think?"[33] In a comedy club, there's laughter (unless Jon Lovitz is onstage),[34] you can lean in close and share a private

---

[31] Do *not* be afraid of charcuterie. Look it up if you don't know what it is; I promise you'll be pleasantly surprised.

[32] Yeeaahh, *Film Vault*! Named one of iTunes' Best Podcasts of 2010, by the way. Did I mention it's free?

[33] The worst question you can ask: "Wait . . . I thought you said you *didn't* put butter on this popcorn?"

[34] This joke was originally supposed to say, "Unless Tom Leykis is onstage," but my editor cut it, saying, "Nobody knows who that is," which was more satisfying than the actual joke.

laugh at a joke that hits close to home, and there's something called a two-drink minimum. Yes, fellas, you and your date are *required* to order drinks when seeing a comedy show. It's the law.[35]

So I had an epic, three-part date planned. I called and told Christie I'd pick her up a few minutes late, which was uncharacteristic of me, but ended up being beneficial. I would not learn this until months later, but Christie had been on another date earlier that day. It was a lunch date with (she later claimed) a guy she wasn't really into. Looking back, I'm glad I didn't know that she had been out on another date beforehand because I'd inevitably get drunk and start slipping in catty questions like "How's the fish? Is it as good as the salad you had at lunch with your other date, *you whore?!*" So like I said, good thing.

Also, I may have wilted under the pressure of knowing that I had the valuable "Dinner Date." In poker, this is known as a position raise. It's a cliché, but it's a cliché for a reason: Avoid lunch dates whenever you can. A "Lunch Date" should be called a "Let's-Get-This-Over-With-ASAP-So-I-Can-Go-Home-and-Change-Into-Something-Sexy-for-my-Real-Date Date."

The date went off magically. Christie may or may not have rolled her eyes at the comedy club when I told the ticket taker, "Yes, I'm Bryan Bishop, and [dramatic pause] *we're on the list.*" But it went great. We even went for an impromptu cocktail after the comedy club, making it an eight-hour date. It also set things up perfectly for a second date, which Christie agreed to.

I was convinced that Christie and I should start dating regularly (she had mixed feelings). Every couple has to face a few milestones before they can move on to the next step in their relationship: first road trip (more on that later), first fight (*much* more on that later), and first casual date. Just hanging out. But not the movie date from college that was really more of a "Hey, wanna watch half of this movie before I try to reach up your blouse?" kind of date. No, this casual date had to be a little more planned out.

---

[35] Calm down, MADD. Coffee and bottled water count, too.

Fortunately, we both had a common (casual) love: USC football. Not that our love of the Trojans was casual, but we could love our team while *being* casual. During the week, Fox Sports Net ran a program called *Trojan Rewind*, which consisted of sideline footage from the previous week's game, as well as interviews, behind-the-scenes clips, and more. It was basically USC football porn. So we set up a midweek dinner date at my apartment that included Tito's Tacos (an LA institution), Shiner Bock beer (because I knew she had lived in Dallas), and a recorded episode of *Trojan Rewind*. This was a make-or-break date for us because this is what I *liked* to do. Too many relationships are built on the faulty foundation of someone (usually the guy) pretending to be someone he's not, or pretending to like things that he hates, or vice versa. You can always tell who these guys are by how quickly they respond to emails about poker night. If they eagerly reply "Yes!" before you've even let go of the send button, then they've got a problem on their hands. If they forget to even respond, then they're in a good relationship. Or they're a sociopath. Or both.

The casual date went great. Oh, sure, there was a chink or two in the armor; Christie, for example, considered Shiner Bock to be "fancy beer." To me, it's okay, but far from fancy. I found out that her beer of choice was Miller Lite. You will probably think I'm joking, but this was nearly a deal-breaker for me. In the business world, this is called a fireable offense. Thankfully, I broke her of this habit, and our relationship blossomed.

Just to be fair, here are the top habits Christie says she's glad she broke me of:

1. *Fifty percent off happy-hour sushi*—"Hey, you've saved yourself a few bucks. Use it to pay your food-poisoning hospital bill."

2. *Wearing ringer T's*—"People your age wore other age-appropriate things, like button-downs or polo shirts. You had [and still have] a rainbow of ringer T's in every color combination known to man."

3. *Eating cold cuts from the 99-cent store*—"I didn't even know they sold food at the 99-cent store, let alone that anyone would buy processed meat for ninety-nine cents. Needless to say, I broke you of that habit immediately. It was for your own safety, really."

In all seriousness, none of these things were potential deal-breakers for me. I only cared about the beer thing in a half-joking way. I was so into Christie that she could have preferred shotgunning Franzia straight out of the box and I probably wouldn't have cared. In reality, there were only two things about any potential girlfriend that I really cared about: If she came from a good family, and if she was polite to restaurant servers. At dinner on our first date, Christie was exceedingly gracious to our server, saying, "Thank you," each time she refilled our water and listening attentively as she described the specials. That's how you can tell a lot about a person's character: how they treat people who are in a subservient role to them. If they ignore them, make unreasonable requests, or—even worse—act rude, save yourself a ton of time and headache and just break it off right there.

Christie also came from a fantastic family. I finally met them after we'd been dating for a couple of months, and I breathed a massive sigh of relief when they turned out to be not only normal, but also pretty great people. Her parents, Don and Sheryl, had been married since 1976. They had two children: Christie and her younger brother, Christopher, who was still in college when I met him. Yes, you read that right. Chris and Christie. Brother and sister. It's not even as if the whole family has C-names. As I said, their parents are Don and Sheryl. I've asked Don and Sheryl before what the hell is up with their kids' names, and they say that they loved the name Christopher and wanted to give the name to their first child, but when it turned out to be a girl, they settled on Christie. Oh. Well, that explains it.

Most couples have an amusing story about their first fight. They also usually have a delightful anecdote about the first time they told each other "I love you." Our two stories happen to be the same. I was hanging out with my friend John and his sister, who was in town from Missouri. For some reason, she wanted to see a taping of *The Tonight Show with Jay Leno.* This sounded like a massive pain in the ass for several reasons. I was not a fan of *The Tonight Show.* It was located on the other side of town. It was approaching rush hour. There was no parking lot—just street parking. It was hot as hell that day in Los Angeles, and you have to stand in line outside (sometimes for hours) just to get tickets.

But we went anyway and had an average time. Afterward, the plan was to meet up with Christie, who had a regular nine-to-five job and couldn't meet us until later that evening. So we went out for dinner directly after the taping. As we sat down to dinner, Christie called. I told her we were just about to eat and she was welcome to come join us; we'd save her a seat. Apparently this was the wrong answer, and she replied with something snippy like "Whatever, I'll just meet you guys after." So we had our dinner, then went to the pre-arranged bar to meet up with Christie.

Let's just say things were awkward. Christie was pissed that I hadn't waited for her to get off work to eat dinner. Her point (which was fair) was that waiting wouldn't have made much of a difference for us, timewise, but she was starving and definitely wanted to join us for dinner. So by the time she showed up at the Mexican bar, Cabo Cantina, she was starving *and* furious. Not a good combo! I suggested she order something off of Cabo Cantina's menu. Residents of Los Angeles are laughing as they read this because Cabo Cantina is not a place you order food from unless/until you're *really* drunk. Which she wasn't. Things got worse from there, until Christie basically said, "Whatever, I'm going home to get some real food." I walked her to her car, which was parked on Wilshire Boulevard, one of the busiest streets in LA. I asked her what was wrong, and she laid it all out. She finished with something to the effect of "Damn it, Bryan, I love you!" I was taken aback. I was *not* ready for the L-word, but she hit me with it the way Michael Jackson hit the *Motown 25* audience with the moonwalk for the first time. *Whoa, where the hell did that come from?!* My response was straight out of the "what *not* to say when your girlfriend says 'I love you' for the first time" playbook:

"I . . . I L you," I stammered.

L. Not *love.* The letter *L.* I'm not sure why I thought saying "I L you" would be more appropriate than admitting, yes, I indeed loved her, too, but let's just say there's a reason Hallmark hasn't come out with a line of "I L you" greeting cards. Something in my primitive, drunk, self-preserving brain told me, "Don't be a fool and say you *love* her! Think about what that could *mean*!"[36]

I don't even remember how we made up. I'm sure it involved a heartfelt apology on my part. The truth was, I did love Christie. I knew my days of looking for the perfect woman were over. Deep down, every guy secretly loves the Quest. We've been trained our whole lives to seek out the One; our soul mate; the person we were meant to be with. We're defined by it—the way we dress, the way we shave, the car we drive, going to parties, going to bars, rom-coms, ballads . . . everything in our adult lives is in some way tied to the mythical pursuit of finding the perfect partner. So when you find the perfect person—as I did with Christie—the feeling is a little scary. I remember specifically thinking after only a couple of dates, "Well, the search is over." But "the search is over" doesn't sound that romantic. What I should have said right there, on Wilshire Boulevard, across the street from Cabo Cantina, was "I love you, too."

Beyond the obvious (marriage), this story has a happy ending: We both eventually had such a laugh over "I L you" that we started to use it as our shorthand for "I love you." Even today, we'll text each other *ILU* or sign off chat sessions with it. I sign almost all of my cards to

---

[36] Here is Christie's version of the events of that night: "I was pissed because I was starving and you told me you'd all wait to eat with me. But then you all ate, didn't tell me, and *then* didn't tell me which bar you were going to, and I was driving around aimlessly and couldn't get in touch with you. You then forced my hand at Cabo Cantina. After we were done, you and I went to eat at Wahoo's Tacos—I did *not* storm out and say I was going home to get 'real food.' That's a lie. We ate at Wahoo's and you didn't understand why I was mad about you eating without me. One topic turned into another, and finally it was about the fact that we had been dating for five months and you hadn't said 'I love you' yet. So I blurted it out instead and you responded with 'ILU.'"

Christie with *ILU* at the end. It's one of the thousands of reasons I love her: because she can take an awkward situation and turn it into one of our favorite inside jokes.

December 2007. Christie and I were on vacation in Big Bear, California. A fresh show had fallen overnight, so I woke up early and scrawled our new favorite inside joke on the porch. *(Bryan Bishop)*

The next gauntlet we had to face: our first road trip. Everyone travels differently. Taking a road trip when you've just started dating is like hooking your relationship up to an EKG: You'll find out pretty quickly how much stress it can take. The only thing worse is traveling internationally with another couple.[37]

So we did what everyone in Los Angeles does for a road trip: We drove to Las Vegas. The only catch: I was relatively poor. Certainly much poorer than a twenty-eight-year-old working in the entertainment industry should have been. But I was still committed to having a fun time in Las Vegas. Adam Carolla would often ask (yell at) me,

---

[37] DON'T DO IT. EVER.

"How do you afford such an extravagant lifestyle on such a meager paycheck?!" First of all, the joke's on you, buddy, because you're the one who's paying me. Second, I do it two ways: keep a low overhead and always be on the lookout for a great deal.

Here's what I mean by low overhead: I shared a modest apartment with a buddy from college. We got a decent amount of space for a relatively low rent. The catch? The apartment building was on Washington Boulevard, a major street in Los Angeles, bordered by a Laundromat on one side, a 99-cent store on the other, and resting on top of a liquor store that was so expensive my roommate and I called it the INconvenience Store. Here's how you know it was expensive: We were two ex-frat guys from USC living literally on top of a liquor store and *we hardly ever went there.*

I also drove a cheap car (or truck, as it were): a 2000 Chevy Silverado 1500 . . . short cab, of course. That way I never got roped into driving my friends around for a night on the town.[38] It was a decent truck, certainly better than I could normally have afforded. But I bought it used from a family friend who was an electrician and owned a fleet of them. Every few years, he'd buy a bunch of new trucks and update his work fleet. Then he'd take pity on me and sell me a used one for well below market value. For me, this was the perfect marriage of "low overhead" and "looking out for a great deal."

Vegas presented another opportunity for a great deal: My college buddy Todd lived in Vegas. His family owned a penthouse condo at the top of the MGM Signature towers that they rarely used. I stayed there with him once and it was tremendous. His offer: Stay here anytime you like. *Anytime* turned out to be "this weekend, when I'm trying to impress this girl named Christie." So it was settled: We were going to take my cheap truck on a road trip to my friend's free room in Las Vegas.

This would be our second trip to Las Vegas together, and our first one that we took alone. A few months earlier, *The Adam Carolla Show*

---

[38] I did move more than my fair share of futons, though, so it probably evened out in the karma department.

had done a live broadcast from the Palms Hotel, and Christie had flown out to join me for the weekend. On that trip I'd attempted to introduce her to the game of blackjack. What ensued is a never-ending source of amusement for me, and a long-running inside joke for Christie and me.

It was a weekend, so the lowest limits we could find in Las Vegas were $10-minimum-bet tables. Three things you need to know about Christie: First, she is very smart. So the basic rules of the game should have posed no problem for her. Second, she earned a comfortable income at the time, so $10 per bet did not present an astronomical amount for her to wager. Third, she is *extremely* risk-averse when it comes to games of chance, especially if she can potentially lose money. I only knew about the first two things.

We sat down at the blackjack table, and of course we lose our first couple of hands. Christie wins her next few hands, at which point she turns to me and whispers, "Let's leave now!" I looked at her stack of chips; she was up maybe $10. Maybe. I laughed and said no, we'd play a little more. We played for about thirty minutes, never winning or losing much either way. After about half an hour, I can tell Christie is getting increasingly agitated, so we collect our chips and head to another table. By this point, Christie has had enough of gambling. I play for a little while longer, but as anyone knows, it's not fun when your girlfriend (or boyfriend or whoever) is standing behind you not playing. You feel bad. So we went to the cashier, cashed in our chips, and headed back to the room.

Once we get back to the room, Christie (who, full disclosure, may have had a cocktail or two) collapsed to the ground in tears. Shocked, I knelt down to console her. "What's wrong?" I asked, concerned.

She sniffled. "I lost fourteen dollars!" she cried.

It probably didn't help that I exploded into laughter. "You make six figures!" I exclaimed. "You drank fifty dollars' worth of free cocktails while you played! You *spent* fourteen dollars. Think of it that way!"

She was inconsolable. Eventually she calmed down and I convinced her to see the hilarity in the situation. I'm happy to report now, years later, Christie has advanced into the ranks of intermediate gambler. On a recent work trip to Las Vegas, she even played blackjack *on her own*! (dramatic music sting). I know she played on her own because she called me from the casino floor, saying, "Okay, I'm standing near a blackjack table. . . . I think I'm going to go play. . . . God, I'm so nervous. . . . Okay, I can do this . . . [deep breath] . . ." And you know what? She won $100. I've created a monster.

So a few months after my work trip to Vegas, Christie and I said, "You know what? We had so much fun out there doing the live radio show, let's go again, but just us this time!" And as I said, we decided to make it our first road trip together. The drive from my apartment to the MGM is a 282-mile, four-and-a-half-hour trek through mostly desert. The scene in *Swingers* where Mikey and Trent drive to Vegas is funny for a reason: It's true. You start out with piss and vinegar, singing along with the radio, making plans for how you're going to spend your winnings. Smash cut to three hours later, and you're adrift in an ocean of sand, static on the radio, and your buddy passed out in the passenger seat.

Luckily, God (or, if you're a tech nerd, your version of God, Steve Jobs) blessed us with the iPod,[39] so we were all set with my custom playlist (more on these in a later chapter). Plus, it was supposed to reach a toasty 108 degrees in Las Vegas that week—perfect for roasting by the pool.

We were a half hour into our journey—literally, we had just gotten out of downtown LA—when I noticed the air-conditioning was putting out warm air. I cranked it up a couple of notches, but all that came out was more warm air. We had a problem.

A normal person would have turned his truck around and said to Christie, "We're taking your car." But I was determined to take Christie on a date. And what kind of a date is it when the guy says with his tail between his legs, "I guess we have to take your car . . .

---

[39] Jobs 3:16—"For God so loved the world, He gave them His only begotten MP3 player, and whosoever listeneth shall not have to put up with annoying radio DJs, but shall have everlasting music."

you know, if that's okay?" So I broke the news to her that the AC seems to have stopped working. And here's where I fell in love with Christie a little more: She said, "Okay, no big deal!" and rolled her window down. I know plenty of girls (certainly none of *my* friends' wives) who would have said, "Oh, hell no" or "Drop me off at the next bus stop." But not Christie. Determined to have a good time, she soldiered on, despite the oppressive triple-digit heat. And it was oppressive; at one point we both leaned forward to let the hot outside air rush in and dry our sweaty backs.

When we got to Vegas, I dropped my car off at a mechanic's and asked them to fix the air-conditioning for our drive home. I don't remember why, but they were unable to fix it in time, so we had no choice but to drive back home a few days later with no AC. We decided to wait until nightfall to make the trek, since the temperatures had "dropped" to a brisk eighty-eight degrees. And you know what? We both laughed about it. The whole way home, we joked about the absurdity of it all. How we had to let the hot outside air dry the sweat off our shirts. How we had to walk across a mile of 108-degree Las Vegas blacktop from the mechanic's to the Wynn hotel. And how we tried to seek shelter from the heat by ducking into the Wynn's employee entrance, only to be turned away, back into the Las Vegas midday heat, once we couldn't produce our employee badges.

Not long after, the decision was made to move in together. The only question was, my place or hers? We both lived in two-bedroom apartments in Los Angeles, about seven miles away from each other. Both apartments offered pros and cons.

The biggest thing working in Christie's favor was that her apartment was in a better part of town. It was across the street from a park, a block away from two major streets. Also, she lived alone in a two-bedroom apartment, so there was ostensibly room for me to move in right away.

However, since she lived in a nicer section of Los Angeles, her rent was more expensive than mine. Plus the building's physical structure left something to be desired. Christie would tell anyone who listened, "If there's a major earthquake here in LA, come to our apartment first because the building will have collapsed on us and we'll be buried beneath the rubble." Worth considering.

My apartment was significantly cheaper, plus the landlord was great, a jovial guy named Frank who only ever wanted to talk movies when he came by. Landlords of cheap apartment complexes in Los Angeles will do whatever repairs they can do themselves to save a nickel, but Frank was actually a capable handyman, so repairs got taken care of quickly and efficiently. Also, the building was more aesthetically pleasing.

The eight-unit complex had a little courtyard, with a big, lush tree, which was used almost every weekend for a Mexican *quinceañera*. A *quinceañera* is basically the Mexican culture's equivalent to our sweet-sixteen party. Judging by the ten thousand *quinceañeras* that took place in my apartment complex's courtyard during the eight years that I lived there, here's how one goes: The girl gets dolled up in an ill-fitting hand-me-down pink dress while her older relatives drink cheap Mexican beer out of twelve-packs and her cousins/siblings/amigos run around screaming until the man with the hot-corn cart[40] shows up selling cobs of corn smothered in mayonnaise.

Also, it was located directly on Washington Boulevard, one of the busiest streets in the city. Also, I had a roommate who hadn't exactly planned on moving out. And there was an alley in back where drunk men liked to throw up in the morning. And there was no dishwasher. And there was no laundry. But did I mention the rent was cheap?

Astoundingly, Christie actually considered moving to my place. (I fooled—err, convinced—her by saying, "With rent so cheap, we can save money for a house!") It nearly worked, but one morning she woke up from a night spent at my place and got ready to leave for the gym (I was already at the radio show). It was 5:45 a.m. and still dark outside. She walked through the Alley Where Men Vomited to get to

---

[40] You read that right. In LA we don't have ice-cream trucks, we have men in cowboy hats who push around carts full of hot corn. Tinseltown, ladies and gentlemen! The place where dreams are made!

her car and encountered a staggering, drunk man who was bleeding from the head. I know what you're thinking: "How do you *know* he was drunk?" Fair enough. The possibility exists that he wasn't drunk (he wouldn't submit to a Breathalyzer test), but he was definitely bleeding. In his defense, Christie says he was friendly (apparently he smiled at her[41] as she scurried past him). But it was the straw that broke the *burro's* back. No way was Christie moving into my neighborhood now.

So I packed up my things and moved into Christie's apartment. In retrospect, this was a wise decision. It was a slightly better place in a much better neighborhood. Plus, given everything I was about to go through healthwise, it offered a few distinct advantages. But more on that in a future chapter.

Over the next few months, our relationship blossomed. Everything in my life, it seemed, got better once we fell in love. In Christie, I had finally found a partner who complemented me perfectly, who improved upon all of my weaknesses. For example, I wasn't blessed with natural business acumen and I'm a generally poor negotiator; Christie has a master's degree from Northwestern in integrated marketing and has great business instincts. When we met, Christie had a near-perfect credit score, but I had no idea what mine was or even how to check it. Christie helped me open a couple of credit cards to improve my score. She did such a good job that we recently discovered—to her horror and my delight—that my credit score is actually now higher than hers.

Once we had lived together for a while, the talk turned to marriage. Honestly, I don't even know if there was ever a discussion of "Should we get married?" It was more like "When do we get married?" Little was ever forced with Christie and me. In fact, I'm pretty sure we hired a wedding planner and picked a date before I even bought a ring and popped the question.[42]

---

[41] I'm putting the over/under on the total number of teeth this guy had at 7.5.

[42] The question being "Why the hell did you pick out such an expensive ring?"

I proposed in Napa Valley, in the heart of California's wine country. Christie had taken me up there for my thirtieth birthday, but I decided to turn the tables on her and propose. One night, after a long day of wine tasting, I decided the moment was perfect. I snuck out to the trunk of my car and retrieved a Sharpie and a champagne cork from a bottle we'd drunk earlier that day. Around the base of the cork, I wrote the words *Will you marry me?* Then I went back inside and got ready to spring my trap.

The cork. *(Bryan Bishop)*

Only, during the time I had been outside, Christie had changed into her pajamas (sweatpants and an old, gray Northwestern T-shirt) and was reading the sports section of *USA Today* on the bed. "Ugh," she said, "I feel terrible. Too much wine and champagne."

So the moment was perfect.

"Hey," I said, examining the cork I had just written on, "there's something written on this cork."

"Really?"

"Yep. Somebody wrote something on the bottom. Check it out."

I lobbed the cork to her across the room, underhanded. Later, this story would become twisted as "He *threw* a cork at me!" But, no, I *gently* lobbed the cork (again, underhand) at her. Besides, I needed to fish the actual engagement ring out of the pair of dress shoes I had hidden it in.

Christie read the cork: "It says, 'Will you marry . . .'" She trailed off. She looked at me, then back at the cork. An honest-to-goodness double take. By this time, I had the ring in my hand and was approaching the bed where she was sitting. She squealed—no joke, an actual squeal—and hid under the covers. Yes, this was her reaction to an imminent proposal of marriage: She hid.

Christie, newly engaged, in her pajamas, on the bed, with a ring box on one side and a copy of *USA Today* on the other. Her mom is on the phone. *(Bryan Bishop)*

She threw back the covers. I was already on one knee. "I know most people say, 'Will you make me the happiest man on earth and marry me?'" I said. "But the truth is, you've already made me the happiest man on earth. So all that's left to say is, will you marry me?"[43]

I must have done it right because Christie was crying and shaking. (Either that, or I did it *horribly* wrong.) Either way, she said yes. She called her parents right away, but since we were seeing my family the next day, we decided to wait and surprise them with the news personally.

We were engaged. My brother and his fiancée were getting married a month after us. We had great jobs that we loved. I was going to be a contestant on *Who Wants to Be a Millionaire* at the end of the month. The year 2008 had treated us well, and 2009 was shaping up to be the Year of Bryan & Christie.

---

[43] Fellas, I made all that mushy BS up for the ladies who are reading this book. What I really said was "Marry me, ho. Or don't. Like I give a shit."

4.

Signs of Trouble

or, "Christie, I'm Sick"

For the first few months, whenever I told anyone that I had been diagnosed with a brain tumor, their first question would invariably be "How did you know?" or "What were your first symptoms?" I suspect they were really asking, "Holy crap, could this be happening to me and I don't even know it?!" But I answered their questions anyway; I told them it came on subtly. In late 2008, I was working for *The Adam Carolla Show*, which at that point was a syndicated morning radio show. The show started live at 6:00 a.m., which meant I usually got there a little before five thirty. For most of the year, the sun hadn't risen by the time I arrived at work. Think about how depressing that is and what kind of spiritual toll that takes on your soul. I was speaking with another morning-show DJ who'd been doing it longer than I had at the time. I asked him how he dealt with the hours; his response: "I've been tired for ten years." What kind of way is that for a person to live? It was a dream job, but the early call time was the only part of the job I hated. Well, that and the radio station's incompetent management. But I'll get into that later.

No, wait, let's get into it now. If you ran CBS Radio or KLSX-FM 97.1 in Los Angeles between 2006 and 2009 and you think you're getting off easy in this book, you've got another think coming.[44] My

---

[44] Why do so many people think it's "You've got another *thing* coming?" That doesn't even make any sense. Yet I see it all the time. I blame Judas Priest.

next book will be all about the inept boobs who ran the station at the time, so I won't take up ten-thousand words describing them here. But our program director (a reprehensible ass named Jack Silver) actually kept a pair of binoculars on his desk so he could spy on attractive women who walked outside his corner office.[45] I wish I were making this up. There will be much more on Jack in a future chapter, but for now, here's all you need to know about the sociopaths I worked with: When I got diagnosed with brain cancer, I got emails and phone calls and text messages from just about every friend and acquaintance I'd ever made, most of whom said something super simple like "Hey, buddy, thinking of you." Guess how many of my former coworkers at KLSX reached out to me to see how they could help, or just to say hi? If you guessed a number other than zero, maybe *you* should get checked for a brain tumor.[46]

I had a food routine for the mornings: on the drive to the studio (around 5:15 a.m.), I had a granola bar out of a box I kept behind my front seat. This was my "breakfast." (Are you jealous of the glamorous morning-radio lifestyle now, kids?) By the time the show was half-over (around 8:00 a.m.), I'd need a snack. So I kept a box of Clif Bars in my "office" (really an office belonging to two other guys that I was allowed to have a desk drawer in . . . yep, some guys have all the luck). At a certain point, I began to feel the tiniest bit of numbness on the right side of my lips whenever I would eat the Clif Bar, at which I thought, "Aw, crap, am I allergic to Clif Bars now?" One day, they announced a recall of Clif Bars because of some tainted ingredient. I thought maybe I had gotten a bad batch. I even looked it up on the Internet, but no dice. My bars were not the ones recalled. I chalked it up to being tired. And the truth was, I *was* tired. So it was easily explained away.

That's how it was for all of my symptoms. There was always an explanation. For example, another routine I had was going to the gym every day after work. The gym was located across the street from the

---

[45] This actually happened. *During meetings.*

[46] This doesn't include the staff of *The Adam Carolla Show*. Those guys were (and are) all really supportive.

radio station, and we got a corporate discount. Plus my workday was usually over by ten thirty, so hitting the gym at 11:00 a.m. was an ideal time. It was usually pretty empty. It was also located on the ground floor of a building that was home to such television shows as *The Soup*, *Family Guy*, and *Attack of the Show*. I don't know if it was a celebrity gym or not because there were never any celebrities there. Actually, that's not true. The bald guy from ABC's *Cougar Town* went there almost every day. So maybe it was a "bald celebrity" gym. But I'll tell you who *did* go there: old men. Lots of them. The thing about old men in the gym locker room: they have no shame and *lots* of free time. This is a bad combination for someone such as me who doesn't want to see a ton of eighty-year-old sack. Yet there they'd stand, balls flapping in the breeze, chatting away (usually about politics, for some reason). I saw more old-man junk there than a urologist in Boca Raton.

Occasionally, I'd jump rope at the gym. One day, I was having a ton of trouble clearing the rope whenever I tried to jump. The rope would keep catching on my left foot. Over and over I'd only be able to get in about four or five clean jumps before I'd step on the rope. Eventually, I got frustrated and moved on to the rowing machine. But I remember thinking, "Hm, that was weird." Another time, I was getting a private training session, which included a running portion on the treadmill. Only I kept stepping off the running surface and had to grab the bars and steady myself. The trainer awkwardly said something to the effect of "Um, why don't we move on to the medicine ball." But again, I was concerned.

You might be saying, "How could you not notice these warning signs?!" First of all, stop talking out loud; this is a book. People are going to stare. Second, all of this would always happen at the *end* of one of my workouts, which I explained to myself as "Oh, I'm just working out too hard" or "I'm not drinking enough water at the gym." To wit, on most days I would hit either the sauna or the steam room after I was done in the gym.[47] It got to the point where I was

---

[47] Old Man Sack Central, by the way.

getting light-headed after exiting the heat and returning to normal temperatures. More than once I had to steady myself walking to the showers. But again, this was easily explained. I was just spending too much time in the sauna, I told myself. It was a reasonable explanation.

The thing that tipped me off the most was what happened when I would drink. Early on, I would get a little clumsy when I would drink. Once, Christie and I were having dinner at a friend's house when a rousing game of Rock Band broke out. I was shredding a particularly wild guitar solo (probably Motorhead's "Ace of Spades") when I took one false step backward and fell into their fireplace. Luckily it wasn't lit, and we all had a good drunken laugh over it. Another time, we were visiting my parents for Christmas, and after a couple of cocktails we adjourned to the living room to open presents. I went to step over a pile of gifts and promptly ended up on my ass on the floor. Everyone had a good laugh and said, "Ha, ha, look how drunk Bryan is!" Only I wasn't *that* drunk.[48]

It was around this time that I started to quietly look for a neurologist. All of these "little" symptoms had me freaked out. Plus the numbness in my lips had now spread to other parts of my face and scalp. I looked up my symptoms on WebMD.com and every possible diagnosis came back brain-related: stroke, TIA (transient ischemic attack; basically a ministroke), or multiple sclerosis. In the back of my mind, my worst fear was that I had the early symptoms of ALS, or Lou Gehrig's disease. Although the symptoms weren't a total match, I was still fearful. A few months earlier, an older cousin of mine had been diagnosed with ALS. He was a newlywed in his late thirties, and his diagnosis had hit my family pretty hard. ALS is, in my opinion, the cruelest disease. At least with cancer, there's a glimmer of hope. You can come up with a game plan and you can fight. ALS is terminal. In all cases. Nobody has ever beaten ALS. I don't say this to be callous or melo-

---

[48] It's hard to convince people you're not drunk. Especially if they're drunk themselves. The only thing harder is trying to talk your way out of a mental hospital. "I swear, I'm not crazy!" "Whatever you say, Napoléon."

dramatic; indeed, I saw its effects up close. Worst of all, it affects only the body, so as people become progressively and inevitably more paralyzed, they are keenly aware of everything that is happening to them. Think about that: You are 100 percent aware of your own paralysis. The pall of my cousin's diagnosis and prognosis—basically, certain death—still hung over my entire extended family. While ALS isn't known to be hereditary, it was an obvious concern. So I started researching neurologists online. And by *researching*, I mean "looking under *neurologists* on my health insurer's Web site."

> Here's my first **Tumor Tip** of the book: If you suspect you might have a serious illness and you need to see a specialist, don't look one up on the Internet. If you go to specialists' Web sites (either personal or one through their hospital), you're only going to find information on how amazing they are—awards, degrees, etc. If you go on a Web site that allows patients to review (read "bitch about") doctors, you're only going to find insane complaints ("He sewed my urethra shut!"). Your best resource is your friends and family. Ask around for recommendations. I didn't do this. I picked a few off the health insurer's Web site and called their offices. Because I didn't have a referral, none of them would see me for months. Literally, months. Finally I found one that could see me at the end of April. It was still March.

One Friday, a few weeks later (April 10, 2009), I went with Christie to her office. It was her last day; she'd been laid off earlier that week—a victim of the struggling economy.[49] She had to drop off her work laptop, and afterward, we headed to my friends Kyle and Catie's house for a few beers in the afternoon. This was pretty light drinking—two or three Bud Lights over the course of a few hours. Despite the fact that I'd only had a couple of light beers, I was *hammered*. When I got up off

---

[49] Christie's client was a private-jet company. Not a great industry to be in when the economy is collapsing.

the couch to use the restroom, I promptly fell over. But I had drunk the same amount as everyone else and they were all fine. We decided to head out to get something to eat just a few blocks away, but I was a mess. Christie had to help me walk down the street. Once we got there, I tried to engage everyone in normal conversation, but I couldn't get the words out properly. Frustrated, I shut down and focused on eating my pulled-pork sandwich with a fork (or trying to, at least). Halfway into dinner, our buddy Sean showed up straight from work. After a few minutes he looked around the table and said, pointing at everyone else, "You're sober, you're sober, and you're sober." Then, pointing at me: "How'd you get so drunk?" Everyone laughed—"Ha ha, Bryan's so drunk!" But again, I hadn't drunk *that* much. Certainly not enough to warrant the state I was in.

Christie drove us home (obviously). When we got home, I had "sobered up," and we were both lying on the couch, commiserating about our unemployment. I knew the time had come to tell her that something was up with me, healthwise. But how? Sugarcoat it? Undersell it? Even I didn't know what was wrong with me. Eventually, I just settled on the direct approach:

"Christie, something's wrong. I'm sick."

She sat up. "What do you mean 'sick'?"

I explained my symptoms. I explained how I wasn't that drunk tonight. I explained everything.

"How long have you had these symptoms?"

"I'm not sure. They're all pretty subtle. The earliest I can remember is around Christmas."

"*Christmas?!*" she shouted.

"It's okay, I've been doing some research online." I shared what I'd found online. Big mistake. Apparently hearing that your thirty-year-old fiancé may have MS or may have suffered a stroke is alarming to some people.

"Don't worry, I've already made an appointment with a neurologist," I said proudly.

"Thank God. When is it?"

"April twenty-ninth." Almost three weeks later.

What happened next . . . Look, it's not important *how* angry Christie got. The point is that, yes, she *was* angry. She immediately called Hutch—Dr. Bill Hutchinson, a family friend. Dr. Hutchinson was a top surgeon at St. John's medical center in nearby Santa Monica. Surely he would know someone he could refer us to who specialized in neurology. Sure enough, Hutch knew someone: a kindly, old neurologist whom I'll call Dr. Schwartz. He had been around for a few years, Bill said, but he was a good doctor and well respected. Bill offered to call Schwartz's office in the morning and personally make an appointment for us. We accepted thankfully.

"Thank God for Hutch," Christie said.

"Yeah," I sighed.

Our appointment with Dr. Schwartz was scheduled for two days later. Leo J. Schwartz is old-school. Literally. He graduated from the University of Kentucky in 1964. For historical perspective, that's two years *before* Pat Riley (yes, the same Pat Riley who coached Magic Johnson's Lakers in the 1980s) was an all-American at Kentucky under Adolph Rupp.[50] Schwartz is what NBA announcers would refer to as "a cagey veteran." But he certainly didn't lack for experience. His office was small—tiny, in fact—with just him and his one (equally old-school) secretary, who typed up all of his medical notes on a manual typewriter. That's how you know people are old-school: They don't have a *receptionist*, they have a *secretary*. Let me tell you, when you're nervous upon entering a doctor's office, the staccato clicking-and-clacking of a manual typewriter in the background will put you right at ease.

Dr. Schwartz began with (what I would later realize is) the standard barrage of first-time questions for a patient: How old was I? Was I a smoker? And most important, how long had I been having these symptoms?

---

[50] Adolph Rupp's best player in 1964? Cotton Nash. That's right, Kentucky had a coach named Adolph and a star player named Cotton. Something tells me we won't be seeing this combination again in major college sports.

> **Tumor Tip:** If you're being diagnosed with cancer (or any serious illness), chances are you're being shuttled from doctor to doctor, hospital to hospital. Doctors are supposed to share medical records on a patient, but it doesn't always work out so smoothly. My advice: Always be ready with a timeline and description of your symptoms (as well as a list of any previous doctors you've seen). Write it down and print it out if you have to. You could even send it to their office ahead of time so the doctor can review it. It'll save time, it'll prevent mistakes ("I think that was a month ago . . . maybe two . . ."), and it'll save you the headache of answering the same questions over and over.

He put me through a battery of simple tests: I followed his pen with my eyes, I touched my nose, I lifted my leg while he tried to hold it down. Finally, he asked me to walk across the room, heel to toe. I stumbled and lost my balance on the second step. He said, "Thank you, that's enough," and began writing in his notes. Christie broached the elephant in the room (for us, anyway).

"Doctor, Bryan has a family history of ALS. His cousin was just diagnosed. Is there any chance . . . ?" She couldn't even get out the words.

"No. This is not ALS," he assured us. "I think you have multiple sclerosis."

This was probably the first time in history a young couple were relieved to learn that one of them might have MS. MS is a degenerative disease where the lining (myelin) of the nerves in your brain wears away (demyelination), and you have strokelike symptoms similar to mine. But with medication, an MS patient can potentially live a seminormal life, depending on what type of MS he or she has (there are four kinds, we learned through our research). People live with MS. People don't live with ALS.

"Is there anything else it could be?" I asked. "We found a few other possibilities online. TIA, stroke . . ."

"Not really." He told us he wanted me to get an MRI right away. The scan would tell him exactly what was wrong in my brain, and how far the demyelination had gotten. Then, he said, he would put me on a steady dose of steroids and go from there.

The MRI went smoothly. I remember little about it, other than thinking, "Thank Christ, finally some tests!" I was probably glad to know the doctor had an idea of what the hell was wrong with me. Christie (who came to every appointment with me) and I left the building hand in hand. Her layoff had just taken effect. We were young, engaged, and unemployed and had recently been informed that one of us had a potentially life-threatening illness. So we did what anyone in our situation would do.

We drove to Vegas.

We needed to blow off some steam; to sit by the pool and relax and contemplate a future that might or might not include a debilitating disease. We had no income, but because certain hotels considered me a gambling "enthusiast," we were comped a room at Treasure Island. We spent the whole first day at the pool, where I got another reminder that my physical abilities were being compromised. When I went to get out of the pool, I would forgo the stairs and just lift myself onto the edge of the pool and get out that way. Only I couldn't lift my left leg high enough to clear the concrete lip of the pool, so I scraped and bruised my leg each time getting out. By the end of the weekend, my left shin was so covered in cuts and discolorations, it looked like a Rorschach test.

Christie's younger brother, Christopher, had nothing to do that weekend, and we had a free room, so we invited him to drive out to join us for a night. Our ulterior motive was to tell him the news about my impending diagnosis. He would be a test case, we figured, of how our family and friends might react to the news. The night he arrived, we sat him down in the room and told him we had some serious news.

"Bryan hasn't been feeling well lately," Christie explained. "We've seen a doctor and taken some tests, and it looks like Bryan may have MS." We paused for Chris's reaction.

"Okay." He shrugged.

We explained that, best-case scenario, I'd be on medication for the rest of my life to try to control the symptoms. We asked him if he had any questions or concerns.

"Not really. You look fine, and if they're going to put you on medication, then . . . What are you gonna do?" he asked rhetorically.

Christie and I looked at each other: What *were* we gonna do? Christopher had the right reaction; there's not much you *can* do, outside of the obvious, so why worry? We laughed at his nonreaction to our "news," then we headed out to dinner.

We drove home from Vegas the next day. A short time later, we got a call from Dr. Schwartz; he had seen the results of my MRI. "You don't have MS," he told me. "But I need to see you in my office first thing tomorrow morning."

Our initial reaction was "Yeah, Bryan doesn't have MS!"—followed by "Wait, why does the doctor need to see us right away?" We were more confused than worried.

5.

Diagnosis

or, "Whatever You Do, Don't Google *Low-Grade Glioma*"

We somehow made it through the next day. Looking back, the anticipation of our appointment with Dr. Schwartz should have killed us. We were about to get the results of an MRI test that would finally tell us what the hell had been going wrong with me. But we were probably just too tired from the emotional roller coaster of anticipation/ prediagnosis/acceptance/misdiagnosis. Getting diagnosed for a serious illness is sometimes not so much about pinpointing what's wrong, but eliminating what *isn't* wrong.

Dr. Schwartz had eliminated multiple sclerosis. That was the good news. But what was left? Had I had a stroke? Something worse? Did I have some brain-eating disease brought on by too much lunch meat consumed from the 99-cent store?

We arrived at Dr. Schwartz's office early in the morning of Thursday, April 23, 2009. The familiar rat-a-tat-tat-tat-*ding!* of his secretary's manual typewriter greeted us as we walked in. We checked in and attempted to distract ourselves by reading the back issues of *Us Weekly* that had gathered on his waiting-room table.[51]

Finally, he calls us in. We sat down. Christie, armed with a pen and

---

[51] Without a doubt, my favorite regular feature in *Us Weekly* is their photo spread "Stars: They're just like us!" It's a handful of photos of celebrities doing "normal" things such as buying gasoline, with captions exclaiming, *They fill up at the pump!* Only in the photo, Justin Timberlake is pumping fuel into his $250,000 Ferrari. Which is *nothing* like "us." Do you have a quarter-million-dollar Italian sports car? Me neither. STFU, *Us Weekly.* Stars are nothing like us.

notebook, was ready to write down everything Dr. Schwartz said. He began to explain that while he initially thought I had multiple sclerosis, I did not. (We were somewhat relieved.) But in the brain-stem, an area where MS typically occurs, was a growth or "lesion."

Christie and I looked at each other: "Lesion?" We weren't sure exactly what he was saying. Dr. Schwartz explained that I had something called a "brain-stem glioma," which sounded far worse when pronounced with his Eastern European accent. Almost like a James Bond villain.[52] We asked the obvious follow-up: "What is a brain-stem glioma?" He kind of chuckled and leaned back in his seat. This wasn't his area of expertise, you see, so he was referring us to his colleague at the Angeles Clinic, who was more of an expert for "these kinds of things." Schwartz had already made an appointment for me, but his colleague couldn't see me until Monday afternoon. It was Thursday.

Now I was really confused. *Angeles Clinic? These types of things? What the hell?* The words *brain tumor* were never used. Nor was the word *cancer*, at least not apropos of my diagnosis. We asked a few more basic questions, but Dr. Schwartz was no help. At one point, he said, "Now, I know how you young people are, but don't go home and look this up on the computer."

You have to know me and (especially) Christie to know how absurd this directive was. Christie's job title was strategic planning director. Basically, she was a professional researcher. She revels in research. Before I even officially proposed to her, for example, she had researched wedding venues, florists, photographers, and a wedding planner. By the time we were engaged, half the wedding was already planned.[53]

After instructing us *not* to look up information on the potentially serious condition he had just informed me that I had, he leaned back in his chair. "Do you have any plans for the weekend?" he asked. "I am going to be pruning my roses."

---

[52] "You've defeated my henchmen, 007, but let's see if you can defeat my *brain-stem glioma*!"

[53] You might think I'm joking, but considering that I was about to be diagnosed with cancer during the planning, it ended up being extremely helpful.

He was trying to make small talk after telling us he was sending me to the specialized glioma center. Christie was aghast. Trying to come up with a possible defense for him in my mind, I assumed Dr. Schwartz had exhausted the extent of his brain-stem-glioma expertise and was trying to change the subject to a more pleasant topic. We wrapped up our appointment, and his secretary handed us the (typewritten, of course) report from the MRI. It concluded:

> IMPRESSION: T2 bright findings expanding the right pons suspicious for low-grade glioma. Demyelinating disease is unlikely to have this appearance. Mild right maxillary sinus mucosal thickening.

We read it over and over on our way home, trying to decipher it. "Demyelinating disease," we figured, was MS. But what the hell did "suspicious for low-grade glioma" mean? Did that mean "we suspect a low-grade glioma"? Or "this is suspicious [read: unusual/atypical] for a low-grade glioma"? We called Hutch and put him on speakerphone in the car so we both could talk to him. His secretary put us straight through to him; he said Schwartz had shared his findings with him and he had been expecting our call.

"How are you holding up?" he asked me specifically. Strangely, this was the first time in this whole ordeal that I had felt panicked. How am I holding up? Is there a reason I shouldn't be holding up fine? Remember, we still didn't understand exactly what a "brain-stem glioma" diagnosis meant. But Hutch obviously did.

"I'm fine, I guess," I told him. "We have an appointment with Dr. Harold Kumar at the Angeles Clinic on Monday."[54]

"I don't know him personally," Hutch said, "but if Schwartz referred you to him, I'm sure he's good."

We ended the call and arrived home. I don't think more than five

---

[54] Obviously, this is not his real name. The publisher's lawyer suggested I change the name. As in, "If you'd like to actually get paid for writing this book, I suggest you change his name."

minutes passed until we were looking up *brain-stem glioma* on the Internet. We quickly saw why Dr. Schwartz had told us not to.

We started reading Wikipedia's entry *Brainstem glioma*. Under "Prognosis" it said:

> Brain-stem glioma is an aggressive and dangerous cancer. Without treatment, the life expectancy is typically a few months from the time of diagnosis. With appropriate treatment, 37% survive more than one year, 20% survive 2 years, and 13% survive 3 years.

Tumor Tip: *Google and the Internet can be your best friend or your worst enemy, depending on you. Your natural inclination (obviously) will be to look up whatever ails you. But keep this in mind as it pertains to statistics: They include everybody. If you run across a statistic that says "80 percent of people with this condition die," remember that everyone is included in that 80 percent. Old people with compromised immune systems. Babies with no immune systems. People who live in remote areas and can't get access to top medical care. People who don't have health insurance and can't get access to top medical care. Religious fanatics who are convinced God will cure them and who don't want access to top medical care. It's a cliché, but it's a cliché for a reason: You are not a statistic. You are you. If you beat cancer, for example, then 100 percent of people in your specific situation beat cancer. Think of it that way.*

You know that feeling when you get really bad news? Your body gets supercold, yet you start to sweat anyway? That's what I felt immediately. Christie sprang into action, like a mom who lifts a car off her infant. "You call the cancer center right now," she said. "You tell them you're coming in there today to see Dr. Harold Kumar."

"But Dr. Schwartz said my appointment was for Monday—"

Christie cut me off. "Right now."[55]

---

[55] Is there any doubt she's going to be a hell of a mother?

I called the cancer center. I explained to the receptionist that, yes, I knew my appointment was for Monday, but it was *really important* that I get in there to see the doctor today. I might have made up something about being out of town on Monday, which wasn't entirely untrue; Christie and I were flying up to the San Francisco Bay Area the next day for a wedding shower that my mom was throwing for Christie, and we were flying back on Monday. So we *would* be out of town, at least for part of Monday.

The receptionist paused. "Can you be here by two thirty?"

We looked at our clock: 2:00. "Absolutely," I told her, and we hurried to our car. Luckily the St. John's Angeles Clinic was only a few miles away, in a nondescript building on Wilshire Boulevard—or at least as nondescript as a giant yellow building can be. As we pulled up to the building at two twenty, we realized that we had driven past it hundreds of times without even knowing what it was. We had suspected it was a condo building or something. And now, we thought, it was about to play a huge role in our lives. Further cementing the irony was the fact that the clinic was located almost directly across the street from Cabo Cantina, the site where Christie had first said, "I love you," to which I had stupidly replied, "I L you." Life sure has a funny way of coming full circle, doesn't it?

We checked in and sat in the waiting room. This was a much different waiting room from Dr. Schwartz's. This was much larger and was filled with cancer patients. Women without hair. Old men in wheelchairs. Middle-aged people walking around, wheeling along their IV drips of chemotherapy. Kids with surgical masks on, so they wouldn't spread (or catch) disease. If you've never been in the waiting room of a cancer center, there's no way to prepare you for it. You can see all the movies in the world made about cancer, but the first time you see a little girl with no hair, wearing a surgical mask, in a wheelchair . . . ugh. Pure, unadulterated pathos.

I don't remember much from the few moments we spent waiting for Dr. Harold Kumar. I do remember thinking, "How the hell did we end up here?" We had gotten the emotional bends from suspecting something was wrong, to thinking it was MS, to being told it wasn't MS, to learning there was some kind of "lesion" where there most certainly *shouldn't* have been a lesion, to now, sitting in the Angeles Clinic, about to be seen by Dr. Harold Kumar, an oncologist. We were emotional putty at this point.

I could wear out the phrase *Thank God for Christie* in this book, but thank God for Christie; she kept an awesome blog during this whole ordeal. I use the word *awesome* in its truest sense; I am in awe of her for how she managed to do it. I merely contributed the title: "An Inconvenient Tumor (. . . but aren't they all?)"

Taken from her blog, here's how Christie remembers our time in the waiting room:

> We sign in and they tell us to sit and wait. In the lobby, there's a *Sports Illustrated* with the USC offensive line on the front cover. We try to read about Rey Maualuga's draft chances, but why his hurt hamstring will hurt his chances of going in the first round. I read five sentences over and over again. I can't focus. I'm shaking. I don't know what's happening. I'm in shock. I look out the window and across the street at the people sitting at Cabo Cantina . . . what I would not give to be there, having a margarita and being, well, ANY-WHERE but here.

Finally, Dr. Harold Kumar comes out to get us. Dr. Kumar is a youngish doctor with a curious bedside manner. "Bryan and Christie?" he greets us in a soft voice. "We're going to go into the exam room and we're going to have a nice little chat about what's going on." *A nice little chat?* Who was this, James Lipton?

He takes us into an exam room. The first thing he does (after closing the door) is sit on a stool and roll right up next to us. He puts his hand on Christie's knee and says, again in a preternaturally soft voice, "I'm so sorry this is happening to you." His face emotes concern. "I'm so, so sorry."

At this point, it's all becoming too much for me and especially for Christie. So sorry for what? Keep in mind that we have yet to even *see* the results of my MRI. All we've seen is a typed-up report and an entry on Wikipedia that says 87 percent of patients diagnosed with a brain-stem glioma die within three years.

Dr. Harold Kumar hands us a pamphlet. In his defense, it was a nice pamphlet.[56] He starts circling words, phrases, and diagrams. Key words such as *pons* (a part of the brain-stem) and *inoperable* are bandied about. The whole experience felt as if he had memorized a worksheet titled "Good Bedside Manner" the night before. The words made sense, but the rhythm was all off. Like when you talk to a customer-service call center in India. It felt that much like a script. Almost like Medical Mad Libs. Finally, I get fed up with the information overload and the endless medical jargon.

"Doc," I said, "realistically, what are we looking at?"

He paused, then in a soft voice said, "Typically, in these cases, I say six months to a year."

At that moment, for the only time in this whole ordeal—before or after—I thought to myself, "Holy shit."

My very next thought, and I am not exaggerating, was "Well, that's not going to be me."

Don't get me wrong, I was seriously worried. I realized instantly that I had a serious, life-threatening illness. That I had cancer, and that it couldn't be operated on, given the tumor's location in the brain-stem. But my gut reaction—whether it was nurture or nature, who knows—was to say, "That won't be me."

Christie must not have had the same gut reaction because she was instantly a mess. She went into an emotional conniption. Just hysterical, heaving sobbing. I don't remember what immediately followed, or how we left it with Dr. Harold Kumar, but the next thing I remembered was sitting in his receptionist's office, making follow-up

---

[56] Who am I kidding, it's not much of a defense.

appointments and scheduling a CT scan. Picture the scene: me, sitting in one chair, dazed. Christie, sitting in another chair, hyperventilating with tears. And Kumar's receptionist, on the phone with the insurance company, trying to get a CT scan approved.

Looking back, it was strange that they had us sit in the receptionist's office instead of the exam room. I suspect they wanted to get us away from the rest of the patients. *That's* how uncontrollably Christie was sobbing.

Dr. Harold Kumar poked his head into the office to check on us (I guess). He saw how upset Christie was and again told us how sorry he was. Christie forced out the words between sobs: "We . . . we're . . . getting . . . married . . . in . . . two months."

"I know," he said softly. "It's just not fair." Then he turned and left. This didn't help Christie; in fact, it may have made things worse. A nurse gave her a paper bag to breathe into because she was hyperventilating so severely.[57]

Kumar's receptionist made the CT appointment for me on Monday. I didn't know it at the time, but CT (computed tomography) scans are generally not prepared by many oncologists, who prefer MRI (magnetic resonance imaging) scans. Some studies suggest CT scans increase your risk of cancer as much as 2 percent.[58] None other than the great Dr. Drew once told me, "You don't want to get too many CT scans."

> **Tumor Tip:** You're probably thinking I'm going to say something like "Insist on getting MRIs instead of CT scans." You're right; if your doctor still uses CT scans, my advice is to bid him "Good day" as you tip your stovepipe hat at him. But my tip is this: Occasionally, you're going to have to ingest something medicinal, and the nurse is going to ask you, "What flavor would you like?" Think about going to the

---

[57] And you thought that only happened in movies.
[58] So, by my math, I had a 102 percent chance of getting cancer.

dentist; whenever they do some kind of elaborate dental work on you that involves some special liquid, they offer you a cornucopia of flavors: root beer, piña colada, wild cherry, etc. Always opt for mint. It's the easiest flavor to replicate. Worst-case scenario, it ends up tasting like toothpaste. Everything else just tastes like a medicine-y version of the thing they're trying to imitate.

The worst twelve hours of our lives had begun. Next up: the unenviable task of telling our families the bad news.

6.

The Worst Phone Call of My Life

or, "Mom and Dad? I Have Some Bad News"

When you set out to tell people you have cancer, you begin with the best of intentions. You envision a five-to-ten-minute phone conversation in which you break the bad news gently, assuage the person's fears, and generally leave it on a hopeful (if not upbeat) note. It rarely goes this way. I thought I would set aside an hour and told myself, "I'm going to call between eight and ten close friends or family members and tell them the news." What ends up happening is, everyone you talk to (because he or she loves you) winds up asking a hundred questions (all the same questions, it turns out) and each conversation ends up taking twenty minutes. It's not necessarily a bad thing, and it's not anyone's fault. But it's extremely taxing, especially when you've got a lot of other things on your mind, such as "When is my next appointment again? What pills do I take in the next hour? Am I going to live to see my next birthday?"

> ***Tumor Tip:*** *Don't do what I did and insist upon telling all your loved ones about your diagnosis personally. My intentions were good, but the next thing I knew, two days had passed and I'd only had time to tell about six people. Plus, word spreads like wildfire among your friends and family. They'll naturally want to talk about it with each other; it's part of how they cope. If you do as I did and say, "Do me a favor, let me be the one to tell people," then you're only making*

people feel guilty when they inevitably ask someone, "Did you hear about Bryan?" Let your close friends and family be your conduit for telling everyone else. It'll make your life much easier, and it will give them a chance to talk openly and freely about it, too.

Christie and I drove from Dr. Harold Kumar's office at the Angeles Clinic straight to her parents' house, where she grew up. I think her primordial gut instinct in a time of such utter panic was to retreat to where she felt the safest. I don't remember anything about the car ride to her parents' house, other than Christie held it together remarkably well. Looking back, we were probably both in shock. I'm sure she was.

We parked and went straight inside. Her mom, Sheryl, was outside in the backyard, smoking (ironically). Through her sliding glass doors, she saw us come in unexpectedly, so she put out her cigarette and came in to greet us. As she did, Christie lost it. She'd been holding it in the whole car ride over, but she couldn't hold back the tears anymore. The look on Sheryl's face was unforgettable—I'll never forget the look of sheer, panicked *concern* for her crying daughter. In an instant, Sheryl's expression went from "I wonder what they're doing here" to . . . there aren't any words to explain her look. In that instant, Sheryl was a mama bear, and her cub was hurting.

Christie was hysterically sobbing within seconds, so Sheryl wrapped her arms around her. All Christie could get out between her heaving breaths was "They said . . . he only has . . . six months . . ."

Christie's brother (who was living at home at the time) must have heard the commotion and put two and two together, because he sheepishly sauntered out of his bedroom to see exactly what was going on. When he saw his big sister in such a state, he just gave her a long hug. Strangely enough, in that traumatic moment, I knew I was making the right decision by marrying Christie. Her family was like mine: close, tight-knit, and supportive in times of need.

Just then, Christie's dad, Don, came home from work. Don owned a power-tool shop in West Los Angeles that his father had started in

1955.[59] Like Sheryl and Christopher, Don knew that Christie and I were seeing doctors and getting tests for some strange neurological symptoms I'd been experiencing. So when he arrived home from work in his Westwood Power Tools shirt and jeans and saw us all in the living room looking devastated, he knew.

Here's what you need to know about Don Clough: Picture Tom Brokaw only more . . . actually, never mind the *more* part. Just picture Tom Brokaw and you're 80 percent there. Similar hair (white, neat). Similar temperament (even, taciturn). Similar voice (low, authoritative). I wouldn't call him antisocial—he's not; he's exceedingly thoughtful and considerate—but his favorite activities are solitary. He loves fly-fishing. He *loves* photography. I don't know if he "loves" researching things on the Internet, but he does it for hours at a time, so he must get some satisfaction from it. A casual observer might describe him (somewhat accurately) as a man of few words.

Don sat down and we told him the news. Christie was still crying, but not as uncontrollably. The conversation was about telling *my* parents the bad news. It wasn't so much how, but when. The obvious answer was immediately, but the issue was a little more complicated, I explained. My parents were on a yearly vacation at a cabin in Truckee, California, a mountain town near Lake Tahoe. They were vacationing with three of my dad's high school friends. This served as a sort of annual emotional "spring cleaning" for them; I knew how much they looked forward to the times in Truckee when they could just unplug and get away from their everyday stresses. Plus, the friends they were vacationing with lived all over the West Coast, so it's not as if they saw them often. Plus, Christie and I were scheduled to fly up there the very next day for a bridal shower my mom was throwing for Christie, so, I figured, we'd just tell them then. This is the kind of news that is better shared face-to-face, right? Who wants to get this

---

[59] Westwood Power Tools in Culver City, California. Amazingly, we would later find out that Adam Carolla himself had once bought a palm nailer there back when he was a carpenter in the late eighties.

kind of news over the phone? Talk about feeling ineffectual: you're in a cabin in the woods, nowhere near your home, friends, or family.

On top of all that, I pictured the scene in Truckee at that exact moment: There was probably some Boz Scaggs or old Chicago playing throughout the house. I pictured my mom, under a blanket, laughing. I pictured my dad, standing over his barbecue, stoking his coals to the perfect temperature. I pictured them in their happiest place, surrounded by old friends, and . . . I didn't want to ruin it for them. I knew this moment would change their lives (probably for the worse), and I didn't want to be the cause of it.

I tried to convince the Cloughs. "Look, we'll see them tomorrow in person. I'll tell them face-to-face. I don't want to ruin their vacation."

The room fell silent. Finally, Don, the man of few words, spoke up in a deep, quiet, cracking voice: "I think you should call your dad."

I went to their spare bedroom and called my parents. Sure enough, when my dad answered the phone, music was playing in the background. I cringed as I heard the revelry in the house and said, "Can you get Mom on the phone and go somewhere quiet? I have some news to share."

Confused, they went into a quiet room. As simply as I could, I told them I had cancer.

Predictably, they were devastated. I hadn't even told them that I was having symptoms, let alone seeing doctors and getting tests. The conversation didn't last long. They were probably too shocked to think of questions to ask me. I assured them that I was fine—as fine as could be—and that I would see them tomorrow, as planned.

They convinced me to call my brother and tell him the news. Initially I resisted: I'll see him tomorrow, I'll just tell him then. No, they insisted, call him now. I hung up with my parents and called Adam. He picked up right away. After exchanging pleasantries, I got right into it: "I have some bad news."

He paused. "Okay . . ."

"I've been diagnosed with a brain tumor."

Either he thought I was messing with him or he didn't want to believe it, or maybe both, because his first reaction was "Come on!"

"I'm serious."

"Come on!" he said more emphatically. But I could hear he was worried. This wasn't "Come on!" as in "Stop joking," this was "Come on!" as in "*Please* tell me you're joking."

I told him how I was going to fly up there tomorrow, as planned, and we would see each other then. Adam's own fiancée, Sarah, was attending Christie's bridal shower that weekend, and my dad, Adam, and I were scheduled to meet with my wedding DJ to go over the day's music.

I gave Adam the rundown of my situation and left it at "I'll see you tomorrow, we'll talk then."

"Okay. I love you, man."

You have to know Adam Bishop to know this wasn't something he said to me often. Or ever. Adam Bishop doesn't emote. But in this instance, I knew him well enough that I could tell he was pretty shaken up.

"I love you, too, buddy," I said.

7.

Telling Adam

or, "So, I Won't Be Able to Come to Work
on Monday . . ."

After breaking the news of my diagnosis to my parents and ruining their vacation, I pragmatically decided that my next call had to be to Adam Carolla.

Adam was my boss but—inasmuch as your celebrity boss can be—he was my friend. He and his wife, Lynette, had been at our out-of-town wedding in Napa . . . well, actually, they were *invited* to our wedding and had indeed shown up, but arrived late to the ceremony and thus missed the part where Christie and I actually got married.[60]

Still, I felt that I had to tell Adam about my diagnosis right away. I hadn't spoken to him in a few weeks; our morning radio show had been canceled less than two months before, and he was deep into preproduction for a CBS television pilot he was about to shoot. The show, called *Ace in the Hole* costarred Pam Adlon (the voice of Bobby Hill on Fox's *King of the Hill*) and Windell Middlebrooks (the Miller High Life guy). I was scheduled to start work as a production assistant (a PA) on the pilot on Monday.

It was Thursday afternoon.

You may be asking yourself, "Why were you taking a job as a lowly PA? Hadn't you just been Adam's on-air sidekick for three years on a

---

[60] More on this in the chapter about our wedding.

popular syndicated morning show in the country's second-biggest market?" Good question.[61] In show business, a PA is an entry-level job. It's where a lot of directors/cinematographers/fluffers start when they're just out of college. I was thirty years old. Plus, a few years prior I'd done a stint as a segment producer on Adam's last TV show on Comedy Central. This represented a major step backward, careerwise. But I did it for two reasons.

First, keep in mind that this was April 2009. We were deep into a recession (some economists were even predicting another Great Depression). The economy was in horrible shape, and jobs were hard to come by. Especially radio jobs. Our entire station had flipped formats from twenty-four-hour-a-day talk to a nearly-DJ-free pop station, and that meant that the LA radio job market was suddenly flooded with "talent,"[62] most of whom had many more years of experience than I did. So a PA job, while laughable, was still a job.

Second—and I think this is an important lesson for any youngish person aspiring to do anything in show business—there's a lot to be said for showing up to work early, kicking ass, and being first in line for that promotion. I think the corporate term is *outperforming*. I've had it explained to me thusly: "Make yourself indispensable." If they can't get by without you, you have all the negotiating power. So while it's important where you come in, it's more important where you end up.[63]

Remember, too, that Christie had just been laid off as well. No money was coming into our humble home. Couple that with no prospects on the horizon, and a two-week PA gig sounded pretty good. Plus, there was the tempting promise that "when the pilot gets picked up by CBS, there will definitely be a job in it for you."

---

[61] Yes, I just congratulated myself on my own made-up question.

[62] Anyone who listened to our old talk station knows I'm using that term euphemistically. Maybe "flooded with candidates" is a better way to put it.

[63] For motivational-speaking engagements, contact my manager at 310-838-3333.

I didn't realize two things: First, this is what producers tell young, naïve, eager people to get them to work cheaply. (They would ask them to work for free, but I'm pretty sure that's illegal.) Second, Adam—and I think even he'd admit this—was about to go on a bit of a cold streak, at least as far as "the industry" was concerned. Again, this was early 2009. Adam hadn't fully formed the podcast that would someday be named the World's Most Downloaded Podcast by *Guinness World Records.* The radio show had just been canceled, the CBS pilot would not be picked up (spoiler alert), and unsuccessful pilots at NBC and Fox were soon to follow. Adam himself will tell you that success in Hollywood is cyclical. This just happened to be the lower end of the cycle.

I didn't know all this on April 23, 2009, nor would I have cared. All I cared about was telling my boss—who had looked out for me on so many occasions, including this one—the bad news. I called his house, and surprisingly, he picked up. Getting Adam on his home phone on the first try is a less-than-fifty-fifty proposition, but this time, he answered.

"Hello?"

"Hey, Adam, it's Bryan."

"Hey, how's it going?"

"Well, I'm afraid I have some bad news actually."

"Why? What's up?"

"I won't be able to come in to work on Monday. Or any day, actually."

"How come?"

"I've been diagnosed with a brain tumor, and I have to start chemotherapy and radiation that day."

Now, Adam's not prone to wild displays of emotion. Nor did I expect him to cry out to the heavens, "Why, God?! Why not me?!" But his reaction—the sound he made—I'll never forget it.

"Ooohhhh," he groaned. "Oooohhhhhhhh."

I don't even know if you'd call it a groan. It was almost a wail. It's the sound I imagine I'd make if I was playing poker and I bet the deed to my house on four aces but lost when my opponent turned over a royal flush.[64] Just a punch in the gut mixed with a knee to the groin.

He asked all the standard questions—what was the prognosis, where was I going for treatment, etc.—Adam is very analytical like that. Then he said something I'll never forget:

"Bryan, I will be your guardian angel. I'll be your white knight. Anything you need, I will pay for it. I'll sell a car if I have to."

You have to know Adam to appreciate the significance of this gesture. *He'll sell a car.* That's like a normal person saying they'll sell a child. Actually, it's not, because most people's children wouldn't fetch $1.2 million at a Barrett-Jackson auction the way Adam's Datsun 510 would.[65] To say he loves his collection of classic cars is not doing justice to the word *love*. He longs for them. This is a man who sat by his front window all weekend in anticipation of the delivery of his latest purchase (a Lamborghini Gallardo), only to be crestfallen when it didn't arrive until *Monday*! (Insert dramatic music sting.)

> **Tumor Tip:** *Adam's offer was significant for another reason: When someone is diagnosed with something like cancer, the best thing they can do in the short term is not worry about the little things—what's for dinner? When's the water bill due? My advice to anyone who wants to help a friend who's recently been diagnosed with cancer or some other serious illness: Get cookin'. Literally, volunteer (insist) to bring over a pan of lasagna, or some premade smoothies, or a Subway gift card. Because when your day is suddenly full of appointments with doctors, radiologists, and neuro-oncologists, the last thing you need to be thinking about is "Where's dinner coming from?"*

---

[64] Ladies, ask your dad what that means.
[65] Ladies, again, ask your dad.

I don't remember how the call with Adam ended, but before it did, I mentioned that Dionne Kirschner—the nice woman who was responsible for most of the hiring and associated paperwork on Adam's pilot—would need to be told that I wouldn't be at work on Monday. She had been helpful (and friendly, a rare combination in Hollywood) in getting me set up with all the necessary paperwork for the PA job. I volunteered to call her, but Adam insisted he would tell her the next day when he saw her on the set. Here's Adam's story of what happened:

Dionne is one of the most compassionate people in the world. I show up the next morning, and I'm devastated by this news. But I was attempting to keep a poker face on in front of her because we're going to do our first table read that day, and it's supposed to be comedy-mixed-with-hope. And everyone's nervous.

So I go in to Dionne's office the following morning because I have to tell her you won't be starting that day, and it's the world's worst timing because there's a three-hundred-pound teamster/transportation guy there who's picking out the car that my character will drive in the show. I come walking in, and she's such a sweet soul—she's five feet tall—and I go, "Hey, Dionne . . ."

And she says, "Oh, there's this guy here who wants to show you the cars that your character's going to be driving." [Adam was playing a driving-school instructor on this pilot.]

I tell her (stammering), "Um, my friend Bryan . . ." And I didn't want to get into it, so I just said, "Bryan is not going to be working, he's not going to show up on Monday, and . . . he's just . . . he's not." I knew I couldn't take it. So I said, "He's not going to show up Monday."

And she said, "Oh, why not?"

"He has a medical condition," I said, "and he can't work."

And she went, "Oh, what does he have?"

And I went, voice cracking, "He has . . . a brain tumor!"

And I break down into a heap. Her eyes start welling up, and she breaks down into a heap. And the tears are pouring. And we're hugging, and we're crying. I mean, I talked to him last night and he said he has six months to live! "He's thirty, he's getting married in two months!"

And the teamster guy is going, "Uh, we couldn't find a blue Saturn, but we found a white Saturn . . ."

And I'm saying, "I'm sorry, I'm sorry," and we're both just a pile of tears.

Dionne's crying, saying, "I know from cancer, my grandfather started St. Jude's . . ."

And the big teamster guy is standing there going, in a comically deep voice, "Should I leave?"

"No, no, no!" I'm crying. "Don't leave!" And she's the kind of person who would cry if I told her one of my kids made a solid bowel movement earlier that day.

So I'm sobbing and pointing at the cars he's showing me on eBay, going, "That one [sniff] . . . in white. But it should be a '95 because [sniffle] they changed the body style in '94."

And he keeps going, "I'll come back! I'll come back!"

And I'm like, "No!," because I feel bad, and Dionne's bawling, and we're still hugging.

And the guy's like, "I'll leave."

And I say, "You don't have to. I can point. I'm just sorry, I feel like an idiot. I'm just sorry." And I'm bawling my brains out, and she's bawling her brains out, and the poor teamster guy was standing there in between us.

In one of those weird, only-in-Hollywood coincidences that Adam alluded to, Dionne's grandfather was the late, great Danny Thomas. Thomas was the star of *Make Room for Daddy* (also known as *The Danny Thomas Show*), which ran for more than a decade on ABC and then CBS in the 1950s and '60s. He was a contemporary of such television legends as Lucille Ball, Andy Griffith, and Dick Van Dyke.

Thomas may be most famous for his TV work, but his real lasting cultural impact? He founded St. Jude's Children's Research Hospital. Named after St. Jude, the Catholic patron saint of hopeless causes,[66] the hospital had treated thousands of children for cancer. And now the founder's granddaughter was set to be my boss.

By the way, Danny Thomas's real name? Amos Muzyad Yakhoob Kairouz. Sounds like a delicious goat-based shawarma plate. Apparently, in the fifties and sixties, you couldn't have any kind of ethnic diversity in your name whatsoever if you wanted to be a performer. You would be amazed at the list of showbiz luminaries who changed their birth names to a more "Anglo" (read: white) stage name. Guys such as Tony Bennett, Dean Martin, Bobby Darin—basically any Italian guy who ever recorded "Mack the Knife"—changed their name to something less "threatening."[67] Compare that to today, when you can be born Russell Jones but end up a millionaire as Ol' Dirty Bastard.

Adam made two other calls that day. The first was to Dr. Drew Pinsky, his former cohost from *Loveline*. Drew, unlike the quacks masquerading as "doctors" on TV, is a real doctor. Or, as Adam puts it, an "airplane doctor." He calls Drew that because, if you had a heart attack on an airplane, he could actually help you and potentially save your life. Could you imagine Dr. Phil's bloated face being the last thing you ever saw? Or Dr. Laura standing helplessly over your lifeless corpse as you drifted into the afterlife?

When Adam told Drew of my diagnosis, Drew made that pained sucking sound you make when you rip off a Band-Aid: teeth clenched, sucking in air and saliva. The international sound for *uh-oh*. The thing about Drew is, he will give it to you 100 percent straight. The man has absolutely no bedside manner. That's probably due to years

---

[66] This is not a joke. My God, there's a patron saint for everything. How would you like to have been at that fantasy draft? "Welcome back to the Patron Saint Draft. St. Jude, you have the second-to-last pick. Still available are Hopeless Causes and Mutilated Child Pornographers. Do you want a second to think about it?"

[67] Why audiences would have been "threatened" by an Italian singer is beyond me. "My God, that man has a the voice of an angel. I'm so moved by this performance." "Yeah, but his parents are from Sicily." "*What?!* Grab the kids, we're leaving!"

of running a rehab clinic and trying to tell junkies how close they are to actually killing themselves. A few years prior, in my twenties, I'd had gallbladder surgery. I was understandably nervous, so I asked Drew about it.

"Where are they doing the surgery?" he asked.

"Daniel Freeman Memorial Hospital in Inglewood."

"Ha," he chortled. "Good luck!"

Good luck! This man is a doctor!

Adam asked Drew if it was bad. Or rather, how bad was it.

Drew basically said, "It depends. If it grows, it could be really bad. Is it growing?"

"I think that's how they found it in the first place," Adam said.

"Then it's bad."

A few years before, a close friend of Adam's wife had been diagnosed with pancreatic cancer. Adam immediately went to Drew, knowing he'd get a straight answer. Drew's matter-of-fact response: "Death sentence. She'll be gone in six months."

Five months later, she was gone. The night she died, Adam gave a short but heartfelt tribute to his wife's friend while signing off *Loveline*. For the first ten years that I knew Adam, it was the only time I saw him cry.

The second call he made was to Dr. Bruce Heischober, his friend and sometimes fill-in for Dr. Drew on *Loveline*. Bruce is an emergency-room doctor and as such has to know a little bit about everything medical related. Adam comically refers to Bruce as "good lenses, bad frames." Meaning, he has all the information (good lenses), but it's poorly packaged (bad frames). Like the best (yet ugliest) glasses you can buy.

Bruce, it turns out, had a sister who was diagnosed with the exact same type of tumor as mine ten years ago: an inoperable brain-stem glioma.

"Oh, yeah?" said Adam, already gun-shy from his talk with Drew. "What happened to her?"

"Oh, she lives up in Pasadena with her husband and kids," said Bruce. "I can give you her number if you want."

Pasadena! Husband and kids! Not only was she still alive ten years after she was diagnosed, but she was living a normal life just a few miles away.

It was our first glimmer of hope, and, boy, did we need it.

8.

Always Bet on Black

or, Everything I Know, I Learned from Watching
Wesley Snipes Movies

The next few days were a bizarre whirlwind of mismatched activity.
Doctor visits. A wedding shower. PET/CT scans. An appointment
with our wedding DJ. A trip to the nail salon. Luckily for Christie, I
let her come with me to the nail salon.

Once the initial shock and raw emotion of sharing the news with
our families wore off, we immediately shifted into business mode.
Most people's reaction to the news of a loved one's being diagnosed
with a major illness—outside of disbelief—is "How can I help?" Our
parents were no exception. Between all of us furiously googling, it
didn't take long for us to come across the name of Dr. Keith Black. Dr.
Black is *the* neurosurgeon for brain tumors. You could say he wrote the
book on it, literally: Dr. Black had recently published a book about his
experiences called *Brain Surgeon*. He'd recently been profiled in *Time*
magazine, which said:

> Of the 5,000 or so neurosurgeons working in the U.S. today, 4,900
> concentrate mostly on the spine and deal on average with only five
> or six brain tumors a year. Of the 100 who routinely work inside the
> skull, perhaps 50 specialize in blood-vessel repairs rather than tu-
> mors. Only the remaining 50 can be considered brain-tumor spe-
> cialists, averaging 100 surgeries annually. Along with a handful of
> others, Black averages more like 250 such operations a year. His re-
> ferrals come not only from the U.S. but from Europe, the Middle

East, South America, Japan and Australia as well. A tumor that is inoperable for the average neurosurgeon is not necessarily inoperable for Black.

When you're in my position, any ray of light is, to borrow a phrase from the great comedian Larry Miller, "like God's flashlight." No matter how dim it might be, it's shining pretty brightly from your perspective. And as I said, everyone wants to help, however they can. Dr. Black worked at Cedars-Sinai Medical Center in Beverly Hills, just a few blocks from where Christie and I were renting an apartment. Christie's mom lit up; she had a close friend from high school who was a major donor to the hospital and could surely get us an appointment right away with Dr. Black. We excitedly shared the news with my parents via telephone; my mom mentioned that a kid I knew from childhood was now a pharmaceutical rep in Los Angeles and maybe he knew someone on Dr. Black's team who could fast-track our case. Even Adam Carolla got in the act; he called me back a short time later that afternoon and said, "I talked to Dr. Bruce, and apparently there's a really good doctor over at Cedars you should see. His name is Dr. Black."

So all the signs were pointing to Dr. Black. This seems like a good time to give you a fair warning: I'm going to talk a little bit about God in this book. Not a lot. But a little. I'm not a religious person. I'm not even a particularly "spiritual" person. In fact, that's one of my biggest pet peeves—when someone says about themselves, "I'm not religious, *per se*, but I'm very spiritual." You'll hear this a lot in Los Angeles; I doubt it's said very often in the Bible Belt. I don't pray. I've never talked to God, and He's never spoken to me. I'm not an atheist, one who rejects the existence of God. I'm more accurately described as agnostic—one who believes the existence of God is unknown and, more important, unknowable. Atheists are as annoying as the people who claim to be spiritual, and more arrogant. How can you possibly *know* that there is no God? It's equally absurd to *know* that there *is* a God. It's like a person who *knows* that there are no such things as aliens. Look up in the sky at night. See all of those stars? Each one is a *galaxy*, complete with constellations and innumerable planets. We literally don't know how big our universe is, but you're telling me you know for a fact that nothing is living up there? How incredibly arrogant is that? You can *believe* it, but claiming you know it for a fact is just as absurd as the guy who claims to have a personal relationship with God.

So here's the deal: In this book, when I talk about God or the Universe or signs or anything metaphysical, I'm just describing the same thing. I believe that the universe gives you certain signs, and if the tide is carrying you one way as opposed to the other, sometimes it's best to just throw your hands up and go with the flow. It makes sense to me, and if it doesn't make the same sense to you, at least you can know what I mean.

So, as I said, all the signs were pointing to Dr. Black. Our final sign came at—where else?—the nail salon. It was Friday morning, the day after my diagnosis, and the day we were flying up to the Bay Area for Christie's bridal shower. Christie needed her nails done for the shower the next day, and I was like, "What the hell? I'm stressed-out, so I'll let the NASCAR pit crew of Asian ladies rub my feet for half an hour."[68] So I succumbed to the temptations of a soothing foot rub. When I finished, I met Christie at the nail-drying station, where she had started a conversation with a woman sitting next to her. The woman was in her sixties and was dripping with diamonds. Imagine a slightly thinner and far wealthier version of Mike Myers character from the "Coffee Talk" sketch on *Saturday Night Live*. You see, Christie went to a nail salon for rich women, despite not technically being rich herself. It was right in the heart of Beverly Hills, just a few blocks from Rodeo Drive. Before we met, one of Christie's delightful quirks was that she rarely looked at the price tag of anything. Once,

---

[68] Fellas, I know it's a cliché to avoid ever getting a pedicure. Forget about that. Who wouldn't like their feet and ankles massaged while sitting in a comfy leather chair? When I discovered that a pedicure was just a foot massage, it was like the time I discovered *charcuterie* was French for "meat-and-cheese platter." *This is what I've been avoiding my whole life??*

when we were shopping for ingredients for an early dinner date, she went to grab a jar of expensive pasta sauce. I noted that the one below it was on sale and pointed to the price on the yellow sale tag underneath it. She exclaimed, "Oh, *that's* what those yellow tags mean!" In the ensuing years, I've recalibrated her shopping radar to look for sale prices first before buying, but it took some effort.

So Christie is talking to Diamond Lady at the nail salon, and Christie tells her that we're flying to San Francisco later that day for her bridal shower. Diamond Lady tells us mazel tov, but remarks that we both look a little stressed-out for such a joyous occasion. Christie then explains about my brain tumor and how we just got diagnosed yesterday and how we're both freaking out a little. Diamond Lady takes her hand out of the nail dryer, puts it on Christie's arm, and says, "You *have* to see Dr. Black at Cedars-Sinai." That's how she said it, too—as if she were encouraging a friend to try the special at an Italian restaurant: "You *have* to try the clams at Matteo's. The butter-and-lemon sauce is to die for." (Actually, poor choice of words.) Christie assured her that we were indeed trying to get an appointment to see Dr. Black as soon as we could. Diamond Lady went on, "He's amazing. And you know what?" She looked around and lowered her voice to a whisper. "He's actually black![69] Can you believe it?"

That was the last sign I needed. If the universe had sent this random older woman to reinforce to us—in a Beverly Hills nail salon—that we needed to see Dr. Black immediately, then who was I to argue?

---

[69] As I look back, the notion that Diamond Lady glanced around and lowered her voice, presumably so as not to offend any black people within earshot, was ridiculous. I went to that nail salon a dozen times, and the only black person I ever saw in there was delivering the mail.

9.

Dr. Black

or, The "Rock" Star Brain Surgeon

Christie's bridal shower was a success. But while she was being showered with gifts and well-wishes, I was dealing with a much more important life-or-death issue: going over our wedding playlist with our DJ, Chad. Chad had been the DJ at two of my friends' weddings,[70] and both times I thought, "I *have* to book this guy for my wedding." Chad was put on this earth to be a DJ at parties. He just *gets* it. For instance, when we had our face-to-face meeting, he asked me about the songs I didn't want played—my Do Not Playlist. I started to name a few songs that I hated whenever I heard them at other people's weddings, and he cut me off: "So, you want the 'no-cheese' factor?"

Yes, I told him, that's exactly what I was trying to say. For the record, here's the complete list of songs I emailed to him and ordered him not to play, under any circumstances:

"YMCA"
"Macho Man"
"Celebration"
"I Will Survive"
"Love Shack"
"Macarena"

---

[70] One of the couples is now divorced, and at the other wedding my girlfriend at the time poured a beer on my head in an elevator.

"Boot Scootin' Boogie"

"Hey Ya!"

"Mambo no. 5"

"Livin' la Vida Loca"

"Smooth"

"Material Girl"

"Fight for Your Right"

"I've Had the Time of My Life"

"Superfreak"

"I Love Rock 'n' Roll"

"Smells Like Teen Spirit"

Easy on the disco

No Lenny Kravitz

No Madonna

No Bob Marley

Little did I know, a song would be released in less than a month that would go on to ruin every wedding for the next two years: "I Gotta Feeling" by the Black Eyed Peas. You know the song: "Tonight's gonna be a good, good night!" over and over. It's the one your creepy uncle or your drunk aunt is jumping up and down to, spilling her drink on your nephew. There's so much to hate about this song. First of all, it's grammatically incorrect. *Gotta* is colloquial slang for "got to," not "got a." So the title is essentially saying "I got to feeling." But why even bother with a title? Why not just cynically call it "The Wedding Song That Your Mom Likes" if you want to be more accurate? Thankfully, Chad is a smart man and didn't have to be told not to play it at our wedding.

On Monday morning, the plan was to fly back home to Los Angeles and pretty much go straight to the Angeles Clinic, where I had a PET/CT scan scheduled. Only one of my contacts had come through: My childhood friend Ryan, the one who now worked as a medical-device sales rep in Los Angeles, had actually done some business recently with Dr. Black's office. He had sold them some medical supplies and was friends with one of Dr. Black's nurses. I got in touch with Ryan—we hadn't spoken in a few years—and he listened as I explained my situation: I had a brain tumor, I was seeing a doctor at St. John's whom I wasn't too sure about, and I wanted to see the best doctor in the business for this sort of thing. "Let me see what I can do," Ryan said, and we hung up. Within an hour, he called back. His friend, a nurse named Theresa, had gotten us an appointment for Monday afternoon. It was Sunday.

Instantly, I was overwhelmed with gratitude. I didn't know exactly what I was feeling, but my buddy JD—my best man, whom I had met at Northwestern—has seen his dad go through (and beat) esophageal cancer and explained it to me thusly: "When you have cancer, it's like you're at the bottom of a hole, and you just want to get out. Only it's too big for you to just climb out easily. But every good thing that happens—no matter how small—is like a rock in the side of the hole. You climb up, grabbing one little rock at a time. Had a good doctor's appointment? That's a rock. Feeling a little better today? That's a rock, too. Before you know it, you've climbed out of that hole, one little rock at a time. You just need to find the rocks." I thought about JD, his dad, and those rocks a lot over the next few months. Considering that it usually takes months to book an appointment with Dr. Black, getting an appointment with him on such short notice was one of our first rocks.

I'd never been so excited and anxious for a doctor's appointment as I was for my appointment with Dr. Black that Monday. I remember waiting for my flight back to LAX in SFO's Virgin America terminal and staring at my phone, wondering why time wasn't moving faster. We landed and drove straight to the Angeles Clinic so I could have my already-scheduled PET/CT scan. My appointment with Dr. Black was scheduled for immediately afterward in a nearby part of town. We could have left as soon as my scan was over and made it in plenty of time, but I wanted to bring a CD copy of the PET/CT scan with me to my appointment. I wanted Dr. Black to have every available piece of information about my condition at his disposal. This was the best brain surgeon in the country. Not bringing the results of a scan would be like asking Michelangelo to paint your ceiling but, sorry, we don't have any blue paint. You're only doing yourself a disservice in the long run.

> **Tumor Tip:** *If you're going from doctor to doctor seeking a second (or better) opinion, always have a copy (on disc) of your medical scans or tests. The place where you get the scan technically has to give you a copy anyway, so just ask for one and keep it with you. When you go to a new doctor, hand it to his nurse and have them make a copy for themselves.*

After my PET/CT scan, I was excited, anxious, and in a hurry, so I probably sounded like an impatient jerk when I kept asking the poor technician, "I'm sorry, but do you have those discs yet?" For some reason, when you're in a hurry, saying "I'm sorry" actually makes you sound like a bigger jerk. But finally, I got them—the discs of my PET/CT as well as my MRI—and we made the short drive from the Angeles Clinic in Brentwood to Cedars-Sinai Medical Center in Beverly Hills. It kind of felt as if we were going up the Yellow Brick Road to meet the Great and Powerful Oz.[71]

Cedars-Sinai Medical Center has a reputation as a rich person's hospital, and it's not hard to see why: They're in a nice part of town, they charge a ton for parking, and they fund-raise like nobody's business. A lot of celebrities have given birth there, and a lot of celebrities have died there. Frank Sinatra died there. So did Elizabeth Taylor, Johnny Carson, and Notorious B.I.G.[72] Upon checking in at Dr. Black's office, we were reminded again why he's considered a baller in the medical community: He doesn't take insurance. At least not for

---

[71] "If I only had a brain . . . that wasn't riddled with cancer!"

[72] Sadly, Carson and Biggie's careers did not overlap, missing each other by just two years. Thus robbing us of one of the greatest moments in television history: Carson uttering the words, "Ladies and gentlemen, Notorious B.I.G."

our office visit. And it wasn't cheap. As I pulled out our checkbook, I shrugged and said to Christie, "Hey, you get what you pay for."

> **Tumor Tip:** What I should *have* done was put it on a credit card. Or better yet, designated a credit card solely for medical expenses. If you're facing cancer or some other major illness that's going to require ongoing medical care, get yourself a credit card that offers you some rewards: cash back or airline miles or hotel points. Number one, you're going to want to get something back for all the money you're inevitably going to spend. Number two, it helps to keep all your medical expenses in the same place, so you can easily find them if you ever need to. Also, if you spend enough—and if you have cancer, you will—you'll probably be able to write off a portion of your medical expenses on your taxes. It's much easier to total everything up when you use the same credit card to pay for everything.

Dr. Black's waiting room was quiet, very Zen. For the first time in several days, we actually relaxed a little. We filled out the requisite paperwork and waited. A few minutes later, Theresa, the nurse who had helped us get our appointment in the first place, came out to say hello. Even though we'd never met, it was nice to see a friendly face in the waiting room. We were still pretty nervous and anxious, after all.

After a few more minutes, another nurse came out to get us. It was time to meet the Man. She put us in an exam room, and a few minutes later Dr. Black himself breezed into the room. After building him up so much in my mind, it was like seeing a celebrity. He looked like a cross between a young Bill Cosby and an old Tiger Woods. He was even followed by a nurse whose sole job was to take notes on whatever was said around him. She followed him around the way Flava Flav followed Chuck D. She was his hype man.[73] That's another sign that you've made it as a doctor; you have a nurse in tow who simply writes

---

[73] At the end of our appointment, I half expected Dr. Black to drop his stethoscope and walk out, like a rapper dropping his microphone and walking offstage after a concert.

down what you say and hear, in case it's important (and it probably is). I was the tiniest bit starstruck. He shook our hands, pulled up a stool, and began talking to us in a low, quiet voice. Even the tenor of his voice was Zen. It was a little louder than a whisper, but still very soothing.

We were immediately at ease. Dr. Black asked us if we'd seen the MRI of my tumor. We looked at each other; actually, no, we hadn't. It was such a bizarrely obvious thing that we'd forgotten to ask anyone if we could see it for ourselves. Who demands to see proof of his or her cancer, anyway?[74] He escorted us into a viewing room, where he had the full MRI on display on a large computer screen. It was revelatory. What we had seen of my tumor up until then had essentially been a few still photographs; this was like seeing a full animation. He showed us where the tumor was in my brain. He explained how it was affecting me and what my symptoms meant. He illustrated the different areas of the brain that were affected by my tumor. He said something about "the pons" and "glial cells." My eyes glassed over. Thank God Christie was furiously taking notes. I looked at the images he was describing. Sure enough, there it was: a malignant little egg in the middle of my brain. I remember thinking it looked like a cloud or a puff of smoke, as if it could be sucked out if we could just get in there.

We adjourned back to the exam room. In his calm, measured tone, Dr. Black explained that he was 99 percent sure this was a low-grade glioma. It was a classic case, he said, and it might have been there for years or even decades. However, based on the tumor's location in the brain—in "the Beverly Hills of real estate," according to Dr. Black—you don't want to operate on it. The chances of something—anything, even the tiniest thing—going wrong are just too high. The tumor was smack in the middle of the part of the brain that controls everything—motor functions, cognitive functions . . . even breathing. So the tiniest slip of the knife, and you could be pretty badly

---

[74] "A brain tumor? Prove it!"

messed up. It's not a forgiving region of the brain, it turns out. You don't even want to biopsy a tumor in that part of the brain since it carries a 1 to 3 percent chance of bleeding, which can cause serious permanent harm, such as paralysis. So matters were a little more complicated. We had a brain tumor we couldn't get to, in a part of the brain where we couldn't perform a biopsy. So, he continued, the plan was to use chemotherapy and radiation, together, in hopes of halting its growth. "In this game," Dr. Black said, "a tie is a win. We don't have to get rid of this tumor. We just have to stop it. We just want a win or a tie."

To that point, it was the most optimistic thing we'd heard a doctor say about my tumor. He went on, saying he was going to make us an appointment with his neuro-oncologist, Dr. Jeremy Rudnick, for the next day. Since Dr. Black was a surgeon, and my tumor was inoperable, this was sort of the end of the line with him, so to speak. He left us with this: "No one wants to have a brain tumor. But if you have to have one, this is the one to have. It's bad, but I've seen much, much worse."

Another rock.

IO.

Dr. McHottie and Dr. Redneck

or, The Rest of the Dream Team

The next day, I had my first appointment with Dr. Jeremy Rudnick. Christie and I were actually excited to meet with him—partly because he was an actual "expert" in brain cancer[75] and partly because we were finally *doing* something. It had been almost a week since Dr. Harold Kumar (now known as Dr. Doom in our house) had basically issued me a death sentence, and we still hadn't heard anything from him or his office. Which was especially strange because I'd had a PET/CT scan the previous morning—that he ordered—to determine if my cancer had metastasized. That is, if it had spread throughout my body. Needless to say, we were anxiously awaiting the results of said test.

We checked in to Rudnick's office and waited. His waiting area felt less like a doctor's office and more like a rich guy's study. You half expected to see an old guy with a beard, a pipe, and a tweed jacket in the corner, reading the *Saturday Evening Post* or some other publication that no longer exists. The walls were all lined with dark wood. Paradoxically, a TV was showing *Good Day LA*, a mindless morning show out here in Southern California. Maybe it was intended to put the patients at ease by dulling their minds, but I suspect it was on for

---

[75] We looked him up on the Internet and an independent Web site listed brain concern under his areas of expertise. His other areas of expertise listed: central nervous system cancer, central nervous system neoplasm, and epidemiology. Now who wants to party?!

the front-desk staff. A nurse came out and showed us to an exam room. On the way, we passed a giant plaque on the wall. Actually, *plaque* might not be accurate, since it took up the entire wall. We passed a monument—a shrine, if you will—erected to honor the major donors who had helped fund Cedars-Sinai's Brain Tumor Center. At the top of the plaque, in giant letters, read JOHNNIE L. COCHRAN, JR. BRAIN TUMOR CENTER. I thought to myself, "Oh, yeah, that's right, Johnnie Cochran died from a brain tumor." Sure enough, in 2005, he had died of a brain tumor. In 2007, Cedars opened their new Johnnie L. Cochran, Jr. Brain Tumor Center. The center was launched with over $5 million in donations, with Dr. Black right in the middle of it all. He and Cochran had been friends, apparently even vacationing together with their families. Dr. Black's name was on the plaque, presumably as a major donor. So were a number of A-list celebrities: Some of the names on the plaque:

Pauletta & Denzel Washington
Eddie Murphy
Tyler Perry
Byron Allen
Martin Lawrence & Family
Keisha & Forest Whitaker
Will & Jada Smith

As I read through the list of illustrious Hollywood names, I began to notice they were all from a certain . . . demographic. You guessed it: They're all actors over the age of forty.[76] As it dawned on me that the only thing connecting them was a very general, very broad classification, I realized, it's so great to be part of a "team."[77] If this book makes me rich, I'm going to hit up every famous bald guy with glasses

---

[76] If you thought I was going to say, "They're all black," that makes *you* a racist.
[77] Cynically, my first thought after reading the list was "I guess Don Cheadle either didn't get a call or said no thanks."

to donate to the National Brain Tumor Society. You hear that, Moby and Steven Soderberg? Get those checkbooks ready!

After a short wait, Dr. Rudnick and his physician's assistant, Rebecca, came in to see us. He struck me as a younger doctor, in his thirties perhaps. Rebecca seemed to be about the same age, possibly younger.[78] I had never heard of a physician's assistant before, and I'm still not 100 percent sure what one is. Rebecca was like Rudnick's right-hand man, but she's not a nurse. She can do most things a doctor can do, include write prescriptions. Rudnick's demeanor was disarming; he was affable but serious, detailed but not convoluted. He started with all the usual questions—not because he didn't know what was going on with me, but because he wanted me to *know* what information he knew about my medical situation. I explained everything—from my symptoms to my series of tests; from Dr. Schwartz to Dr. Harold Kumar to Dr. Black. "Okay," he said when I had finished, "what did the other doctors tell you?"

"Dr. Harold Kumar said we were looking at six months to a year."

Rudnick leaned back in his seat. I can't describe his look any other way than to say he looked . . . offended. As if someone had shoved a plate of rotting fish under his nose. "Oh," he said slowly, "I would take that with a *big* grain of salt."

With that, I was sold on Dr. Rudnick as my doctor. He didn't talk badly about Dr. Harold Kumar—"He's an idiot, he doesn't know what he's talking about"—and he didn't make any outrageous promises—"We can cure you, we have the technology here." He didn't need to. Rudnick was exactly what I was looking for in a doctor: younger, with a can-do attitude. Don't tell me *why not*, tell me *how*. Even if the odds are against us, tell me how you would beat this thing. And that's exactly what Rudnick did.

---

[78] I found out later that Rebecca is eight years younger than Rudnick. I'm *sure* she appreciates the part where I estimated that she was about the same age as him.

Tumor Tip: *Find a doctor that you're comfortable with. It seems so simple, yet I see it all the time: People stick with their crappy doctor because, hey, the devil you know. I even saw it with my own father-in-law. Christie's dad, Don, has had a congenital heart defect since he was a child. A year or so ago, he required an aortic-valve re-placement—a pretty major surgery—and had to fly all the way to Cleveland to have it. Unfortunately, Don was seeing a crappy doctor back home in Los Angeles who was mismanaging his condition. Don would complain endlessly about him, but he would never see another doctor, despite our pleas. "Please go to Cedars," Christie would plead with him. "They have great doctors and they've been so good to us." But Don would just brush off or ignore her dozens of attempts to convince him to see a better doctor. Why? I suspect it was something as simple as that he already knew the parking lot at his current hospital, or he was already familiar with the route to get there. Something insanely simple like that can prevent a lot of peo-ple from seeking out the best possible medical care. Do yourself a favor: Don't let anything stand in the way of your finding a doctor you're comfortable with. You don't have to like him or her, he or she just has to inspire confidence in you.*

Rudnick inspired confidence. We ended up spending almost three hours at the hospital that day, asking him questions, viewing my scans, and getting an idea of what treatment would be like. My bar-rage of questions was endless: Would I be on an infusion of chemo-therapy? (No, I would take pills orally.) Could I still go on my bachelor party? (Yes.) Could I still drink alcohol? (Yes, just not to excess.) Could I get my chemotherapy pills at any pharmacy? (No, it's a spe-cialty medication.) What if the treatment doesn't work and my tumor continues to grow? What then? (We still have one or two "big guns" in our arsenal that we can use if it comes down to it.) We asked Dr. Rudnick if he'd seen my type of condition before (a potentially stupid question, but one that had to be asked). He said yes, all the time. In fact, it was most of what he saw, being that Dr. Black exclusively sent him inoperable cases like mine. And although Dr. Rudnick said my tumor was uncommon, accounting for only one out of every fifteen or twenty tumors he treated, it wasn't rare. We asked who in Los Angeles would be considered an expert on my type of tumor—again, potentially stupid, but we were in cover-all-our-bases mode.

He smiled a little and said sheepishly, "Well, me." It maybe looks a little arrogant when you read it, but the way he said it was "You've come to the right place." Brain tumors were Rudnick's *thing*. Kumar, by comparison, was more versed in melanoma, yet he treated every kind of cancer, including brain tumors. Think of it this way: If you want a great steak, you don't go to a short-order cook. He's in the back of a diner, cranking out eggs Benedict, spaghetti marinara, and steak. You want to go to the best steak house in town, where *all the chef does* is grill steak.

Then Rudnick tried his hand at a joke: "The good news is, you won't lose your hair!"

I looked at him for a second with a straight face, then said, "Leave the comedy to the professionals, please." He laughed. We all laughed. I continued, "You do what *you* do best, and I'll do what *I* do best, and together we'll get through this." The ice was broken. Even Rebecca, the physician's assistant, laughed, and she can be a tough nut to crack. I would not want to play poker with her.

Rudnick explained that we'd be meeting with Dr. Amin Mirhadi, a radiation oncologist at Cedars, to go over the plan for my radiation treatment. Rudnick left the room to fill out some forms and start making my arrangements for treatment. Rebecca began to brief us on where we would be going and whom we would be seeing. "You go down to the basement level and tell them you're there to see Dr. Mirhadi—"

"I'm sorry," Christie interrupted, "Dr. Mirhadi?" The pronunciation of his name (Mer-HOTTIE) was peculiar. "Like, Dr. McHottie? Kind of like in *Grey's Anatomy*?"[79]

---

[79] It was a popular show at the time, and Dr. McHottie was a big reason why, at least among female viewers. The only things I ever knew about *Grey's Anatomy* were Dr. McSteamy, Dr. McDreamy, the chick from *Old School*, and that Katherine Heigl's character had a brain tumor, ironically enough.

"That's right," said Rebecca. "All the nurses call him that. All the doctors have nicknames here. Dr. McHottie, Dr. Redneck . . ." She gestured toward Rudnick.[80] We laughed—his name *did* sort of sound like *redneck*. "I'm Rebecca Whore," she said in a self-deprecating reference to her last name, Naor. She made us an appointment with Dr. Mirhadi for the next day.

I joke about Dr. Black's being a rock star, but Dr. Mirhadi is as close to a rock star as a doctor can get. In our first conversation with him, we first went over my course of treatment—how much radiation I would be getting, how often, what kind of side effects I could expect, etc. The whole thing. We learned some fun facts. Did you know that the unit of measurement for radiation is called a gray? Did you also know that SPF lotion used on your skin can reduce the amount of radiation by 1 or 2 percent? Me neither. As soon as I learned that, I went from a daily SPF-on-the-head wearer to a lotion-free existence. Hey, why chance it? Christie asked far more questions than I did and would later on ask me why I wasn't asking more questions. I was a little overwhelmed, for one, but mostly I just wanted to get started. Once I mentally committed myself to a course of action—in this case, getting radiation and chemotherapy treatments from the team at Cedars—I'm out of question mode and into let's-get-this-going mode. Every moment spent talking about treatment was another moment spent not getting treatment. But I appreciated Mirhadi's (and the rest of the team's) taking the time to explain everything to us, however painstakingly.

Once all our questions were answered, we transitioned into a friendly getting-to-know-you conversation. At one point, he actually made the joke, "Well, at least you won't lose your hair!" Turns out Mirhadi is a Southern California native. He's from Orange County, and he grew up friends with Mark McGrath, the musician.[81] Mirhadi's also close friends with Joseph McGinty Nichol—better known as

---

[80] In reality, Dr. Rudnick is as much of a redneck as Dr. Mirhadi is a hottie, if you catch my drift.

[81] I actually had to think about how to reference Mark McGrath. If you went to college in the late nineties as I did, he's the lead singer of Sugar Ray. But now, that's almost a footnote to his career. What should we call him? Musician? Entertainer? Game-show host?

McG, the film director. He's best known for directing the first two *Charlie's Angels* movies, but he's also directed *We Are Marshall*, *Terminator: Salvation*, and *This Means War*. Mirhadi explained that he and McG are such good friends that McG always names a minor character in his films after Mirhadi. I was intrigued; not only am I a film buff, but I love the *Terminator* series,[82] and McG's movie *Terminator: Salvation* was about to be released in less than a month. My nerd-boner was fully engorged. *Now* I had questions. Mirhadi had already seen the film, and sure enough, he "played" a pilot who gets killed. He then explained that he was going to be gone for a week in the middle of the month. Why? No, not to attend some critical cancer summit where the cure we've all been praying for was being developed. He was flying to Europe with McG for the overseas premiere of the movie. I laughed; only in LA.

After our sit-down with Mirhadi, he showed us to the room where I would be getting my radiation therapy. It was weird, like getting to tour the front lines of a war during a cease-fire. You know there's going to be a battle there soon, and you know there are going to be casualties. You just hope your side comes out as the victor. He introduced us to a radiologist named Sinead. Sinead was a firecracker—fully Irish, complete with a thick brogue. You got the impression that you wouldn't want to get into a drinking contest with her.[83] She's the kind of employee every hospital needs one or two of: welcoming, friendly, with a positive attitude. She put us at ease, and we hit it off right away. She, too, was a USC football fan, and like us she tailgated at all the home games.

She brought me back to get fitted for my custom mask. All brain tumor patients who receive radiation therapy have a mask made for them. The mask's job is to hold your head perfectly still while you got zapped by the radiation beams. Since the area they're zapping is so small and so incredibly precise, they can't afford to have you accidentally move your head, even by an eighth of an inch. The mask

---

[82] Except for the third film. That was garbage.
[83] Or maybe you would.

starts off looking like a tennis racket with plastic netting. First you lie down on a table. Then the mask is dipped in superhot water, to get the plastic nice and pliable. Then the tennis racket is placed over your face—right on top of your nose—and streeeetched all the way down to the table. It doesn't hurt, but it doesn't exactly tickle, either. The mask then hardens, and the result is a 3-D mold of your face that they keep and pull out when it's time for your radiation appointments. Sinead explained that some people like to decorate theirs, as a way to sort of personalize it. She showed me one that obviously belonged to a little kid and was colored to look like Spider-Man. I know she was trying to be upbeat and put a smile on my face, and I appreciated the effort, but seeing a mask made for a little kid . . . ugh. It was a harsh reminder that brain cancer affects everyone, regardless of age, gender, or income. The idea of a *kid* with brain cancer having to go through all of this upset my stomach.

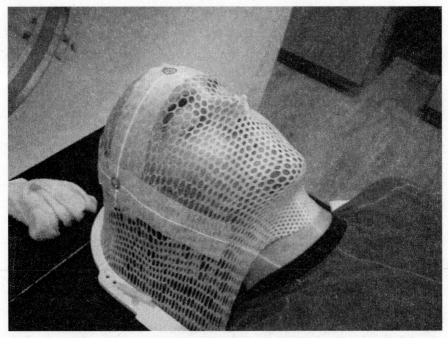

My radiation mask. Notice the plastic "bolts" affixing it to the table. Radiation on your brain is so precise that the technicians can't have you moving at all. *(Christie Bishop)*

Sinead then showed us the actual machine that would administer the radiation. It was encased in a room with a giant lead door and a bunch of signs and stickers warning pregnant ladies to stay away. Sinead was so excited about the machine that she was giddy. Almost like an accountant would get geeked out over a new version of some tax software. It was made by a company called Varian, and apparently it was the latest, most high-tech radiation machine on the market. "And," Sinead said, "she's fully loaded." Her excitement could barely be contained. It was refreshing to see someone who worked around so much pain and suffering to be that enthusiastic about her job.

As we left the radiation area, Sinead leaned in and whispered to Christie, "He's going to *sail* through this." Maybe she could tell Christie was nervous (much more nervous than I was). Maybe she thought Christie was overwhelmed by all the machines and tests and plastic masks. Maybe she was lying to Christie and was just trying to cheer her up. Either way, it helped. A lot.

We wrapped up at the hospital and headed home. It had been a long day, but a satisfying one. No more tests, no more meeting new doctors, no more new-patient forms, and no more explaining everything from the beginning to every new person we met. Plus, I was finally among doctors whom I not only felt comfortable with, but confident in.

A couple of days later, I experienced a fitting ending to my interaction with Dr. Harold Kumar, the doctor who had ham-handedly delivered my grim initial prognosis. He called me on a Friday—more than a week after telling me I might have as little as six months to live. When the phone rang, I recognized the number.

"Who is it?" Christie asked as my phone rang.

"It's Dr. Doom." That's what we had started calling Kumar. Seemed appropriate after the hopeful experience we'd had with our new doctors at Cedars-Sinai. I answered the phone.

"Hello, Bryan, it's Dr. Harold Kumar. I'm just calling to give you the results of your PET/CT scan and talk about a course of treatment."

I should have gone off on him. What I *should* have said was "You have some nerve. First you freak me and my fiancée out by telling me I could be dead in six months while failing to mention that you're not an expert in brain cancer. Then you wait a week to call me again to *start* talking about a course of treatment? According to you, that's 4 percent of the time I have left on earth, you insensitive clod! And how could you assume that I haven't seen my own PET/CT scan already? Not only did I get a copy the day that I was in your office for the scan, do you really think I'd just be sitting at home, twiddling my thumbs, hoping for the phone to ring with news of how my scan looks?"

But I didn't say any of that. Civility got the best of me. "Oh, that's okay," I simply said. "I'm already getting treated at Cedars-Sinai. I start chemo on Monday."

Straightforward and professional. But it must have stung. Radiation and chemotherapy can cost hundreds of thousands of dollars, depending on the hospital and the patient's insurance, and the Angeles Clinic wouldn't be getting any of it.

He took a long pause. "Well," he said tersely, "I'm sorry we won't have the opportunity to treat you."

"I'm sorry, too."

"Your PET/CT scan came back normal. There's no other cancer in your body."

"Okay, great," I replied. "Thank you."

We hung up. And that was the last I ever heard from Dr. Harold Kumar.

II.

The Worst People I've Ever Met

or, My Mount Rushmore of Douche Bags

After my last interaction with Dr. Harold Kumar, I felt I had enough evidence to convict him of being a world-class douche bag. He wasn't guilty of first-degree (premeditated) douchery; more like aggravated douche-slaughter. Either way, in just a short time, he earned himself a spot atop my Mount Rushmore of Douche Bags. My Mount Douchemore. His douche-y résumé:[84]

Gave me six months to a year to live without prefacing that it would be the absolute worst-case scenario. Offered no treatment options or possible solutions upon delivering my prognosis. Failed to explain that he isn't an expert in my area of illness. After delivering my death sentence, did not contact me for a week, despite his office having the results of a body scan that would tell me whether my cancer had metastasized. When he did finally contact me with the results of said test, he had the impudence to assume I was still waiting patiently for him to follow up with me and suggest a course of treatment. When I told him that I had already started treatment at a competing hospital, he had the further temerity to act butt-hurt[85]

---

[84] I tried to get my agent to work in a clause where I would get a bonus every time I used the word *douche* in this chapter. The publisher wouldn't go for it. Good thing, because I'd be into the thousands by the time this chapter is over.

[85] *Butt-Hurt (BUT-hert)*: 1. An inappropriately strong negative emotional response from a perceived personal insult. Characterized by strong feelings of shame. Frequently associated with a cessation of communication and overt hostility toward the "aggressor"; 2. A person who may be

about it and say tersely, "Well, I'm sorry we won't have the opportunity to treat you."

Dr. Harold Kumar had joined a small but illustrious fraternity of assholes. They all got to where they are today by taking different routes, but in the end, they earned their place atop Mount Douchemore. The other illustrious members:

Jack Silver, Program Director for KLSX-FM (97.1, Los Angeles)

Fans of *The Adam Carolla Show* are already familiar with the infamous Jack Silver. When I was given the chance to be an on-air part of the show, my first character was Fake Jack Silver. Fake Jack was a parody of Real Jack, only it was hard to comically exaggerate his character flaws while staying believable because the Real Jack was so over-the-top. My character began as me just goofing off in our daily postshow production meetings. Our producer would throw out an idea for the next day's show, Adam would sign off on it, and I'd pipe up (in Jack's raspy voice), "Not enough cooch, peeps!" This was an almost direct quote from a day earlier, when the Jack Man (as he called himself)[86] burst into our production meeting and greeted us with his trademark "What up, peeps?!" He said this all the time. It became one of the catchphrases for Fake Jack Silver. He then criticized a comedy bit we had done earlier that day, explaining, "I'd really like to see some more cooch!" Teresa Strasser, our female cohost, who was sitting a few feet away, nearly gagged and put her head in her hands in disgust, to which Jack simply said, "My apologies to the ladies in the room!" Adam later described Teresa (on the air) as having been "ear-raped" by Jack Silver.[87]

We had an annual Halloween party/broadcast from the Playboy Mansion that we called "Blotto in the Grotto." For the record, the

---

a whiny little bitch, sad, upset, or pissed off about an event or something that occurred. *Ex: She got all butt-hurt because we didn't invite her to go shopping with us.* SOURCE: UrbanDictionary.com.

[86] Sure sign of a douche bag: He gave himself a nickname. That it was an awful nickname only heightened his douchiness.

[87] I'm pretty sure this is the first cancer memoir to include the term "ear-raped."

Playboy Mansion is *way* overrated. It feels like a corporate party space / animal sanctuary haunted by the ghost of James Caan.[88] The girls in attendance would be dressed in skimpy outfits, and the guys would mostly be dressed in clever outfits. True to form, Jack wore a series of inappropriate costumes, culminating in the year he dressed as a Free Breathalyzer Test. And where was the nozzle? Right over his genitals, helpfully labeled BLOW HERE. This was actually a step up from the previous year, when Jack dressed as a jar of pickles, indicating, of course, his penis was a pickle. *This was our boss.*

The Jack stories are endless.[89] People who worked under him trade Jack Man stories like a combination of Vietnam POWs and the old guys at the beginning of *Broadway Danny Rose.* Jack delighted in firing people, especially part-time staffers. "Bulleting them," he called it, and always with a chuckle. He kept a set of binoculars on his desk in his second-floor, corner office so he could check out attractive women walking down the street. He would do this all the time, sometimes in the middle of a meeting. He would draw diagrams for our writer, Mike Lynch, to (literally) illustrate how comedy worked. He constantly fought with Adam's agent over whether to provide peanut butter as a snack for the staff. Not peanut-butter-and-jelly sandwiches. A single jar of peanut butter. Jack actively and openly "wanted a little less of" three comedians we'd recently had on the show: Joel McHale, Louie CK, and a young, quirky comic named Zach Galifianakis. Jack gave them all a big thumbs-down at the time. Read that list again. Three of the world's biggest comics—one in TV, one in stand-up, and one in the movies—got the "Thanks, but no thanks" treatment from Jack. Yet he worshipped marginal talents such as Tom Leykis and Danny Bonaduce and constantly pleaded with Adam to be more like them, which is like David Kaczynski's dad asking him, "Why can't you be more like your brother, Ted?"

---

[88] Wait, what? James Caan is still alive?

[89] I emailed Angie, our former producer, to see if she remembered any hilarious or bizarre stories about Jack. Her response: "Just seeing his name in the subject line made my skin crawl. Yuck." Congratulations, Jack. That's your legacy.

But I could forgive all the personal stuff if Jack kicked ass at his job. He did not. Jack was in charge of the station in the midnineties, when they were lucky enough to syndicate Howard Stern's wildly popular morning show. Jack rode that wave of success to a number-one ranking in the Los Angeles market. This typifies one of my favorite phrases: He was born on third base and he thinks he hit a triple. Once Stern left for XM satellite radio, the station began its inevitable slide back toward mediocrity. Jack had not developed any new talent, nor had he surrounded *The Howard Stern Show* with any compelling programming. So when the golden goose left and took his eggs with him, it was only a matter of time before the station sank. Just over three years, to be exact.

But here's the crazy part, and the part that reveals Jack's ultimate incompetence: Podcasting was in its infancy when *The Adam Carolla Show* took over for *The Howard Stern Show* on the West Coast (2006). We were only syndicated in a dozen or so markets (there are hundreds of "markets," or geographical regions, in the United States alone), yet the demand for our show came from all over the world. Adam had developed a national radio following by previously hosting *Loveline*, which was syndicated throughout North America. To keep up with the demand, KLSX began posting *The Adam Carolla Show* online, for free, in tiny segments. The show became very popular online, and we were seeing a large number of daily downloads. In fact, more people were listening online than over the traditional airwaves.

Jack would come in every few months and yell at us about our poor ratings. The ratings were only for the Los Angeles radio market, and they didn't include any online numbers. When he would finish delivering the bad news, Adam would reply with something to the effect of "Yeah, but our downloads are really high," to which Jack would invariably respond, "Nobody cares about downloads!" In his feeble mind, online was a dead end: They couldn't (or wouldn't) sell advertising there, and besides, no physical ratings were gained from the downloads. We could all see the writing on the wall: If the show was going to survive, online would be its salvation. But explaining that to Jack was like explaining to a stegosaurus why the weather was getting warmer all of a sudden.

Fast-forward to the present: *The Adam Carolla Show* is the number-one podcast in the world, as verified by none other than *Guinness World Records*. The show makes enough money to pay a staff of a dozen or so employees and turn a profit—all online. Jack, meanwhile, is on his third radio job in as many years, having descended into the no-man's-land of AM radio. He had the soon-to-be most downloaded podcast in the world—not number one in the city, not number one in the country, but number one in the world—right in the palm of his hand, and he let it slip away. Or rather, he threw it away. I get to use another one of my favorite old-timey phrases here: "penny wise and pound foolish." Jack valued pennies (ratings in the Los Angeles radio market) over pounds (significantly more listeners around the world). Somewhere, I hope Jack is enjoying his empire of pennies.

Professor Ed Cray, USC Annenberg School of Communication and Journalism

A little background: Starting at about the age of twelve, I became a journalism nerd. I loved journalism the way Kevin Smith loves *Star Wars* or like a fat kid loves cake.[90] I wrote dozens of stories for my tiny local newspaper throughout middle school—for free—because I loved reporting. My beat consisted of my middle school's volleyball and basketball teams, as well as covering a few other "big local events," such as the town fair. All I wanted out of life at that point was to be the next great sportswriter. Some kids wrote letters to their favorite athletes; I wrote letters to my favorite columnists in the *San Francisco Chronicle*. When I found out the editor of *The New York Times* had gone to the high school I was about to enroll in, I wrote *him* a letter asking for career advice. I was fourteen.[91]

---

[90] I guess we could just simplify this and say "the way Kevin Smith loves *Star Wars* cake."
[91] I'm still waiting for a reply, Bill Keller.

Me, at age twelve, writing a sports "column" on my grandparents' old typewriter. *(Bishop Family)*

By the time I got to high school, I had two goals: become the editor of my high school's newspaper and get in at a university known for its journalism school.[92] I became my high school paper's editor in chief, won the school's award for Most Effective Writer, and was accepted to USC's Annenberg School of Journalism. It was the best journalism school this side of the Medill School of Journalism at Northwestern University in Illinois (or, more accurately, the best journalism school where it doesn't snow).

USC requires all of its journalism majors to enroll in Journalism 201: The History of News in Modern America. It's an introductory class, basically, a US history class taught through the lens of journalism. I loved history. I loved journalism. I loved trivia. This was right up my alley. It was taught by a white-bearded, tenured professor named Ed Cray.

Ed Cray ruined this class the way an infant with dysentery ruins a

---

[92] A third goal, "Don't get stuffed in a locker by a senior," quickly fell by the wayside.

diaper. Actually, that's not fair to the infant; the kid has no idea what he's doing.

Early on in class (possibly even on the first day), a TA explained that we would be graded on three things: one midterm exam, one final exam, and one written paper. The exams would exclusively cover what Professor Cray lectured about in class. The grading for the exams was a little strange: You would be given a handful of essay questions along the lines of "Explain how 'yellow journalism' impacted Hearst vs. Pulitzer." Then you would be awarded a point for every "fact" you included in your answer. We were explicitly instructed *not* to make our answer simply a list of "facts," but to write a cogent, well-thought-out essay that defended our position. Furthermore, the entire class was to be graded on a curve, so the person who achieved the highest score (i.e., the most number of facts) would get the highest grade, and so on.

When it came time for the first exam (the midterm), I was psyched and ready. I remember writing several passionate, persuasive, detailed essays in my blue book that day. I walked out of the exam room with a skip in my step; maybe *I* would get the highest score in the class. With over a hundred students enrolled in the class, it was a long shot, but here's what I had in my favor: I was an effective writer (hence the award I had received the previous year). I had a great memory (to wit, I would win $100,000 on *Who Wants to Be a Millionaire* just ten years later; it's unlikely my memory got *better* in the ensuing decade). I was a good test taker (I had scored 1290 on my SAT test less than two years earlier). So I was naturally optimistic.

When I got my test back during the next class, I hurriedly opened it to read the glowing praise that was sure to be peppered throughout. Instead, to my horror, all I saw were a series of check marks, one by every name, date, and place I mentioned. I flipped through my "graded" exam, looking for feedback or any sort of critical evaluation. Instead, all I found were check marks. No commentary. No criticism. No *words*. They were only counting facts.

I turned to the last page where a grade should ostensibly have been, but all there was was a number: the total number of facts I had listed. I was enraged. I looked around the class and saw the same realization dawning on the rest of the students. It was like a wave of dejection was washing over the classroom. I was apoplectic. WHY DID YOU TELL US TO WRITE AN ESSAY?! WHY EVEN BOTHER? YOU CAN'T SAY "DON'T JUST LIST FACTS" AND THEN GRADE US SOLELY ON OUR ABILITY TO *LIST FACTS*! To add insult to injury, it didn't take long to figure out who had scored the highest on the test (in a competitive academic environment, it never takes long). It was a girl whose score blew all the rest of ours out of the water. She showed someone her test; it was a list of facts in paragraph form. The words made almost no sense; it was basically one run-on sentence after another, each one jam-packed with facts. But there were dozens and dozens of check marks throughout her blue book; she got so many points for her list of facts, it was almost as if it were colored red.

To that point in my life, I had never been so crestfallen. Few things are more cruel in academia than establishing a set of rules or criteria and then changing them on a whim, without notice. In the real world, they have laws against this. The cops can't arrest you and say, "Remember that thing we said was legal? That's illegal now." The only two possible explanations for what was happening in Professor Cray's class were, either he knew about the bait-and-switch grading, for which he should have been severely disciplined; or he *didn't* know, and his TAs had total control over the grading, for which he should have been fired for letting the inmates run the asylum. Alas, he was a tenured professor, which meant outside of a child-molestation scandal, he pretty much couldn't be fired. And given his laissez-faire attitude toward something as important as his chosen profession, the possibility of such a scandal seemed remote.

That was the moment that journalism was ruined for me. Another exam was to be taken at the end of the semester, but the die had been cast. I had an awful taste in my mouth from the experience. Soon after, I was emotionally checked out of journalism; the course of study

I had put years of my life into was no longer something I wanted to be associated with. I felt (rightly so) that the game was rigged. Professor Cray had taken something I loved and made me hate it. He ruined journalism not just for me, but he was ruining it for the whole Annenberg School. Here's what I mean: USC will relentlessly pimp its notable alumni whenever and wherever possible. If you're on their Web site or flipping through an alumni publication, you can't get far without being reminded of USC's notable (read: rich and famous) alumni: Ron Howard! George Lucas! Neil Armstrong! Frank Gehry! Judge Wapner![93] Celebrities from every walk of life . . . except journalism.[94] Why not journalism? Are the best and brightest students being lured away by competing universities? (No.) Are the best and brightest students simply enrolling in other majors? (No.) The fact is, professors such as Ed Cray are hindering their development. He's taking smart writers and neutering them of their talents. Journalism (as we know it) is obviously dying a slow death, but the Ed Crays of the world are hurriedly shoveling dirt on its still-warm corpse.

Bernie, the Father of My First Girlfriend

Everyone else I've enshrined so far on my Mount Douche-more has, more or less, been incompetent in some way. My last honoree was a bully, and a dick.

My first girlfriend was a sweet, innocent soul named Samantha. Samantha was petite before petite was in. During the time we dated, she weighed between 99 and 101 pounds. Not because she didn't eat; she ate like a champ. I once saw her consume an entire I Declair[95] at

---

[93] Strangely, O. J. Simpson no longer appears on these lists.

[94] You could make an argument for Lisa Ling, the excellent TV reporter, but I'd argue she's more of a television personality now than a journalist. And, more important, she started her on-camera career at Channel One News at age eighteen. So it's not like USC "molded" her into a great journalist. But even if I conceded her, that's one. Just one.

[95] Claim Jumper is a sort of Wild West / Gold Rush–themed restaurant. The I Declair was a play on words: *I Declare* meets an éclair. Get it? Ah, dessert humor. I guess after ingesting three thousand calories, anything seems funny.

a Claim Jumper restaurant. For the uninitiated, the I Declair was a giant éclair stuffed with Bavarian cream and topped with vanilla ice cream, hot fudge, and whipped cream. It's as if an éclair were raped by a hot fudge sundae and its overbearing parents forced it to keep the baby.

Samantha was blessed with an active metabolism. I was not. Yet we ate the same food when we were out on dates, which probably explains how I got so fat. It's true; by the time Samantha and I broke up, she was still about 100 pounds, yet I had reached 228 pounds. I was twenty-four years old.

Samantha and I started dating in college, back when I weighed about 180 pounds. We dated exclusively for over five years. We were each other's first serious relationship, and we lost our virginity to each other. It was sweet and innocent. Samantha was a great first girlfriend, and, I think, I was a pretty good boyfriend. But only a couple of years into the relationship, there was no spark. This was possibly due to my putting on weight faster than Marlon Brando on the set of *Apocalypse Now*. But Samantha and I did everything together, and we cared for each other very much.

She was from New Jersey and returned home every winter for Christmas and Hanukkah (her mother was Catholic and her father was Jewish, so she got to celebrate both holidays). One day, we were chatting on AOL's instant messenger, which we did often when we were apart. She mentioned that her dad was hilarious; he could be a comedian, she said. To which I replied, "A Jewish comedian? Imagine that!"

Now, this is not a racist joke. Nor is it even a racial joke. Hell, it's not even a joke. It's simply a whimsical observation that Jews are extremely prevalent in the world of comedy. This is not my opinion. This is a fact. Don't believe me? Ask Sarah Silverman. And Gilbert Gottfried. And Woody Allen. And Jerry Seinfeld. In fact, ask *anybody*.[96]

---

[96] You can also ask Sacha Baron Cohen, Milton Berle, Lewis Black, Albert Brooks, Mel Brooks, Lenny Bruce, George Burns, Red Buttons, Sid Caesar, Andrew Dice Clay, Billy Crystal, Rodney Dangerfield, Al Franken, Shecky Greene, Buddy Hackett, Andy Kaufman, Jerry Lewis, Richard

Why am I belaboring this point? Because right at that moment, Samantha's dad, Bernie—whom I had not yet met, but had heard a lot about from Samantha—walked up behind her and said, "Who are you talking to?" He read my "joke" over her shoulder, said, "Hm," in a terse, pointed way, and walked away without saying anything. His disapproval was obvious to Samantha.

"That was bad, Bryan," she typed to me in our chat window. "That was really bad." She explained how her dad happened to be there right at that instant, and how she could tell he was upset.

I protested, "How is that even remotely offensive? He's Jewish, he should *get* the joke!" But there was no turning back. From that moment on, I was a bad person in Bernie's mind. I would later learn how wildly overprotective he was of Samantha; she was a delicate, precious flower in his mind, and I was the fat slob who was robbing her of her virginly virtue. He would never accept me, and every time we did meet face-to-face, he went out of his way to be a jerk to me.

The best (and last) example I can remember was at Samantha's graduation dinner. She had just graduated from USC, and her family had flown out from New Jersey to be there. They hosted a small dinner at a local restaurant. Samantha and I had been dating for over three years, and I was as fat as she was thin. When we went out, we looked like the number 10. All night at dinner, Bernie gave me grief about my weight. The coup de grâce was toward the end of dinner, when just a small amount of food was left on the table (dinner was family-style) and everyone was discussing whether it was worth it to wrap up the leftovers to take home.

Bernie piped up loudly in his nebbish New Jersey accent for everyone to hear, pointing at me, "Just give it to the garbage disposal over here!" Everyone laughed uneasily, including me. What I should have said was "Hey, dick, I've been nothing but an exemplary boyfriend to your daughter. Why are you going out of your way to torment me?"

Lewis, Howie Mandel, Jackie Mason, Gilda Radner, Carl Reiner, Paul Reiser, Don Rickles, or Joan Rivers. Actually, a lot of those people are dead, so you can't actually ask them. But still.

Instead, I just kind of laughed it off. Bernie was paying for Samantha's celebration dinner, and it would have ruined her night if I had made a scene. But Bernie was a bully who preyed on an easy target: an intimidated, fat, balding college kid who had the nerve to fall in love with his youngest daughter.

Now, please don't think I have thin skin, or that I'm the kind of guy who can't take a joke. Anyone who follows me on Twitter[97] knows that I will retweet almost anything negative said about me, as long as it's clever or funny. At my bachelor party, my friends threw a roast for me in which they told horribly insulting jokes at my expense. I loved it. So don't think I'm overly sensitive. If anything, I'm less sensitive than the average person. To wit, once, sometime after Samantha and I broke up, I embarked on a series of self-improvement projects. One, obviously, was to lose weight. I did, dropping fifty-five pounds to a trim 172. Another was to sign up for something called a Nohari Window.

A Nohari Window is an online survey where you email a whole bunch of friends a link to an anonymous web page. On this page, friends can pick out five or six words (from a list of fifty-five) that best describe you. The only catch: They're all negative. A lot of my friends thought this was masochistic and refused to participate. I assured everyone that I was a big boy and was prepared for whatever they had to say. Besides, it was anonymous, and the results were only going to benefit them—they'd be getting a (hopefully) improved friend!

The words one can choose on the survey range from *incompetent* and *hostile* to *needy* and *unethical*. They call it a Nohari *window* because the results give you a window into your soul. When the results came back, four words stood out as having been selected the most, as my most commonly agreed-upon flaws: *self-satisfied*, *smug*, *distant*, and *withdrawn*. I had suspected *self-satisfied* would be on there; when you set up your window, you actually pick out four words for yourself

[97] @BaldBryan. This will be especially hilarious in 2021, when Twitter is just a distant memory.

that you see as your own biggest flaws. *Self-satisfied* was one of mine.[98] *Smug*, I would argue, is pretty much the same thing (and, of course, I'd be right. Just like always).

I was prepared for *smug* and *self-satisfied*, but *distant* and *withdrawn?* I didn't think of myself that way. But my friends—the ones who knew me best—thought of me that way, so it must have been true. Perception really is reality, so if others perceive it to be true, then it's true. I made myself a commitment to not be distant or withdrawn anymore, and I think it worked. I doubt anyone would call me that now. I would like to do this experiment again someday soon and compare the results to what they were almost a decade ago. I don't think *distant* or *withdrawn* would show up this time. *Smug* and *self-satisfied* . . . well, let's just say those are an ongoing battle.

---

[98] The others I (wrongly) predicted for myself: *inane*, *loud*, and *predictable*. Would a *self-satisfied* person say that about himself??

12.

Best-Case Scenarios

or, My Trip to the Sperm Bank

I was all set up for treatment to begin on Monday, May 4, 2009. We had met all of our doctors, been prescribed all of my pills, and toured all of the hospital's facilities. Only one more medical situation had to be . . . "addressed": a trip to the sperm bank. Radiation, my doctors explained to us, can cause sterility in males, at least temporarily. Even if my sperm production returned to normal postradiation, there was the issue of chemotherapy. I was going to be on chemotherapy indefinitely, my doctors told me—remember, my tumor was inoperable. So, best-case scenario, chemotherapy and radiation would keep my tumor at bay for the rest of my life.[99]

Christie and I thought about it. Here we were, a young couple, due to get married in less than two months. We again pictured the best-case scenario: I would get treated for my brain tumor, we'd get married, and once I bounced back to full health, we'd go about the business of living a normal life—a house, a puppy, and eventually children. But if I was going to be taking chemotherapy forever, then we had to scramble and do some quick preplanning. As one of our doctors warned us, "You don't want to get pregnant when you're on chemotherapy, and you *really* don't want to have a chemo baby." The tone in his voice and the look on his face when he said it told us enough. He didn't have to explain.[100]

---

[99] It's kind of scary when the "best-case scenario" doesn't sound all that great.
[100] Personally, I pictured the grub that Geena Davis gave birth to toward the end of *The Fly.*

So Christie started calling around town to some sperm banks (or, as they're euphemistically known, cryogenic facilities or reproductive centers). Here's all you need to know about sperm banks: They're all expensive, and they all say they're the best. When, in fact, they're all pretty much the same. Some are just a little . . . "classier" than others.

We chose one based partly on its proximity to our apartment and partly its being the cheapest. (Keep in mind, neither of us had a job and we were expecting the worst in terms of our sure-to-be-monumental medical bills that were going to arrive imminently.) Plus, they were able to see me that same day, so off to the sperm bank I went. Christie asked if I'd like her to come with me (get it?), but I told her no, this was the one appointment that she did *not* need to come to. (Seriously, get it?) She seemed relieved.

I checked in at the sperm bank and was greeted by an attractive young nurse. Of course she had to be attractive. Because this story wasn't shaping up to be awkward enough on its own. She explained how the process worked. It's a pretty simple process, as you can probably imagine: masturbate into a cup, screw the cap on, and return it to the front desk. Only she kept using overly clinical terms to describe what I was supposed to do. She kept instructing me to "produce a sample." "Produce a sample into the specimen jar, and once you've produced a sample, screw the cap on tightly . . ."

I decided to have a little fun with her. I held the empty cup up. "Now, how exactly am I supposed to produce this 'sample'?"

Her eyes widened. "Well, uh . . . you just . . ."

I let her off the hook. "Just kidding."

She laughed uncomfortably. She showed me to one of the private rooms where patients produced their samples. It was small. Very small. It was more of a booth, really.

She started to give me the "tour" of the five-by-ten-foot room: "Here you'll find all of the . . . *materials* you'll need." She gestured at a small nightstand that was presumably filled with porn. On top of the nightstand was a roll of paper towels, some K-Y jelly, and a tub of

Purell.[101] On the wall was a small television with a DVD player at-
tached. As she stammered her way through her instructions, I could
sense that she was extremely uncomfortable with this part of the process. But why? It's not like any guy has ever gotten this far into the
process only to say, "Wait, you want me to do *what*?!"

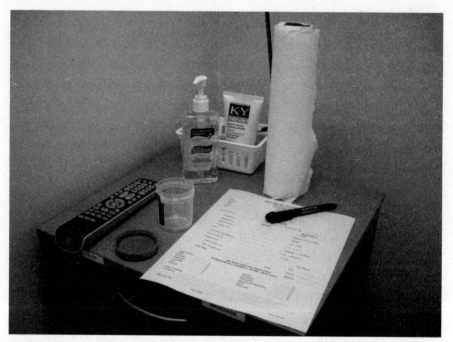

This is what greeted me in my private porn room. Really sets the mood, doesn't it? *(Bryan Bishop)*

She left and closed the door behind her. It was just me and my empire of porn. Curious, I opened the drawer to the nightstand. What
kind of porn do they have at these kinds of places, anyway? I quickly
got my answer: every kind. Sperm banks like to cast a wide net when
it comes to porn selection, apparently, because every major fetish and
predilection was covered: girl-on-girl, Asians, MILFs, busty beau-
ties, you name it. I pictured the poor (probably female) intern who

[101] For all you young masturbators out there, *never* get those last two items mixed up. Take it from
me and my stinging shaft. BTW, "Me and My Stinging Shaft" is a nightclub act I hope to launch
someday in Las Vegas. It's more of an adult-themed show. Sorry, kids.

was tasked with buying all the porn for the office. She probably felt the pressure we all feel when our boss tells us to buy lunch for everyone in the office. You don't know what kind of sandwich everyone likes and dislikes, so your boss tells you, "Just get one of everything!" Strangely, given that we were sort of close to West Hollywood, there was no gay porn in the drawer (I said *strangely*, not *sadly*). Do gay men not go to sperm banks? Or do they have their own fabulous reproductive centers?

Luckily, both magazines and DVDs were in the porn drawer.[102] Being more of a "movie man" than a "magazine man," this was great news. I opened the first DVD box and looked inside, but the disc was missing. "Must still be in the DVD player," I thought. I opened the next DVD box: no disc. I opened all the DVD boxes and found the same thing: all of the discs had been stolen. Who steals porn? From a medical facility?! The resale value can't be high, so that ruled out crack addicts looking to score some quick cash.[103] Who then? Desperate patients who are down on their financial luck? But if you can afford a DVD player (not to mention the cost of cryogenic sperm storage), you can probably afford monthly Internet, in which case you don't *need* porn DVDs. The *world* is your porn DVD! I finally decided the DVDs were stolen by business travelers who used their work computers on road trips and thus couldn't download porn. So their only option was to pack a few adult DVDs in their carry-on. That's the *only* possible explanation.

Thankfully, one DVD was left, and it was in the DVD player. I turned the power on, and the DVD started playing from where the previous guy had turned it off. You don't see that as often these days, but back in the day of VHS cassette tapes, there was something called the splooge point. Once a guy was "done" watching a porn video, he'd hit stop and eject the tape. Rarely would anyone rewind the tape to the beginning. When he'd pop the tape back in at a future date, it would

---

[102] The *porn drawer* is a good name for some slutty girl's vagina.

[103] I was also in a Beverly Hills sperm bank, so that further ruled out crack addicts looking to score some quick cash.

start playing from the point where he'd left it off the time before—the point where he "splooged." Hence the term the *splooge point.*

Well, I was treated to what had been the previous gentleman's splooge point. The DVD played, I took care of my business, and I started to zip up and adjourn. Then I got a great idea for a practical joke.

I'm a big fan of victimless practical jokes. Obviously, there's a victim in every practical joke, but I mean jokes where nobody gets hurt (physically or emotionally) and nobody loses his or her job, for example. A joke where everyone laughs at the end, the victim says, "Ya got me," and we all move on with our lives. I'll give you an example:

Once, when we were in our early twenties, a bunch of us were hanging out at my friend JD's house, drinking beers and watching cheesy horror movies. As we started to watch *Pumpkinhead* (yes, THAT *Pumpkinhead*), it quickly became obvious that the kids in the movie were all going to die, one by one, until only one was left. I think about seven kids were in the movie, and there were seven of us. We decided, arbitrarily, that we would each get assigned a kid from the movie, and whoever's kid died fifth, that person would lose the bet. The penalty for losing: You had to go outside of the apartment and yell, at the top of your lungs, *"I am a registered sex offender!"*[104] Well, you can guess what happened: My kid died fifth, so I had to go outside into JD's residential street and yell, *"I am a registered sex offender!"* Just before I did, I clarified the rules with JD and everyone: As long as I say the words *I am a registered sex offender,* the bet is fulfilled?

Right, they all assured me. So I walked out into the middle of the street and got ready to yell. All the guys and girls who were in the house gathered on the stoop to watch me humiliate myself. I paused for a second, then let rip in my loudest voice, *"My name is JD and I am a registered sex offender!"*

Everyone laughed (even JD, who realized I had beaten him on a

---

[104] I didn't say it was especially clever. What do you want? We were drunken idiots.

technicality). I had said the words—shouted them, in fact. I just added a little bit that turned me from the victim into the victimizer. Best of all, no real harm was done, and we went back to watching Pumpkinhead pick off the rest of the kids.

Back to the porn booth. I rewound the DVD to its most . . . "explicit" point. I mean, the part of the movie (excuse me, *film*) with the most vigor. Then I pressed stop once (when you press stop on a DVD just once, it starts playing again from that exact spot. Which is what had just happened to me). Then, in a move of diabolical genius, I turned the volume on the TV up to its maximum level. Then I turned the TV off. If my prank went according to plan, the next unsuspecting guy who innocently pressed play on the DVD player would instantly be greeted by the deafening roar of filthy, vigorous lovemaking. Better yet, he would flood the rest of the office and the waiting room

Good clean fun. *(Bryan Bishop)*

with said sounds. I pictured the panicked gentleman furiously fumbling for the remote control as the "actress" moaned and screamed obscenities. Embarrassing, yes, but harmful? No way. He'd never see any of those people again. Best-case scenario: He'd think it was a clever practical joke (which it was).

13.

Chemo, Day One

or, A Journey of a Thousand Miles . . .

Monday morning, I woke up ready to start my treatment. Or, at least I thought I was. That night, at 10:00 p.m., I was to start taking my oral chemotherapy pills—Temodar, to be exact—and the next morning I would start my six-week cycle of daily radiation. But first, I had a to-do list.

One of my greatest fears is being disorganized, especially in times of crisis or considerable stress.[105] Thus, I had a long list of tasks, appointments, and errands to fulfill before I could start my pill-taking routine with a clear conscience.

First, we needed groceries. Not the crap we normally eat; I had a burning desire to eat healthy, organic produce. So off we went to Whole Foods, known for their organic, locally sourced fruits and vegetables. We loaded up on everything from fresh-pressed juices to raw kale to prunes. Our doctors had warned me about the potential for (read: probability of) constipation, and I was going to head that shit off at the pass—pun intended.

Next stop: Crate & Barrel, or, as we were calling it, the Wedding Registry Depot. Friends and family had been getting us gifts off our registry for Christie's shower, but a couple of them had arrived broken, despite their insanely elaborate packaging. No wonder that store

---

[105] Please don't tell this to a single mother in Africa whose greatest fear is not being able to find clean drinking water every day.

charges so much—someone has to subsidize all that padding. So we headed to Crate & Barrel and exchanged our broken red Mario Batali pizza stone for a new one.

Once we crossed that crucial errand off the list, it was off to a CVS pharmacy to fill a whole bunch of prescriptions. A lot of the pills that our doctor had prescribed were available over the counter, but he had recommended the prescription-strength version of a few of them. We got . . .

1. *Steroids: minimizes swelling (and symptoms) of the brain caused by the tumor and radiation (take twice daily).*

2. *Antacid: prevents acid flare-ups from steroids (once daily).*

3. *Prescription-strength fish oil: Who knew they even made this? Helps open the blood-brain barrier so the chemo can pass through and get to the tumor (once daily).*

4. *Zofran (antinausea): protects the stomach from getting upset when taking chemo pills (once daily). I knew this was serious stuff when Christie and I were watching Deadliest Catch one night and one of the cameramen became dangerously seasick. When he wouldn't stop vomiting, they broke out their secret supply of Zofran. I exclaimed to Christie, "Holy crap, that's the stuff that I'm on!"*

5. *Ativan: antianxiety. I didn't think I was anxious, but the doctors assured me that it was better to have it, just in case (one pill as needed).*

The one thing we couldn't get at CVS was the actual chemotherapy. It's serious medicine and is classified as a Category D drug, or whatever the hell it is. Basically, you have to get it from a specialty pharmacy—in my case, an online pharmacy that would ship it to me in temperature-controlled packaging overnight. When it actually arrived, I felt like Nicolas Cage in *The Rock* handling VX gas.

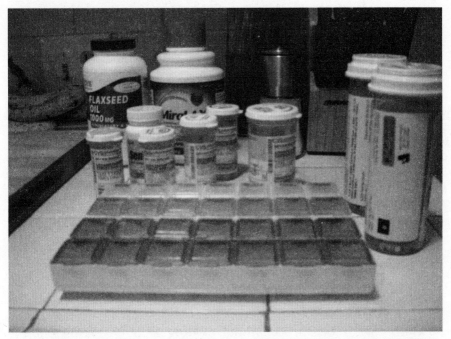

The collection of pills and medications I ended up with after just a couple of days. *(Christie Bishop)*

Then it was on to Costco, where we'd be loading up on some "supplies" we'd need for my cancer battle, including bulk packages of some over-the-counter medications. Specifically, multivitamins and flaxseed oil. You know, like the kind Barry Bonds took.

Tumor Tip: If you're going to take a daily multivitamin (and you probably should), might I suggest you take a children's chewable? Most of them actually have enough vitamins in them for an adult's daily recommended value, and they have the distinct advantage of tasting good. Most adult (nonchewable) multivitamins taste like . . . well, multivitamins. Not good. Chewables, on the other hand, make you want to take them regularly. So don't punish yourself just to get your daily intake of vitamins. Switch over to the chewables ASAP and prepare to have your pill-taking life changed forever.

Finally, we returned home. We put away all of our gifts, groceries, and pills. It was about dinnertime, and Christie was ready to wind down. Not me. "Let's make pizza!" I urged her. She raised her eyebrows at me weakly, as if to say, "Really?" Yes, really. I wanted to put our new pizza stone to use to make some healthy homemade pizza, topped with some of the organic veggies we had just bought.

Pizza making is a rewarding, albeit time-consuming, process. But what the hell else did we have to do? Stare at the clock, waiting for 10:00 p.m. to come, when I could start taking my chemotherapy pills? Hell no. A couple of hours later, we were fed; our new pizza stone had been broken in. *Now* Christie was ready to wind down. And, she thought, so was I. Wrong again. I jumped off the couch. "We need to clean this place."

She looked at me. "Really? Now?"

"Yes," I said. "*Now.*"

With that, I began vacuuming, folding laundry, taking out the trash . . . basically, everything Christie had begged me to do for the previous year. In my mind, I was thinking, "I'm going to start a routine tonight—the most important routine of my life. And I *cannot* do it properly if my life isn't perfectly organized." Of course, the idea of one's life being "perfectly organized" is ludicrous, but things like unfolded laundry or an overflowing trash can were, in my mind, going to prevent me in some way from beating cancer. You could call this line of thinking ridiculous, but if someone believes something so wholeheartedly, and it can put his or her mind at ease, is it necessarily wrong?

Christie, God bless her, helped out in my insane crusade to organize our home. Then, ten o'clock rolled around. Time to take my chemo pills for the first time. My doctors had instructed me to take them at the same time every night. I'm sure *at the same time* meant "within a half an hour either way," but I wasn't leaving anything to chance. I was taking my pills at 10:00 p.m. every night. I adjourned to the bedroom and picked up the comically large bottle of pills. The pills themselves weren't especially large—about the size of a normal gelcap—but they were split up into pill bottles the size of flashlights.

Each bottle had just that day's dose inside, so there was *no way* you could accidentally take too many pills.

I read the instructions printed on the label, which tell you to wash your hands immediately after touching the pills and to never let a pregnant woman handle them. Yet here I was, about to swallow them. Bottoms up! I took the pills one at a time and washed them down with water. Big mistake. Water alone couldn't mask the awful flavor. The pills were coated in a disgustingly flavored serum, presumably to prevent little kids from accidentally taking mommy or daddy's chemotherapy. In these scenarios, I wish there were an option to say, "Not only do we not have kids, we don't know anyone with kids, so please spare me the childproof cap and the foul-tasting coating for the pills. Thank you." I learned from my water mistake that night; I started washing my pills down with Gatorade.

I sat there, on our bed, the pills barely in my stomach. I braced myself for an overwhelming wave of nausea. "Here comes the sickness that you see in movies," I convinced myself. It was a cliché, but it was a cliché for a reason, I figured. Doctors freak you out about it, too—"If you throw up the pills after taking them, do not take more pills. Call your doctor," they say. I sat there for a few minutes, breathing deeply. I felt . . . normal. As if nothing were different. The anti-nausea pills I had taken an hour earlier seemed to be doing the trick. If anything, the only thing I was feeling was anxiety—self-induced. I went back into the living room.

Christie looked up at me. "So? How do you feel?"

"Fine," I replied. "Normal. Good."

We went to bed. If I'd accomplished anything that day, it was wearing both of us out. We'd had a full day, thanks to my anxiety. We went to bed and slept a full, good night's sleep. We needed it; the next day was Day One of radiation.

14.

Radiation

or, "I Wonder What She Has"

I can't properly explain how I felt when I woke up on the morning of my first day of radiation. Not because I don't remember or because I blocked it out. It's because I don't exactly know what to compare it to. It'd be like trying to explain to a Vulcan what love is.[106] The closest thing I can compare it to, maybe, is the clichéd feeling that the "nervous groom" feels on the day of his wedding: "Oh, crap, this day is really finally here. . . . All the planning and worrying has led to this. . . . God, I hope I don't throw up. . . . I could run, but what good would that do? . . . It'd only make things worse. . . . Let's just get this over with. . . . Best-case scenario, this all goes smoothly and I live a normal, uneventful life from this day forward."

Yes, I had all these thoughts that morning. From the time we pulled up at the parking lot of the hospital's cancer center, I kept thinking, "This is wrong, we don't belong here." Like the fat prisoner at the beginning of *The Shawshank Redemption:* "I don't belong here! I wanna go home!" Then the other inmates chant at him, "Fresh fish!" And he gets beaten to death by the guards.

We checked in at the front desk. The receptionist explained the labyrinthine path we'd need to follow to get to the radiation area of the hospital. Then, seeing that we were already overwhelmed with confusion, he called over Jerry, a porter whose job it was to show new

---

[106] This isn't even close to the nerdiest analogy I'm going to make in this book, so be warned.

patients around. Jerry was a tall, lanky black man with a warm, infectious energy. He was bubbling with enthusiasm, which seemed incongruous with the place he worked at. He took us to the elevator, then down the winding ant farm of hallways that led to the radiation waiting room. I remember thinking it'd take a trail of bread crumbs for us to ever find our way out of there; thank God for Christie's superior sense of direction.[107] It felt as if we were Clarice and Dr. Chilton was leading us down to the dungeon to meet Hannibal Lecter.[108]

Once we got to the dungeon—err, waiting room—it felt oddly out of place: a little oasis in a desert of slick, sterile hospital life. It was a tiny beehive of activity: A few patients were lined up at the check-in desk. A few more patients were sitting in the waiting area—some in hospital gowns, some in regular clothes. Some were stepping in and out of little private booths lined along the perimeter of the waiting room. Some were talking to their doctors. Some were young, some old, and some in between. Some looked tired, a few looked anxious, and one or two looked angry. All colors and ethnicities seemed to be represented. It was like the world's saddest United Colors of Benetton ad. Either that, or the opening ceremonies to the Super-Depressing Olympics. Yet, despite the obvious sadness, you could instantly feel a sense of community upon walking into the waiting room. Everyone was intermingling. People seemed oddly at ease.

Jerry left us at the desk to check in for our appointment, then we found a pair of seats in the waiting room. We began to take it all in. Personally, I can't put it any better that Christie did in her blog:

> There was a young Hispanic girl, probably about 32 years old, who was accompanied by her sister and her baby. A beautiful paisley bandanna covered her head, as she was clearly losing her hair as a result of treatment. There was an older African American gentleman, with whom I

---

[107] This line probably pleases her more than anything else I could possibly write in this book. For the record, I have a far superior ability to read maps, but Christie has the better natural sense of direction. Ugh.

[108] Yep, that's the third movie reference in as many paragraphs.

have since had the pleasure of getting to know, chilling out in his blue hospital gown. He knew all the nurses and doctors and was as calm and cool as a cucumber. Then there was the neurotic, angry Caucasian woman. She had places to go and things to do. She exclaimed, to no one in particular, that she had been "coming to this center off and on since 2001," and she didn't have time for this. Apparently she had to pick up her daughter from school and radiation was getting in the way. I didn't know how to react to her other than just simply sigh. Finally, there was an older couple, probably in their late 70s, who had clearly been coming to the radiation center for a long time. They were beyond sweet. He was sitting in a wheelchair, while she sat and held his hand from a nearby chair. They were talking to a cancer center volunteer about the friends they used to see in the park "from time to time," and how cancer inevitably got each and every one of them. It was heartbreaking and I had to bite the inside of my cheek to fight back my tears.

I wonder what they thought of Bryan and me that day. We were clutching on to each other in the chairs. Literally, both our hands were wrapped around each other's. The old-timers probably laughed at us, knowing we were newbies. Or they were devastated, knowing we were so young.

For me, it was amazing to see the different stages of acceptance in which each person (and group) seemed to be. I think these stages are something like denial, anger, bargaining, depression and, finally, acceptance. Some people were fine, like "Let's do this so I can get on with my day." Some people were beyond pissed, being rude to the technicians and staff. Some people were clearly exhausted from the fight and just sat, waiting for their turn with the machine. And then there were the newcomers, like Bryan and me and another girl our age, named Joanna. While I don't know what emotional stage Joanna was in, Bryan and I created our own "How the hell did we end up in a cancer center?" stage (okay, I guess that's technically denial). Between Bryan, Joanna and myself, the three of us were the quietest ones in the room. We had signed in at the registration booth with Joanna, so I knew it was her first day. I wondered what her story was, but didn't dare ask (we were too fragile and I could tell she was, too). I wondered when she got the news about her cancer and I wondered if it was from a good, caring doctor. I hoped she didn't have to go through the "Dr. Doom" experience that we did. I wondered what her prognosis was. But most of all, I wondered why she was all alone. Why there was no one there holding her hand. Had she not told anyone? Did she want to be alone? Or did she not have anyone to come with her? It really made me realize that no matter what Bryan and I were going through or how bad it might get at times, we had each other for support. Every day and every minute, through thick and thin. I think that is the true meaning of unconditional love.

Looking back, we probably stuck out like a pair of sore thumbs that first day. While everyone else was chatting and forming an invisible web of support for each other, we sat alone, huddled together, nervously holding hands. I remember that Caucasian woman who seemed all bent out of shape that her appointment time had elapsed and her kid needed to be picked up. I remember thinking how I would normally have been annoyed by someone like her, but now I just thought, "Man, the stress of it all must really be getting to her. I wonder what she has." I found myself silently saying that a lot from that day forward: "I wonder what he/she has." Sometimes it was obvious—the guy with a fresh surgical scar on his head, for example—but most of the time it wasn't. Thankfully, we came to find out that "What do you have?" is a perfectly acceptable question in the radiation center and can even be an effective conversation-starter.

I remember everyone that Christie wrote about that day, more or less. I remember the nice young couple who had traveled from Jamaica just to get treated at Cedars-Sinai. They were staying in a hotel for a month while the wife received her treatment. I remember Herb and Faye, an older couple whom we became friendly with during our time in the radiation waiting room. While I was in total business-mode when we got to the radiation center, Christie was our ambassador. For the fifteen to twenty minutes that we were apart—me in the back, getting radiated, her in the waiting room—she would write blog entries and make friends. Herb and Faye were two of those friends. They were an adorable older couple. They, too, made note of Jerry's upbeat attitude the first time they ever checked in. When Jerry first laid eyes on Faye, he remarked that she looked "just like Elizabeth Taylor!" To a woman in her sixties, this is a massive compliment, especially when said woman might not be feeling her most beautiful. So Jerry was instantly on their good side. We bonded over that. We also bonded over a bizarre coincidence. Many years earlier, Herb's mother had lived in the same apartment that we currently lived in. Not the same building; the exact same unit. We marveled at the sheer odds. Los Angeles is a huge place, as I mentioned before. And for us to meet under those circumstances—two couples, decades apart, linked by the unlikeliest of coincidences . . . I mean, you either believe in these things, or you don't. The cynic in me was saying, "Wow, that's an unlikely coincidence. Not impossible, but unlikely."

But the believer in me . . . well, I'm not sure what I was thinking. Was it a coincidence that I moved into Christie's apartment instead of the other way around? To be in the shadow of Cedars-Sinai, less than a mile away from one of the world's leading institutions for treating brain tumors? Was it a coincidence that a childhood friend had a connection with Dr. Black, arguably the world's leading brain surgeon? Was it a coincidence that Christie and I had just both been laid off, so we wouldn't have to worry about missing so much work time when we were at the hospital? The answer to all of these things is "Probably, yes." But when you're in a desperate situation and looking for answers to questions as simple as "Why?," a series of coincidences start to look more like a plan, or a path, kind of like the green arrow in those Fidelity commercials.

Radiation itself only took a few minutes. I checked in every morning and was handed one of those red, buzzing pagers that they give you at the Cheesecake Factory or California Pizza Kitchen. When my pager lit up and buzzed, I left Christie behind in the waiting area and headed back to the radiation room. I was greeted by one of three techs who worked the machine. One of them, Len, was a chatty, bald guy who loved sushi. *I* was a chatty, bald guy who loved sushi. It didn't take long for our love to blossom. Len looked like the stand-up comedian Dave Attell, if Dave had chosen a life of clean living and sushi over a life of drinking and whoring. Each radiation appointment lasted a good three minutes longer than it needed to as Len and I bonded over our shared love of raw fish and scalp polish. Los Angeles gets a lot of crap (deservedly so) for its shortcomings—pollution, crime, high cost of living[109]—but has some positives, even beyond the weather. Thanks to the sheer size and diversity of the population, LA has a large number of terrific ethnic restaurants, sushi places being toward the top. Len was a wealth of information about good sushi restaurants to visit. Given that I was committed to eating as healthy a diet as possible while I was on chemotherapy, new sushi recommendations were welcome. Also, we were on a serious budget—the kind couples put themselves on when they're both unemployed less than two months before their wedding. (Admittedly, this is kind of a unique circumstance.) People think of sushi as expensive or even luxurious. It certainly can be, but a lot of great sushi—at least in big cities such as Los Angeles—is pretty cheap. Get a recommendation from a friend who knows, and go get some good, cheap sushi.

Every day, I walked into the radiation room and stood face-to-face with the machine that Sinead had dubbed "the Ferrari of Radiation Machines." The techs would lay me on the slab, faceup, and affix my custom-fitted mask over my face and head. Then they would leave and shut the massive leaden door. The fact that the techs stood in another room, separated by a two-foot-thick lead door, should have alarmed me, but it never crossed my mind. Instead, I lay totally still, with measured breathing, waiting as the machine did its work. I expected some buzzing or maybe even a burning sensation, but I felt nothing. If not for the whirring of the machine's gears as it occasionally

---

[109] Also, police corruption, traffic, illegal immigration, high taxes, unions, failing schools, inept government, potholes, earthquakes, lack of parking, gentrification . . .

changed positions, I'd never even know it was powered on. The only other sounds in the room came from an iPod that the techs left on for the patients, ostensibly to calm them as they received their radiation. I remember there being a lot of Phil Collins and artists of that ilk. At first, I was a little annoyed at the music selection, but then I realized that it must have been a joke—a tongue-in-cheek playlist made partially to calm me down, and partially to amuse me. At least, I hope it was a joke.

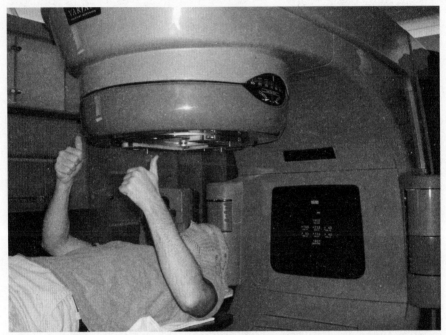

About to get radiated for the first time. This sums up my general attitude at that point in my life.
(Nancy Bishop)

I came out of the radiation room every day looking like Godzilla. The plastic mask they had molded to my face—the one that had started out looking like a tennis racket—fit *very* snugly. Remember, this was a game of millimeters, so they didn't want me moving in the slightest. After ten or twelve minutes of having this thing affixed to my face, I had a crisscross pattern on my face that made me look like a lizard . . . a pink, bald lizard. I could probably have scared the hell out of some kids if I'd just had the motivation to hurry off to the pediatrics ward.

Within just a few days, we counted ourselves among the Regulars at the radiation center. It doesn't take long for you to feel initiated into a fraternity like that one. A week or so later, we saw another young couple checking in for the first time. They were about our age, maybe even a little bit younger. We could tell who was new and who wasn't. The regulars had an ease to their body language; the new couple wore their anxiety all over their faces. She was the one with cancer—I could tell from the patient's wristband she wore. Also, she was the one filling out all the paperwork. Her boyfriend looked on dutifully—I assumed they were dating because neither wore a ring. I found myself wondering if their relationship would last; if he would stick it out all the way through, come what may, or if he would bail. I thought about this, and I realized again how lucky I was to be engaged to Christie. I looked over at Christie; she was typing away on her BlackBerry, blogging. I squeezed her arm. She looked at me and smiled. I smiled back and gestured toward the new couple. Christie looked at them, then at me. She knew what I was saying. She smiled again. I leaned in closer to Christie and whispered, "I wonder what she has."

15.

My Feel-Good Playlist

or, "You've Got to Pay Your Dues If You
Want to Sing the Blues"

During my first week of radiation, I woke up early one morning and couldn't get back to sleep. Despite my best efforts to get organized prior to starting treatment, I still felt that some little things were out of whack. Things that might seem trivial to most (read: normal) people, but were big deals to me. Chief among them: I needed to make a playlist.

I pride myself on having a playlist of songs for almost every occasion. Big-band Rat Pack songs for a cocktail party? Got it. Americana for a backyard barbecue? Got that, too. Embarrassing songs that you love but you wouldn't want to be caught singing loudly in your car with the windows down?[110] You bet your ass.

I woke up with the sudden urge to make a playlist of feel-good songs that I could listen to when I was on my way to radiation, or anytime I was feeling lousy. Rather than go into detail about the song itself, I'll just tell you why it ended up on my Feel-Good playlist. If you are familiar with these songs, great. You'll know what I'm talking about. If you haven't heard them before, do yourself a favor and track them down, then read this section.

---

[110] I seriously have a playlist of these songs. I call them Tool Tunes. Think "Kiss on My List" by Hall and Oates.

1. "It's a Great Day to Be Alive" by Travis Tritt

I don't really like Travis Tritt. He has a mullet. He has a finely mani-cured beard. In 1992, he coheadlined "The No Hats Tour" with Marty Stuart (another guy with a mullet, come to think of it). Most of his songs are best described as meh. But not this one.

"It's a Great Day to Be Alive" was the first song I thought of for this list. Actually, my thought was "I need to make a whole playlist of songs that make me feel as good as "'It's a Great Day to Be Alive.'" It's a what-the-hell song, a song that makes anything seem possible. Not because the singer thinks he's invincible; far from it. At one point he sings, "Look in the mirror and what do I see? / A lone wolf there staring back at me / Long in the tooth but harmless as can be / Lord, I guess he's doing all right." He accepts his limitations and fights on in spite of them.

It's one of the best songs ever to prominently feature a banjo, right up there with "I Will Wait" by Mumford and Sons, "Wagon Wheel" by OCMS, and "The Rainbow Connection" by Kermit the Frog. It also features a lyric that any cancer patient (or anyone going through a difficult time) can identify with: "Sometimes it's lonely, sometimes it's only me / And the shadows that fill this room / Sometimes I'm fallin', desperately callin' / Howlin' at the moon."

Anyone who's faced a tough stretch in life—sickness (be it one's own or a loved one's) or a divorce or some other prolonged traumatic experience—knows the loneliness that the nighttime brings. When the moon comes out and the world goes to sleep, it's just you and your thoughts. Sometimes that can be the worst prison of all; I'm not at all surprised that some people turn to drugs or alcohol in times like those. You *do* feel as if you're falling and desperately calling—for help, for someone who understands, or maybe just someone who'll listen.

2. "Feelin' Stronger Every Day" by Chicago

Chicago is my dad's favorite band. So much so that he even likes Chi-cago's later eighties stuff, when they morphed into Robo-Chicago and started putting out ball-less soft-rock hits such as "So Hard to Say I'm Sorry" and "You're the Inspiration." Now *that's* loyalty.

Forget what you know about that band. *This* song is from the band's heyday, 1973. It was cowritten by Peter Cetera, presumably before his testicles started producing massive amounts of circulating estrogen. The first half of the song is a pleasant-yet-unremarkable breakup song about how they tried, but now it's time for them to "live on the run," yada yada. It's the song's rollicking second half that made it an obvious choice for my Feel-Good playlist.

When the second half of "Feelin' Stronger Every Day" kicks in, it brings the song from a midtempo shrugfest to a horn-infused, all-out jam. It feels as if the rest of the band tired of Cetera's shoe-gazing and said, "Okay, enough of this mopey nonsense, let's jam." The drummer goes nuts, the horn section picks up the pace, and the band yells, "Feelin' stronger every day! (You know I'm alright now!)" about twenty times in a row. If Sigmund Freud were alive (and a rock-and-roll fan) in 1973,[111] he'd have heard this song and said, "Dude, that song is pure *id*."

And that's why it's on my list. Not for any deep metaphorical reason. It's because sometimes, when you're on your tenth round of chemo and your wife is helping you get to another physical-therapy appointment in your ankle brace and walker, you need a song to pump you up so you can say, "Yeah, I *am* feelin' stronger every day!"

3. "It's a Long Way to the Top (If You Wanna Rock 'n' Roll)" by AC/DC

Most people can't get past the bagpipes in this song. I feel bad for those people because to them this song will always be "That song with the bagpipes," instead of "That awesome AC/DC song that rocks and just happens to feature bagpipes."

On it's face, it's just a simple Rock & Roll Life on the Road song[112]

---

[111] I actually had to look up if Freud was still alive in 1973. Yes, I'm an idiot. On the other hand, I *do* have a brain tumor.

[112] Other great Rock & Roll Life on the Road songs: "Turn the Page" by Bob Seger, "We're an American Band" by Grand Funk Railroad, and "The Load-Out" by Jackson Browne.

about all the crap you have to put up with to become a big-time rock star (getting robbed, stoned, beat up, old and gray, ripped off, underpaid, and sold secondhand. It's not hard to see how Bon Scott died choking on his own vomit). But metaphorically, it applies to all of us: Anything worth achieving is worth going through a lot of crap to get there. That's what I thought to myself as I sat with a fistful of chemotherapy, anyway.

Apparently, it's a pretty universal theme: The song has been covered by everyone from Motorhead and Billy Corgan to Hanson and the Wiggles.

4. "Where the Green Grass Grows" by Tim McGraw

If I told most people that I had a Tim McGraw song on my playlist and the song made me get a little emotional, they'd probably think it was "Live Like You Were Dying"—a decent song, but not the one I'd choose. Fun fact (if you consider brain tumors fun): "Live Like You Were Dying" was recorded in honor of Tim's father, Tug McGraw. Tug was a major league pitcher who died in 2004 of (you guessed it) sickle-cell anemia. Just kidding. He died of a brain tumor! What are the chances? And Tug's most famous quote? "You gotta believe!"

This is the only song on my Feel Good playlist that makes me a little emotional. Not because it's a sad song; quite the opposite. It's a triumphant song, about overcoming your current crappy situation ("Another supper from a sack / A ninety-nine-cent heart attack") to live the life of your dreams, whatever that may be—in this case, living where the green grass grows (and the corn pops up in rows, apparently).

But the part of the song that makes the room get a little dusty (in a good way) is when Tim McGraw sings about how he's going to get out of this miserable city ("I don't know who my neighbors are / There's bars on the corners and bars on my heart") and spend his days "pointing our rocking chairs to the west" and his nights "tucked in close to you." I would listen to this song and think, "Hey, that's what I want . . . *I* want to be old someday in a rocking chair, and *I* want to be tucked in close to my wife." Keep in mind that Christie and I weren't even married yet, so the idea of getting to be old and in rocking chairs together wasn't just romantic, it was aspirational.

5. "It Don't Come Easy" by Ringo Starr

Released in 1971, this was Ringo Starr's first UK single after leaving the Beatles. It was a Top 10 hit in both the United States and the UK. It was such a good song that it led to one of the great rock-and-roll urban legends/rumors of all time: Did George Harrison write "It Don't Come Easy" for Ringo and give him full writing credit? As an urban legend, it ranks just behind "Did the lead singer from Three Dog Night really have an erection that lasted two years?" and "Did Rod Stewart really once ingest so much semen that he had to have his stomach pumped?"

Speaking of which, sometimes I like to imagine all of the stars of the seventies getting together for an Urban Legend Fantasy Draft. It'd be like ending up as part of the Human Centipede: You want to end up first, you don't want to end up second to last, and you *really* don't want to be last. Rod's manager would probably be, like, "Well, Rod, the bad news is the guy from Three Dog Night got the first pick, so he's most likely gonna snap up the priapism one that makes him look like an indefatigable sex monster. I mean, he'd be stupid not to. But the good news is you're not picking last. Some young actor named Richard Gere got stuck with that one!"

As for the veracity of Ringo's songwriting, you can understand why the rumor persists among rock aficionados. It was 1970, and George was brimming with talent and confidence. Some (such as myself) would argue that he had the best solo career of any Beatle[113] and was the most eager to break out once the band fell apart. Ringo, meanwhile, wasn't exactly known for his songwriting prowess. His best Beatles songs—"Matchbox," "Act Naturally," "With a Little Help

---

[113] If you want to argue with me, please listen to "Wonderful Christmastime" and "Dear Yoko" on a twenty-four-hour loop first. Then we can talk.

from My Friends"—were sung by him but written by others. By all accounts, Ringo was an affable (if marginally talented) guy; that's how he ended up in the Beatles in the first place (the band's original drummer, Pete Best, was supposedly an insufferable dick that nobody wanted to be around).[114] So when the Beatles broke up because Paul, John, and George thought, "Man, these other guys are really stifling my creativity!," Ringo looked around and thought, "Um, *I'm* not feeling creatively stifled at all. Quite the opposite, in fact."

So George did Ringo a solid. He had a surplus of great songs, so he delivered one to his pal Ringo. And it's a fantastic song. The opening lyric: "You've got to pay your dues if you want to sing the blues / And you know it don't come easy." I vividly remember lying in my bed (both at home and, later, in the hospital) thinking about the lyrics to "It Don't Come Easy." How someday this would all make a great story, but I had to pay my dues first. All of the unpleasantness—radiation, chemotherapy, rehab—it was just paying my dues so that I could someday write a mediocre book about it.

When anyone asks me how I got through it all—the radiation, the chemotherapy, etc.—I can't ever point to any one thing. My wife, my family, my friends, my doctors . . . they all obviously played huge parts in getting me to where I am today. But these songs, which I listened to almost every day early on, helped a lot, too. It feels silly, giving credit to a list of songs. But as Ringo said, you gotta pay your dues if you wanna sing the blues, and these songs helped me get there.

---

[114] This is a piece of advice I'd like to extend to all young people in the workforce: *Start out* as a jovial fellow, *then* slowly become an unconscionable prick. Not the other way around. It worked for me. (Hi-yo!)

16.

Constipation and Other Early Symptoms

or, When the Shit *Doesn't* Hit the Fan

After only a few days of chemotherapy and radiation, I was feeling all right. Normal, even, or as normal as I had been feeling before I started treatment. The chemo wasn't making me nauseous the way you see in the movies. The radiation wasn't affecting me in any noticeable way. Other than being a bit fatigued from the whirlwind of it all, I was doing okay. I was even feeling well enough to attend the taping of *Ace in the Hole*, Adam Carolla's TV pilot for CBS that I was supposed to have been working on. I contacted Dionne Kirschner about dropping by unannounced to watch the show being taped and to say hi to the guys I knew on the staff—head writer Kevin Hench, writer's assistant Mike Lynch, and of course Adam himself. I asked Dionne not to tell anyone that Christie and I would be showing up; none of them had seen me since before I was diagnosed, and I wanted to surprise them.

The taping went well. It was exceedingly long, which should come as no surprise to anyone who's familiar with the television business. If you're a tourist visiting Los Angeles and you want to see a sitcom taping, do everything in your power to watch an *established* show being taped. One whose title you've at least heard of. Shows that have been on the air for a couple of years (usually) run like clockwork. They have the kinks ironed out, and the cast and crew treat it like any regular job: They punch in, do the work, and then they want to get the hell out of there and go home. New shows, on the other hand, do a lot of tinkering: Move this camera over there, try that line this way, do it again and again and again. In terms of taping time, pilots are the worst. And you know what exacerbates all that sitting and waiting and forced laughter if you're an audience member? *If you've just started chemotherapy and radiation for a brain tumor.*

That said, it was a fun time. When Adam looked up and saw me and Christie in the crowd he said, "Hey, Bald Bryan's here." He said it under his breath, to himself, almost as if he were thinking out loud, but because of the microphone on him, his aside was broadcast among the entire crowd. And because the crowd was largely made up of fans of the radio show, a few people shuffled in their seats to look my way. A few of them waved and smiled. They had no idea I was being treated for cancer. They were just happy to see me and my fiancée out supporting Adam.

During the taping, everyone was all-business. Considering it's ostensibly comedy, sitcom pilot tapings are awfully serious. I did get to briefly shake hands with and say hi to the guys I knew[115]—Lynch, Hench, Adam, and his agent, James "Baby Doll" Dixon. Dixon had flown in from New York (where he was from) for the taping. Dixon is, by any measure, a superagent. His clients include Jimmy Kimmel, Jon Stewart, Stephen Colbert, and, of course, Adam Carolla. He is heavily leveraged in the late-night space, as they say, and once Leno and Letterman ride off into the sunset, he'll have cornered the late-night market, inasmuch as anyone can "corner" a market of talent these days.

During the taping, Dixon, who was watching from the wings, leaned over and whispered in his New York accent to Mike Lynch, "Did you hear about Bryan?" Dixon shook his head sadly. "Fuckin' shame." Lynch, who couldn't exactly respond because they were in the middle of a take and needed quiet on the set, thought to himself, "What if I hadn't heard?! This is how and when I find out?!" Dixon's a good guy, but he lacks . . . I don't know, tact? Refinement? Later, after the

---

[115] Saying hello to people you know at a TV pilot taping is kind of like saying hello to your old pal Kobe Bryant during a Lakers game. You might get a quick "'Sup!" in, but it's best to wait until after the game, in the locker room.

taping, Christie and I were shown to Adam's dressing room. We shared a little moment with Adam and Jimmy Kimmel (an executive producer on the show) before everyone else started trickling into the room. Outside of a few phone conversations, Adam and I hadn't seen each other since before I told him I had brain cancer. So it was a nice moment when Adam and Jimmy asked Christie and I how we were doing, how I was feeling, how the wedding was coming along, etc. After a few minutes, some more people started to wander in—writers, producers, friends. Then Dixon comes in smoking a lit cigarette and stands next to Adam, Jimmy, Christie, and me. He takes a few puffs before looking around at the four of us, then says almost sheepishly (for him), "Oh, should I put this out?" The rest of us kind of look at each other as if to say, "Well, you *are* standing next to a guy who was just diagnosed with cancer and is supposed to take chemotherapy in an hour," then Dixon laughed and said, "Ah, who am I kidding, we'll never be back here again!" and took a long drag off his cigarette. He was referring to the physical building. His "Should I put this out?" question was really "Do you want the room to smell like smoke after we leave?"

A few days later, I had a follow-up with Dr. Rudnick and Rebecca. These were scheduled weekly, partly to check my symptoms and see how I was responding to the treatment, and partly to address any concerns I had. So far, I told them, the only thing I was suffering from was mild constipation. This was normal, they assured me. The chemotherapy I was on affected my bowels similar to Vicodin or some other painkiller—it stopped me up. After a quick evaluation, they determined that overall I was tolerating the treatment well. Then it was my turn. They asked if I had any concerns or questions for them. I hesitated. "Well," I started, "this may sound weird, but . . . I've been taking the chemo pills and getting the radiation for a week or so now, and, well . . . why don't I have any side effects?"

Rudnick and Rebecca looked at me, puzzled. "What do you mean?"

"In the movies, you always see people sick from chemotherapy, or fatigued by radiation," I explained. "Then they make a miraculous comeback. But that's how you know the treatment is working: the side effects. So I just wanted to know . . . where are my side effects?"

Rudnick started to smile. "So let me get this straight: You *want* side effects?" He began to laugh.

Rebecca smiled and chimed in with a grin, "You can stop taking your antinausea pills."

"Yeah," said Rudnick. "Then you'll have *allllll* the side effects you want."

We all laughed. It *was* kind of absurd after all; most patients didn't come in to complain about a lack of side effects to their chemotherapy. Usually, it was the opposite.

"Listen," Rudnick continued, "you're doing beautifully. This is exactly what I was hoping for. You're having an easy time with treatment, constipation aside, and I'm really, really pleased." That's all we needed to hear. He gave us the name of an effective over-the-counter laxative, and we left. And as long as we're on the subject of constipation, here are a few thoughts from my . . . experience.

First, ladies and gentlemen, on chemotherapy: Take care of your bowels. Your pooper is a machine that requires daily maintenance. Don't wait until you need a powerful, prescription laxative the way I did. When you start taking chemo, start taking these other things daily:

Water. Seems dumb and obvious, I know. But staying hydrated is the easiest natural way to stay "regular."

Fiber gummies. A few companies make these. They are daily fiber supplements that come in delicious, chewable gummy form. Get the right ones (I prefer Vitafusion) and they taste like gummy bears candy.

Probiotic yogurt. You know those "millions of live cultures" that Jamie Lee Curtis is always prattling on about on TV? Turns out they really do work.

Foods that are high in fiber. I'm not going to tell you what to do. I'm only going to tell you what *I* did. I stopped shopping at the big chain grocery stores. I started shopping at Trader Joe's and Whole Foods. I started buying organic produce and meats and foods made with organic ingredients. And I started reading food labels with more scrutiny, looking for high fiber content. And I found a ton: granolas. Cereals. Whole-grain milk. Energy bars. Beans. Nuts. Seeds. Plus, stores such as Trader Joe's and Whole Foods have a high-fiber version of almost everything. Christie and I went nuts (no pun intended) and bought high-fiber versions of all our favorite foods. Christie even found high-fiber waffle mix.

Unfortunately, I found this bevy of products too late, and I needed pharmaceutical help. We went to our local pharmacy and looked for the laxative Rudnick recommended, Senokot-S (with Colace). It's generic name was senna (with docusate). We went to the laxative section[116] only to find the shelves where the Senokot should have been were completely empty. The store's entire supply was gone. "Huh," I said to Christie, "this stuff must really work if it's all sold-out!" We went over to the prescription counter to talk to the pharmacist. "I'm looking for a product called Senokot-S, but the shelf is empty," I told him.

"Oh, it's been recalled," he said.

"Really? Why?"

"There was some problem with the labeling," he said. "They didn't list some ingredient correctly."

"Oh. So there's nothing wrong with the actual product?"

The pharmacist shrugged. "I guess not."

"Well, do you have any back there that I could buy?" I asked. "I don't really care about mislabeled ingredients."

"I'm sorry, I can't do that," he answered.

"Look, I haven't pooped in days." I somehow thought that hitting him with this embarrassing, revealing information would soften his stance so that I could soften my stool.

He stood his ground. "No, I'm sorry. It's illegal, and I could get fired."[117]

---

[116] For a good time, walk up to a pharmacy employee and ask, "Where is your laxative section?" while holding your stomach and gritting your teeth.

[117] Thank you, FDA, for protecting us against the horrors of mislabeled packaging of effective

Frustrated (and still no closer to pooping), I called Dr. Rudnick and explained the situation. He laughed (which did not help), then offered to fax over a prescription for a serious laxative that I could get from the pharmacist right there. He did, and within a couple of days I had started pooping again. But it wasn't easy.

Just a heads-up: I'm about to describe my feces. If you've never had cancer, you might find this a little TMI—too much irregularity. In which case, feel free to skip ahead to the next chapter. But if you have had cancer, you will find this part familiar. Plus, it can be comforting or helpful to know that someone else has gone through the same experiences as you.

Pooping when you're on chemo is like crapping out a rock. No soft limestone, either. I'm talking about passing a Rosetta stone of fecal matter. Cancer patients love to bond over this stuff, too. When I was first diagnosed, my aunt Judy, who had survived a battle with breast cancer, asked me, "How's the constipation?"

"Not great, actually," I told her.

She lit up. "Oh, Bryan! I used to sit on the toilet for *hours*!" It was the happiest I'd ever seen her, come to think of it.

In the middle of the night one night, after I hadn't had a bowel movement for a few days, I could feel . . . *something* coming on. I plopped myself on the toilet, determined to make something happen. I remember it specifically: I was the only one awake, and I had a big book on the history of the *Peanuts* comic strip to distract me.

Forty-five minutes passed. I wish I could say, "Forty-five minutes of nothing passed," but that would be a lie. Instead, it was forty-five minutes of dread. I could feel something moving. Inching toward the surface. And it was big. And it was probably hard. And it was going to hurt.

I struggled for a few more minutes, then my body told me it was time. Honest to God, I was expecting it to be so bad that I actually thought to myself, "It's okay. If there's any kind of tearing down there,

---

medicine. Here's a much more efficient suggestion: Have all pharmacies put the senna behind the counter, then when you go to buy it, the pharmacist hands you an amended, updated label that supersedes the label on the box. That way, we can all poop (and rest) easily.

we'll just get it stitched up at the emergency room. I'm sure this happens all the time. I can't be the first cancer patient to experience this."

I gritted my teeth. It was time. I made one last big push, and then . . . splashdown. A wave of relief washed over me. I took not one but several deep breaths. It went much quicker than I'd expected. My morbid curiosity got the best of me; I couldn't flush it down without inspecting it first. I stood up and looked behind me. There, in the toilet, was a shot put of shit. Only slightly more oblong. Like a mini-football, or what the head of Stewie from *Family Guy* would look like if he were real and made of feces.

I exhaled deeply. I actually said out loud, "Well, *that* could have been ten thousand times worse." I wiped—yes, there was a little bit of blood. Not from my stool, but from the damage done to my anus.[118] I flushed away the Nerf football I had just produced and went back to bed. If there's a silver lining to this dark brown cloud, it's that now, if a woman ever says something to the effect of "You've never experienced the pain of childbirth," I can solemnly nod and say, "Oh, yes, I have." Proportionally, I feel justified in claiming some knowledge of the pain a woman goes through in childbirth. Let's say a vagina is 75 percent bigger than an anus (give or take). Well, a newborn child is probably 75 percent bigger than the poo-baby I birthed that night. With no midwife or epidural either. Yet I gritted my teeth and survived, which is more than I can say for half the women of the nineteenth century.

I wish I could say that this is the end of the number-two talk, but there's more to come. So all I can say is, thanks for putting up with the unsavory discussion. I promise I won't bring it up again for at least ten chapters.

---

[118] Again, I did warn you to skip ahead.

17.

Sobering News

or, Announcing on the Podcast

Tuesday, May 12, 2009, was a big day. I had radiation in the morning. I took chemotherapy at night. In between, I recorded a podcast with Adam Carolla and Teresa Strasser. Adam had been podcasting ever since the radio station flipped formats, at first out of a room in his house, and later out of a warehouse he owned in nearby Glendale, California. The shows were usually about an hour long, with just him and a guest having a long-form conversation. After about a month or so, he started inviting me and Teresa Strasser—his cohost from the radio show—onto the podcast once a week. It was probably partly out of familiarity and partly because he knew that fans of the recently canceled show would enjoy it. Either way, we reunited once a week to do a show that his buddy, Donny, would record, edit, and post online for people to download all around the world.

May 12 would end up being a major fork in the road in my life. I had been in treatment for a week, yet this was the first podcast I was appearing on since I knew that I had cancer. Adam knew my whole story, as did Teresa. When Adam (via Donny) reached out to me to come back on the podcast, the question was raised, How much, if at all, did I want to reveal about my illness? At this point, I sounded and looked pretty normal, so there was reason to think that I could keep the whole thing private if I wanted to. This happens all the time; think about the time you heard that a teacher or a neighbor or a family friend or even a celebrity died, seemingly out of the blue. You were shocked; "I didn't even know she was sick!" you might say. People keep their cancer battles private all the time, and it's hard to blame them. Some people feel a "deathwatch" scenario when they sense that "everyone knows" that they have a serious, life-threatening illness.

Christie and I talked about it. She said the decision was ultimately mine, but in my mind there really wasn't much of a decision. Talk radio, and now podcasting, is such an incredibly intimate medium; so much more so than TV or movies or even documentaries. For three years, I'd shared with listeners my most intimate and celebratory moments: getting engaged to Christie, or traveling cross-country to be a contestant on *Who Wants to Be a Millionaire*. Adam had helped instill in me a great broadcasting trait: to always be honest. Now, at my lowest moment, I couldn't imagine *not* sharing that with listeners. I could not fathom going on the podcast and pretending everything was okay. And what if things got worse? What if I ended up like every other cancer patient, weak and nauseous and thirty pounds underweight? I certainly don't get recognized out on the streets every day, but it does happen from time to time. Our fans are a technologically savvy bunch. It would only be a matter of time before someone tweeted a picture of me looking gaunt and near death and said, "OMG, WTF happened to @BaldBryan??" Even if that particular scenario never happened, the idea of just one day disappearing from the podcast with no explanation seemed . . . ugh. I mean, just imagine living your day-to-day life harboring a huge secret like this. That's no way to live. Plus, so much of dealing with cancer is putting yourself into a positive, healthy state of mind. And trying to keep all of that inside rather than to openly seek and welcome support . . . well, I wouldn't recommend it.

So that day, I decided to announce my diagnosis on the air. Adam led off the top of the show with it: "A very special podcast for you today," he began. "Teresa Strasser—very pregnant—is back, and Bald Bryan is back. Bryan has some, uh . . . very sobering news. We're gonna discuss it. Teresa and I are aware of it, but I'll let Bryan put it into his own words. What's going on with you, Bryan?"

With that, the spotlight was on me. The show wasn't live; I could have called, "Cut," and said, "You know what, I thought better of it, and I'd really like to keep my privacy about this whole thing." But I didn't. I didn't know exactly what to say, so I just out and said it: I'd been diagnosed with a brain tumor, and I'd been getting chemotherapy and radiation for a week. I rambled on for a minute or so, giving way too much detail way too fast, then Adam jumped in with questions to kind of steer the ship a little. For the next hour, we talked. About everything. Adam is nothing if not inquisitive. He will ask as many questions as you can provide an answer for about a topic that interests him. Teresa is similar in this way; I think curiosity is a trait that all smart people inherently share. How big is the tumor? they asked. How long did I have symptoms? What were the symptoms? Did you feel anything while we were all doing the morning show, and we just didn't know? Did you visit a sperm bank?

At the end of the show, I mentioned that people could stay updated on my story through Christie's blog, AnInconvenientTumor. com. She had been blogging about our journey, mainly for friends and family to keep up with our latest medical news. But now we were inviting the world to follow along (or at least the part of the world that listened to *The Adam Carolla Show*). I got home from the podcast that night and let out a deep sigh. "Okay," I said to Christie as we hugged by the front door, "it's done. Now the whole world is going to know." We thought we knew what we were in for. We were wrong.

We woke up the next morning to find our in-boxes jammed full of emails—well over a hundred between us. People from all over the world, expressing hope, concern, love, and general well-wishes. I read every one of them and even got a little emotional on more than one occasion. People wanted to share their stories—stories of survival, stories of hope. People talked about their dads, their moms, siblings, and friends. A couple of people even told me about their children who had been diagnosed with a brain tumor, and how they're doing great years later. Maybe it's stupid, and maybe it's a cliché, but it felt as if my soul were getting fed every time I read someone's heartfelt email of hope and survival. With every message, Dr. Harold Kumar's six-months-to-a-year prognosis faded a little more into the background of my mind.

The pervasive theme of the messages I woke up to that morning—whether they were emails, tweets, or comments left on Christie's blog—was "I don't know you, we've never even met, but I feel like you're my friend." Here's how Christie put it when she wrote a blog post later that day:

> We woke up and found hundreds and hundreds of emails in both our in-boxes. Your responses, unconditional support and words of encouragement literally made us break down and cry. Now for me, that's no big deal because I'm crying at the drop of a hat these days. But for Bryan, well, he had yet to break down. He hadn't had his moment yet, and I wondered when it would really hit him that we're truly going through this. That our life now, or at least for the next few weeks, is our new definition of "normal."
>
> It hit him today. The amount of emails, phone calls, texts and tweets we've received is . . . honestly, I can't even think of an appropriate word to describe his reaction. It's unbelievable. It's overwhelming. But most importantly, it reminds us that despite the really crappy things that may happen in life—a brain tumor, for example—the world is still filled with loving, compassionate, generous people. The idea that you have taken the time in your own hectic lives to share your inspirational stories, thoughts and words of wisdom with us is humbling. Beyond humbling. And for anyone that knows Bryan's penchant for describing himself as "self-congratulatory," well, he is anything but that right now. I really think he's in shock from all of this. He never knew—no matter how many times I told him—how much he truly touched people's lives through the radio show as well as just being the friend and amazing man that he is. Hopefully he'll get that through his big bald head now. :)

At that moment—wading through hundreds of messages from strangers—I began to understand the power of the podcast. Yes, it took something horrific like cancer to kick-start it all, but here were countless well-wishes—with more pouring in by the hour—from people I'd never met and probably never would. The only thing connecting us, really, was a microphone on one end and a set of headphones on the other. And in between were just words and ideas.

Looking back on that day, I'm amazed that there was even a question as to whether I'd choose to be public or private with my cancer battle. I can't imagine doing this without the outpouring of support from the show's fans. Each message I got—whether it was that first day or at any time after—was like another tiny rock—a pebble, if you will—that was going to help me get out of that hole I was in.

18.

Barbara's House of Healing

or, Alternative Therapies

After announcing my diagnosis on the podcast, I had a lot of people recommend a lot of different kinds of alternative treatments. They ranged from meditation to hypnotherapy to Reiki to just smoking a ton of weed. Some people even recommended all of those things.

I consider myself to be an open-minded person. On the scale of "skeptic" to "believer," I fall somewhere in the healthy middle. I'd never given much thought to (let alone tried) alternative therapies such as Transcendental Meditation or even yoga, but the people who did them regularly seemed happy and well-adjusted, so who was I to argue with the positive effects? In the days following my diagnosis, I began to seriously consider dipping my toe in the waters of alternative "healing" practices.

About a week after I was diagnosed, some of our friends got together and planned an impromptu get-together/fund-raiser for Christie and me. It was held at our friends Matt and Jen's house, and about thirty or so of our close friends showed up. They called it Beers for Bryan, and the idea was for people to "buy" beers throughout the night and "donate" the money to us. Our friend Catie even went out and bought a piggy bank for the event and decorated it with inspirational messages such as *Feed me . . . NOW!* and *I'm so very hungry.* When we walked into the party, we laughed at this ridiculous porcelain pig. Then we lost track of it for the rest of the night. Unbeknownst to us, our friends must have been stuffing that thing with bills all night, because when we got home and emptied it the next morning, a few hundred dollars were inside.

The piggy bank. We still have it proudly displayed in our home. *(Christie Bishop)*

As we counted the donations (and, I'm not afraid to say, became a little emotional from the outpouring of support), I started to realize something: In times of crisis, people want so badly to help their friends. As I write this, it seems absurdly obvious, but it's not until you're the one in crisis that you get to see this in action. People come out of the woodwork to offer something—anything—they think is helpful. At the Beers for Bryan party, my friend Brandon, who was there with his then-girlfriend Annie, pulled me aside and said, "Annie's family has this house in Lake Tahoe. It's right on the lake, and it's such a peaceful, healing place. If you ever want to go there, just say the word. We'd be happy to take you."

My friend Quinn—who may or may not have been a little drunk[119]—pulled me aside later and said, "I fly to New York every other week for work. I'm literally an airline-miles millionaire. If you ever need to go anywhere . . . see family, whatever . . . just call me."

My friends' generosity reached its comical zenith when it came time to leave the party. With piggy bank in hand, we said thanks to everyone who attended. Forget whatever donations may have been inside the porcelain pig; it was just great to see everyone again. The past couple of weeks had been stressful, to say the least, and spending an evening with all of our friends had buoyed our spirits. Matt, whose house had hosted the evening's get-together, said, "Here, let me walk you to your car." We got outside to his driveway and he hands us a full-size brown grocery bag. "Here," he says, presenting it to us, "I want you to have this."

"Aw, thanks, Matt," I said, opening the bag. "What's in here?"

"It's a bunch of medical marijuana."

A couple of things you need to know about Matt: First, as you may have guessed, he's a marijuana . . . "enthusiast." Second, he has a prescription for medical marijuana, which in California made this satchel of pot perfectly legal. Finally, Matt is a comedy writer who has written for a couple of successful sitcoms. He's a great writer for the same reasons he'd make a horrible stand-up comedian: He's thoughtful, introspective, and reserved. He's also hilarious, which I know because I've read a couple of his scripts and seen a few of his episodes on TV. So the absurdity of his handing me a giant bag full of weed should at least have made him chuckle. You see, I've never smoked pot. It's just never particularly interested me. I don't judge those who do partake, and I think marijuana should be legal for everyone to purchase or grow in small quantities. People ask me, "How do you know you won't like it?" The truth is, I probably *would* like it. I liken it to pornography (stay with me, ladies). Think of any semimain-

---

[119] In Quinn's defense, a lot of our friends were a little drunk that night. Everyone was self-medicating, trying to deal with one of their friends' having been diagnosed with cancer at age thirty and being told he had less than a year to live.

stream, socially acceptable porn fetish: MILFs, or girl-on-girl action. Those don't particularly interest me, either. Would they "get the job done"? Sure, I could get off to them, but I probably wouldn't go out of my way to seek them out. Plus, now that I'm in my thirties, I don't want to ruin my lifelong streak of never having smoked weed. Of course, if my doctors came to me one day and said, "This is the end, you really do have six months to live at this point," I'd probably be on Amazon.com buying a vaporizer that afternoon. YOLO!

Plus, being a stoner (or just a vocal enthusiast of pot) seems like a great way to go through life. Who wouldn't want to be Doug Benson? Dozens of fans handing you pot at every show? Who wouldn't want to be simply handed something he or she loves just because he or she talks about it all the time? That'd be like my fans handing me USC football tickets or a Transformer after every show.[120]

I looked at the bag and laughed. It was filled with edibles of all varieties: pot-infused cookies, brownies, sodas, you name it. Matt explained that he went to the dispensary[121] that afternoon, and because he knew that I didn't smoke, he stocked up on snacks that would get me high. I didn't have the heart to tell him I would probably never get around to trying them; the bag was an expression of love, after all, and I wanted to be gracious. Plus, I had only been on chemo for a week, and I was still anticipating getting nauseous, so I might actually need the edibles at some point.

Christie and I said good-night. Then Matt added, "Oh, I know you had mentioned looking into some alternative therapies. My stepmom does all that stuff."

Now I was interested. "She does? What kind of stuff?"

"All that healing stuff. Hypnotherapy, Reiki . . . I mentioned you to her and she'd love to work with you, if you're interested."

I *was* interested. I imagine the incongruity of someone who wanted nothing to do with marijuana but was deeply interested in alternative

---

[120] Or scalp polish.
[121] That's the fancy name for a pot store, you squares.

healing was a little confusing to him. But I got the name of his stepmom—Barbara—and her contact information before we left.

I contacted Barbara a couple of days later, and within a week we set up our first appointment. At this stage, I was about ten days into chemotherapy and radiation. Christie came with me; she was as interested in all this stuff as I was. Plus, she was in need of some good therapy herself. The stress was starting to get to her; putting on a happy face despite such trauma will do that to you.

We arrived at Barbara's residential home in North Hollywood, just north of . . . well, Hollywood, in the part of Los Angeles known as the Valley. Right away, I was struck by how aggressively *normal* the house was. Matt's dad was a college professor, and the house looked like a college professor's house: neat, quiet, tastefully appointed. Matt's dad met us at the door and said, "You must be Bryan and Christie. Barbara is expecting you; she'll be out in a minute."

We waited in the foyer[122] for a minute, then Barbara came out to greet us. She was a petite blond woman who was dressed kind of like Mickey Mouse in *The Sorcerer's Apprentice*. She welcomed us with big hugs. Barbara had a terrific energy; it wasn't hard to see why she chose to do this kind of work.

She led us into a small room on the first floor. It was sort of a study that had been converted into her "healing room" (my words, not hers). *This* was how I imagined a House of Healing to look: crystals, a CD player, a big comfy recliner, decorations on the wall . . . In what I imagined the world's smallest yoga studio to look like, I sat in the recliner and Christie grabbed a seat in the corner. Barbara began our first session with a lot of background questions—about my illness, of course, but also about my childhood, my experiences with alternative therapies, and my goals for our sessions. She explained that we would be doing three things: positive visualization, guided meditation, and hypnotherapy. The positive visualization should be no problem, I explained, be-

---

[122] Pet peeve: people who pronounce it *FOY-er*. It's *foy-YAY*, you unrefined rube. When you say *FOY-er*, you sound as comically wrong as when Napoleon Dynamite says *quesa-DILL-uh* instead of *quesa-DEE-ya*.

cause I was generally a pretty positive person. The meditation sounded interesting. But the hypnotherapy . . . was she going to swing a watch in front of my eyes and tell me I was getting sleeeepy . . . verrry sleeeepy?

She laughed. No, this would be her taking positive memories from my past and incorporating them into a sort of guided meditation. She would be doing most of the talking; all I had to do was listen, think, and visualize. I began to realize that all of these things that we'd be doing—positive visualization, guided meditation, and hypnotherapy—worked together, rather than as separate therapies. Barbara gave me a homework assignment: Make a list of positive memories from my childhood: sounds, smells, sights . . . the more specific, the better. Before we ended our first session, Barbara asked me about another kind of visualization. "When you picture your tumor," she asked, "what do you see?" I paused. I had never thought about it before. I mean, I pictured a *tumor*, whatever that looked like.

Christie jumped in: "When I picture it, I think of something black with tentacles invading his brain, kind of like the smoke monster from *Lost*, all black and evil and everything." She stopped.

Barbara looked at her with her soft eyes and said (very sweetly), "That's good, Christie, but I want Bryan to answer with what *he* sees."

"Oh. Sorry." Christie slumped her shoulders a little. To me, she looked like a first-grader who had been scolded by her teacher. Which she hadn't. Barbara was as sweet-natured and soft-spoken as they come. But watching Christie, I realized that *she* needed some healing, too. She needed someone to ask how *she* was doing, and what *she* thought the tumor looked like.

> ***Tumor Tip:*** *When there's a full-time caregiver in your life who's not on the payroll—a wife or a husband or a son or a daughter—go out of your way to give that person a forum to talk about what he or she is experiencing. Or just to cry or yell or complain. I can't stress this enough. I didn't know to do this, and it weighed heavily on Christie. No one was asking her how she was feeling. It's understandable for*

everyone to focus on the patient. That's just human nature. But I was doing fine. I felt taken care of. I didn't need all the attention I was getting. Truth be told, Christie could have used some of it. She was doing the majority of the work—taking care of me, essentially, while also preparing for a wedding—without much credit. She was such an incredible trouper that she would never have asked for any, but deep down, I'm sure she (and lots of other people in her position) was thinking, "Doesn't anyone want to know how I'm doing?" Because when you're the caregiver, you're just as much the patient as the actual patient.

We went home and I began working on my assignment. I made a list of positive memories from my youth that Barbara could use in our first actual session in a couple of days. I remembered the smell of my mom's fresh-baked banana bread that used to fill the house. She made perfect banana bread: a tiny bit moist, made with dark bananas too old for snacking, with no walnuts (ugh) and no chocolate chips (gilding the lily, in my opinion).[123] I also remembered the sound of my dad in the shower every morning. My dad woke up for work at five o'clock every morning. He'd shower in a bathroom that shared a common wall with my bedroom. (Technically *our* bedroom, because I was sharing a room with my brother all throughout middle school and high school, remember?) The pipes were inside said wall, so when my dad showered, I would wake up just enough to be soothed back to sleep by the sound of the hot water rushing through the pipes. It was an incredibly reassuring and comforting sound, and it's probably why I find the sound of running water so pleasing to this day. It made me feel safe.

Later that week, Christie and I went back to Barbara's for my first real session with her. She sat me down in her big comfy recliner,

---

[123] Adding chocolate chips to almost anything aside from cookies—pancakes, banana bread, etc.—is just an apology for making an inferior product. "Oh, these are my chocolate-chip pancakes!" Well, then you don't make good pancakes on their own. You can't hide behind a thin veil of chocolate forever, home cooks of America.

turned out the lights, and put on some soft meditative world music. She began with basic relaxation techniques—breathing, mainly, and always being aware of how you feel, from the physical sensations on your body to the air traveling through your nose and into your lungs and back again. When I reached an appropriate level of relaxation, Barbara began to incorporate some of the memories I'd written down for her. She asked me to "smell" my mom's banana bread, straight out of the oven, and to "hear" my dad taking his morning shower through the wall. And although I couldn't "smell" or "hear" them per se, I could easily conjure the memories of how they used to make me feel.

Our session went on for a while. When it was over, Barbara gently brought me back to a more wakened state. "How long do you feel like that was?" she asked as I sipped on some water.

"I don't know. At least twenty minutes or half an hour."

She smiled. "You've been here for over an hour."

I looked at Christie, who was sitting in the corner. Even she looked relaxed, which made me feel even better.

Before we left, Barbara handed me two CDs she had copied for me. "These are guided meditations," she explained. "They're very good. Once a day, you should find a solitary, quiet place and listen to them. Do you have a place like that in your home?"

"Yes," Christie answered for me. "Our second bedroom."

I nodded. "It's perfect."

Barbara smiled. "Great. Listen to one or two tracks at a time. It'll really help."

We got in our car and headed home. We both felt cleansed, as if the recalling of pleasant memories had washed out some of the painful experiences of the past few weeks. Like an auto detail for our souls.

We got home and I immediately went to the second bedroom. I was curious to find out what this guided meditation was all about. I popped in my headphones, shut off all the lights, and lay down on the bed. I started listening to the CDs, and over the next few days I listened to them regularly. Sometimes I listened actively—that is, I listened to every word and considered what the narrator was saying.

Other times, I listened passively, letting my mind wander, using the tracks as jumping-off points that I would occasionally come back to. I started to realize a few things. First, guided meditation—for me, at least—wasn't about deep thinking, or some spiritual journey (although those were nice ancillary benefits when they occurred). Really, it was about quieting my mind. We are so overwhelmed with stimuli these days—it's a cliché, but it's a cliché for a reason—that taking some time to shut it all out and be alone with your thoughts can be a powerful experience. I'm laughing to myself as I write this because (as fans of the radio show will know) we once had Deepak Chopra on for an interview. Adam asked him about some meditation basics, and Deepak first piece of advice was "Take a little time to be quiet." I clipped that small audio bite and made it into a "drop"—a sound effect that I would play whenever Adam got a little long-winded. If he hit minute number five of complaining about taxes, or the LAPD, or "Maneater" by Hall and Oates, I would play Deepak saying, "Take a little time to be quiet," in his trademark Indian accent.

So I took a little time to be quiet every day from then on. I started to realize that I had been meditating for years without even realizing it. One of the benefits of working for a morning show is that your workday is done at 10:00 a.m. In Southern California, the weather is pleasant to great most of the year, so on warm days after work, I would head down to the beach. I took a towel, a can of sunscreen, and a hat, and I lay out near the gentle, rolling tide and fell asleep. I'd nap for about an hour, wake up naturally, and be refreshed, ready to stay up to a normal hour that night. I did this for a few years; if it ever got too hot, I would just cool off by jumping in the ocean for a minute. When the weather turned too cold to go to the beach,[124] I'd fall asleep for my daily afternoon nap to the sound of "Ocean Waves" on my nature-sounds alarm clock. As I lay meditating in our second bedroom, it all came together: I had been so profoundly and positively impacted by the sound of running water that I had carried it with me into my

---

[124] I believe you people in the rest of the country call it fall and winter.

adult life—falling asleep to the sounds of ocean waves, whether it was by visiting the beach every day, or by turning on the sound machine I kept next to my bed.

Meditation also challenged me and gave me a new way to look at the world. One of the discs Barbara gave me was specifically for people with cancer. It had a track called "Affirmations." On it, the narrator instructed you to thank, in your mind, various people and things in your life for the role they'd played in making you who you are and helping you fight your cancer. I was listening actively—thinking along with the narrator, thanking people in my life. Then the narrator said to thank my cancer. *Thank my cancer? Did I hear that right?* The narrator continued, "I tell my cancer, 'Thank you for teaching me to stop and listen. Thank you for reminding me of what is truly important. You can go now.'"

It was a revelatory idea—instead of cursing my tumor, thank it. I began to consider the ramifications. Instead of being in an angry, hateful "Why me?" state, I would put myself into an accepting, welcoming, grateful state. I still wanted my tumor gone, but the idea that it could be a blessing that I was somehow *thankful* for . . . the idea took some getting used to. I mulled it over in my mind. Ultimately, I decided, we can't control what happens to us. We can only control how we react and respond to it. I could spend a lot of energy being upset or frustrated that I had cancer. But where would that get me? No closer to recovery, that's for sure. But if I looked at it as a positive development in my life, no matter how twisted that thinking might be . . . maybe it could portend a positive outcome.

For my next appointment with Barbara, she asked me to visualize my tumor, to see it in my mind's eye and see it getting smaller. I had heard a lot about this type of positive visualization. One of my friends told me about her uncle who literally imagined his tumor shriveling and shrinking to the size of a pea. Another friend told me how someone they knew would imagine the chemotherapy acting like the Doozers from *Fraggle Rock*, working away tirelessly, building infrastructure in the brain. Christie saw my tumor as the smoke monster from *Lost*. But positive visualizations have to be yours and yours alone. Kind of like the totems from *Inception*. If someone else knows yours, it won't work right.[125]

I thought about it over the next few days, especially as I was getting radiated each morning. During those ten or twelve solitary minutes, I would calmly try to organize my thoughts: What's really going on in there? What does my tumor look like to me, and what is it doing? How is the radiation treating it? I searched the recesses of my brain for a cultural touchstone. Being a child of the late eighties / early nineties, I found one in the world of arcade games: *Centipede*.

In *Centipede*, the object of the game was to shoot a fast-moving centipede (obviously) with a laser gun. As you shot and "killed" sections of the centipede, those sections would stop moving and become mushrooms (or something. It was a pretty primitive game by today's standards), which you then had to shoot and destroy. But whereas the centipede sections were one-shot-one-kill, the mushrooms took several shots to destroy. I began to think about my tumor as a giant version of one of these mushrooms, and the radiation as the laser gun. Every morning, I'd get strapped into my "game" while the laser gun blasted away at my giant mushroom-tumor. *Pew-pew-pew-pew*. Blasting away, each shot making it the tiniest bit smaller. I found a couple of links on YouTube of people playing *Centipede*, and I sent them to Barbara. (She was a couple of decades older than I was, so I couldn't just say to her, "Oh, it's like that old video game *Centipede*.") The next time I visited her, she smiled. "Now we have something to work with." From then on, I pictured the game *Centipede* whenever I was lying there, strapped down to the radiation machine.

I really enjoyed my sessions with Barbara, but eventually, sadly, I had to stop going, partly because I couldn't afford to pay her, even though she never asked me for any payment. Still, Christie and I had now been unemployed for months, plural, with no prospects in sight. Plus, our bills were starting to pile up. Not just hospital bills,

---

[125] Or something. God, that movie was confusing.

but health insurance—we were paying for COBRA out of our own pockets—in addition to regular fixed expenses such as rent, utilities, gas, and car-lease payments. But, as you'll see pretty soon, my symptoms were starting to worsen. Soon, I wouldn't be able to drive on my own, speak well enough to be understood . . . or even walk.

19.

"Rock" Bottom

or, The Day We Lost Our Engagement Ring

People with cancer invariably have horribly sad stories that end with "And that was pretty much the worst of it." It's a rock bottom that we all share. Like addicts who tell harrowing stories of breaking their kid's piggy bank to get the $12 worth of change inside to get another fix. These stories are basically our answer to the question "How bad did it get?" I can point to a handful of these moments—most of them sad, some embarrassing, one or two of them scary. This was the first, and it had all three of those. And more.

We got to the cancer center for my daily radiation appointment on the morning of Friday, May 15. We parked our car and hopped in the elevator to take us down to the radiation "dungeon." We held the elevator doors for Jerry, the hospital porter who had become a sight for sore eyes over the last couple of weeks. As I said in a previous chapter, his warm energy was infectious.

"Look at you two," he said. "Always holding hands! I can't wait to find the type of love that you two got."

We smiled and noticed that Jerry's arms were full of plates of sweet treats—slices of cake, cookies, cupcakes, candies . . . his arms overflowed with sugary temptations.

"What's with all the desserts?" Christie asked.

"Oh, it's Employee Appreciation Day here at the hospital," Jerry said. "There's a whole thing going on up on the third floor. Check it out when you're done down here."

Okay, we decided, and left him when the elevator reached our floor. We went through our usual routine that morning: checked in for my appointment, sat in the waiting area, and kibitzed with Herb and Faye and all of our new friends. When I got the call on my buzzer, I left Christie and did my normal twelve-minute radiation therapy. When I was done, I took my lizard face and went back out to the waiting area to Christie. We decided to head up to the third floor where Employee Appreciation Day was taking place and check it out. It was on the other side of the hospital, several hundred yards away, but since it was a nice day (and I needed the exercise), we decided to walk across Cedars-Sinai's campus. So back up the elevator we rode, four or five levels up, until we reached the third floor. Then it was a several-hundred-yard trek through several indoor lobbies and outdoor spaces and across a number of bridges linking the buildings.

The entrance to Employee Appreciation Day. *(Christie Bishop)*

Finally, we reached Employee Appreciation Day. Cedars must *really* have appreciated their employees because it was a carnival-like atmosphere that spread out to about the size of a football field. We decided to walk around slowly and take it all in. Masseuses were giving out chair massages to some of the nurses. Next to the build-your-own-ice-cream-sundae station were towers of cakes and cupcakes, just for the taking. There were face painting and balloons for kids. Jugglers were tossing bowling pins into the air. It was a circus for adults. Christie started to drift behind; she was starting to pay a lot more attention to her blogging, so she was taking tons of pictures. I wandered a few feet ahead on my own, taking it all in. Then I heard Christie's panicked voice.

"Bryan . . . Bryan . . ."

My first instinct was to freeze; I thought maybe I was accidentally drifting backward into a juggler and was about to get hit on the head with a bowling pin. I looked behind me and saw only Christie, looking at her quivering left hand. I hurried over to her. "What's wrong?"

Speechless, she held her still-shaking left hand up to me to show me her engagement ring. The band was still there; the diamond was gone.

One minute after Christie took this picture, she realized her diamond was missing. *(Christie Bishop)*

My mind did more math in the next three seconds than it had done in four years of high school. "Okay," I thought to myself, "where could it be?" I looked around as if it had simply dropped out of her ring setting right there and then. I realized the futility of that idea; we were in the middle of Employee Appreciation Day at one of the largest hospitals in the country. Hundreds of people were walking about; who knows how many had come and gone in the time we'd been there? The diamond was only a couple of centimeters big, and it didn't exactly stand out against the midday concrete. It could easily have been kicked or caught in the sole of someone's shoe . . . it could be anywhere by now. And that's if it even made it up to this floor! It could have fallen out anywhere: in the car, in the parking lot, in one of the elevators we took, in the radiation waiting area, in one of the many lobbies we'd walked through to get to Employee Appreciation Day. When I started to factor in less likely but still plausible scenarios—it fell down an elevator shaft, or it fell into a drainage grate, or someone saw it on the ground and took it—the odds against ever finding this tiny, clear item in a hospital of this size seemed astronomical. If there was even a chance, it was the slimmest of chances.

As I said, I did all of this math in my head in about three seconds. Christie must have done the same math in her head at the same time. Her math probably included the financial implications: The lost diamond represented a few thousand dollars that we, as unemployed, engaged cancer patients, did not have. Buying an engagement ring when you're both employed is a scary enough venture. Now, think about having to replace one when you're in our shoes.

I looked up at Christie, who had tears in her eyes. Not so much tears of sadness (although those were certainly there, too), but tears of terror. Here was a woman in her twenties whose soon-to-be-husband stood a real chance of dying in the next few months. The only thing—the only material possession—that he had given her with the intention of it lasting forever was now gone. Lost. Swallowed up by the very institution that was trying to save her fiancé. First it giveth, then it taketh away.

I grabbed Christie and hugged her. Then she let it all go. Christie cried and cried, partly for the missing diamond—which, as she would later say, "in the grand scheme of things is only a piece of rock"—and partly for the cruel totality of it all. Here she was, a young woman with a great job and the man of her dreams, and it was slowly, systematically being taken away from her.

As I held her as she sobbed, I looked up at the sky. It was a hot May morning, and the sunlight warmed my face. I closed my eyes and tuned out. I breathed deeply and said silently to whoever was up there, "Okay, you've won. You've broken us down. Look at us, we're helpless. We have nowhere else to go. I know people say stupid stuff like 'Everything happens for a reason,' but there had better be a really spectacular reason for all of this. Because right now, I'm not seeing it."

Christie calmed down to the point where we looked at each other and said, "What now?" All around us, the incongruity of Employee Appreciation Day was still in full swing. We were hopelessly adrift in a sea of mirth. The only thing we could do, we decided, was to try to retrace our steps, as futile as that sounded. Our actual steps that day must have numbered in the thousands, easily. Still, we soldiered on, heads firmly fixed to the ground, looking for that telltale sparkle given off by a rogue diamond.

We walked all around the outdoor plaza, dodging jugglers and masseuses, scouring the ground for Christie's diamond. After fifteen minutes or so, the futility of it all began to overtake us. Sadly, dejectedly, we made our way back through the maze of lobbies and corridors to the elevator—our eyes firmly locked to the ground the whole time, in the incredibly remote chance we might stumble across it. Finding nothing, we rode the elevator back to the basement level, where we retreated to the radiation waiting area. It was pretty empty by this time, so we set about searching the floor near where Christie had been sitting earlier. "I was sitting there." She pointed at one of two dozen chairs. "No, not that one. That one over there." We looked under every cushion of every chair, but found nothing.

Then the receptionist, who might have been the only employee still working on the floor, asked, "What are you guys looking for?"

"My fiancée's diamond," I said. "It fell out of her engagement ring." It was the first time either of us had verbalized what was happening. It made our nightmare feel real.

The receptionist's face dropped. Then Len, the sushi-loving radiation tech whom I saw every day, came out from the back. "What's going on?" he asked the receptionist.

"She lost the diamond out of her ring."

Len looked up in disbelief. Christie held up her hand as if to say, "See?"

Len sprang into action immediately. "When did you see it last? Where else have you been in the hospital today? How big is it? Have you told anyone else yet?" He grabbed a Maglite flashlight from the emergency kit on the wall and said, "Follow me." Either Len had a long-standing fantasy to star in an episode of *NCIS* or else he *really* wanted to help us try to find that diamond.

We must have caused something of a commotion because a doctor named Francine came out to investigate all the ruckus. She asked what was going on, and we (Len, Christie, and I) filled her in. She grabbed a walkie-talkie (!) and immediately joined our search party. We had never met Francine before that moment, but here she was, taking time away from (presumably) helping people beat cancer to help us search for something the size of a kernel of corn inside something the size of a football stadium. I thought to myself, "I really, *really* appreciate the effort, but don't they see the futility of it all?"

Still, we retraced our steps, yet again. We went back through the basement level, up the elevator, and through the myriad hallways and lobbies. The entire time, Len was shining his flashlight against the linoleum floor, trying to catch a glimmer of the diamond, and Francine was on her walkie-talkie, communicating with maintenance. It was one of those phone/walkie-talkie combos, so I only heard her side of the conversation: "Has anyone found a diamond in the last hour? . . . That's right, a diamond. . . . Yeah, like the kind you'd find in a wedding ring. . . . No, I'm not joking." After a half hour of retracing our steps, we ended up right in the middle of where all this started: Employee Appreciation Day.

We spread out across the outdoor plaza and searched again. While Christie was scouring the ground, a random middle-aged woman came up to her and asked, "Are you looking for something?"

"Yes," Christie simply said, tears welling up in her eyes.

Then, in a calm voice the woman said, "I have a very comfortable feeling you're going to find it." Then, Christie swears, as suddenly as the woman had appeared, she was gone. Poof—out of sight.

After finding nothing, we reconvened near the plaza entrance. Len looked spent. He was sweating—remember, not only was it a hot day and we were outdoors, but Len was in his full getup of scrubs, what he would normally wear on the comparatively frigid basement floor. He stood there panting, holding his flashlight with his hands on his hips. Francine shook her head. Christie looked dazed, like a POW from old war newsreels. "Guys," I said, addressing the troops, "I really appreciate you dropping everything to help us. Really, I do. But I think the only thing we can do now is file a report with the building's lost and found and hopefully something will turn up."

Francine turned and walked back toward the elevator inside. "I'm going to look inside again." You could tell that she didn't accept defeat easily. I envied her patients.

She left us with Len. He said, "Is there any other place it could be?" We brainstormed that it could be in our car; maybe it fell out as we were parking that morning. Or maybe it was in our driveway. Or in our sink. My mind was instantly overwhelmed with the sheer number of possible places the diamond could have been. It could have been *anywhere*. The worst part was, since we'd most likely never find it, we'd be constantly wondering—for the rest of our lives, perhaps—"Could it have been here? We never checked there. Oh, no, wait, how about here?"

Len said, "Come on, I'll take you down and help you fill out a lost-

and-found form for building maintenance. Who knows, maybe something will turn up."

We walked back inside from the plaza. Francine was standing a few feet away, halfway between us and the elevators, talking to someone on her phone. Then, she took off running toward the elevators. "I think we've got something!" she yelled as the elevator doors closed behind her. Under normal circumstances, I would have gotten intrigued. Excited, even. But we were spent. Beaten down emotionally. When Francine took off running toward the elevator, I thought, "Good luck, Francine. We'll see you back at the radiation center." Christie, Len, and I trudged our way back to the radiation waiting area. Christie may not have known it, but I had silently resigned myself to having to buy her another ring. Keep in mind, we were unemployed, without health insurance, and battling cancer. But I didn't care. Come hell or high water, I was going to make sure Christie had an engagement ring. It might be the last thing she had to remember me by.

We got back to the radiation waiting area and were immediately greeted by the receptionist, who was standing up at her desk. She was wrapping up a phone call and looking at us, her eyes wide. "Okay, they're right here. . . . Okay, I will." She hung up the phone. A smile creeped across her face.

"They found it," she said simply. "They found your diamond."

She started to smile wider. I didn't get a look at Christie, but I imagine her reaction was similar to mine. "Bullshit," I thought. "Someone actually found a clear pebble in the midst of a massive hospital campus? I won't believe it until I see it for myself."

"Francine has it," the receptionist told us. "It's locked in her desk. She'll be right back. Here, you can wait in her office."

We were dazed. If the story seems disjointed here, it's because neither Christie or I can remember exactly how we got back to Francine's office. You could tell me that we floated back there on a cloud of good vibes and I'd probably shrug and say, "Sure, sounds about right to me." We waited for an indeterminate time—it could have been three minutes, it could have been fifteen. We mostly sat there silently, holding hands. We'd spent too much time in doctors' offices, holding hands, waiting for news about our future. A hundred thoughts raced through my mind. I even remember thinking, "What if they found someone else's diamond? What do we do then? Do we try to find *that* diamond's owner?" Clearly I wasn't thinking straight.

Francine came back into her office wearing the world's biggest smile. "Do you want to see your diamond?" she asked rhetorically. We nodded weakly, and she unlocked a drawer above her desk. And there, wrapped in a tissue, was Christie's engagement diamond. It was too much for us. We both started crying. Through her tears, Christie asked Francine if she had an envelope or something we could carry our diamond home in. Christie is a very organized person, but after all we'd been through with this diamond, there was no way in hell she was taking a chance by putting it in her purse or her pocket. Francine started to look around for an envelope, but then had an idea. She reached into a different drawer and pulled out a tiny, white, zippered pouch, labeled *My Rosary*. She unzipped it and pulled out her Catholic rosary and set it on her desk. Then she handed us the pouch. "Here," she said with a smile. "This will keep it safe."

I'll spare you all the religious symbolism that started racing through my mind. Christie and I just hugged and laughed. It was all so absurdly perfect.

Francine asked us, "Would you like to meet the woman who found your diamond?" It's not often in your life that you get asked that question, so of course we eagerly said yes. Francine led us just a few feet down the hall where a small Asian woman dressed in a Cedars-Sinai maintenance uniform was standing next to a rolling trash can. "This is Leila," Francine said. "She found your diamond."

We both hugged her. Hard. Probably much harder than Leila had been hugged by a patient at the hospital before. Christie started to cry again. We both said, "Thank you," probably about a dozen times each. Leila, for her part, just smiled. Honestly, she looked a little embarrassed by all the attention.

The missing diamond and the bag that kept it safe. *(Christie Bishop)*

"How did you find it?" I asked. This was a mystery that I needed to solve *now*, or else it would haunt me forever.

In broken English, Leila explained that she had been mopping over by the water fountain—she pointed to it across the room—and she felt something under her shoe. She looked down, and stuck in the sole of her tennis shoe was our diamond.

I took a second to process it. "She stepped on it," I said in disbelief. "She *stepped* on it."

Francine smiled. "She stepped on it!"

I shook my head. Christie was aghast. "Yeah, I got up to get a drink while you were getting radiated. It couldn't have been for more than a few seconds . . ." Her voice trailed off, the sheer improbability of it all slowly sinking in. "My God, it was right next to the grate," she said, looking over at the drainage grate that led to the pipe system. Had Leila—or anyone—kicked it, or even nudged it, our diamond would have been gone forever, washed out to sea.

We didn't know what to say. After another dozen or so hugs and thank-yous, we left. As we walked back to the elevator for at least the tenth time today, whom did we run into? Jerry, of course, who had been the one to tell us about Employee Appreciation Day in the first place. Instead of having cake in his hands, this time he was pushing an empty wheelchair. He saw us holding hands and waiting for the elevator. He came up to us, smiling. "That's good," he said, pointing to our hands. "More people need to hold hands. There's not enough love in the world."

We explained to Jerry what had happened to us that day—or as much as we could explain in the thirty seconds it took for our elevator to arrive. He listened, wide-eyed at first, then slowly smiled. "I want you to know, it's your love that brought that diamond back to you. It knew where its home was. Now go buy a lottery ticket, because today's your day."

I looked at Christie. "No lottery tickets today, Jerry." I smiled. "We already won."

We drove home in silent disbelief. When we arrived home, I announced to Christie that I needed to meditate in the second bedroom *immediately*. I needed to process the day's events and put them in some semblance of order, to make sense of it all. Christie understood and wished me luck. I drew the curtains, turned out the lights, and quieted my mind. *What the hell had happened to us?* On the surface, it was just a diamond. Neither of us were hurt or injured, and even if we *had* lost the diamond, it was only a material possession. It *could* be replaced, albeit at a particularly high cost. But still, it could be replaced. But to us, obviously, it was more than just a diamond. It had a sentimental, emotional component. A couple's engagement ring is supposed to symbolize the everlasting nature of their love. Now, with my brain tumor threatening to turn "forever" into a very short time, our ring took on extra meaning.

My mind scrambled to assimilate what happened earlier that day. Christie had likened the experience of the loss to a bungee jumper who was free-falling for what felt like forever . . . and then *snap!* You're bounced back to safety. I thought about that, and about how, when we were at our lowest—on the plaza, without our diamond, holding on to nothing but each other—I didn't even feel angry. Or sad. Or anything, other than tired. I had given up. I had let go of all my emotion—my anger, my hate, my frustration. I didn't know whom to be mad at, and I didn't care. All I knew was that only one thing in my life really mattered when it was all said and done, and I was holding her in my arms.

Then something began to dawn on me: *Maybe that's why we lost our diamond.* Maybe I had to feel as if we'd lost "everything" to recognize what was truly important. Maybe I had to experience this lowest of lows so I could someday appreciate the highs. For a brief second, I allowed my mind to consider the overwhelming odds against what had happened: A maintenance worker found our two-centimeter diamond while she was cleaning by stepping on it next to a drainage grate inside a giant, packed hospital on Employee Appreciation Day. I thought about each of those variables and how each had to go *exactly right* for the diamond to make its way back to us. What if the diamond had been kicked by someone else? What if Leila had mopped another area first? What if Jerry had never told us about Employee Appreciation Day? What if Christie hadn't gotten up to get a drink of water?

After about thirty seconds of silently asking myself these kinds of questions, I quit. The variables were boggling my mind. It's almost like asking yourself, "How did I end up here, right now, in this very spot?" Your parents had to meet at the exact time they did, and they had to conceive you at the exact time they did. And their parents did the same, and their parents before them . . . [126]

As I said earlier, I'm not a particularly "spiritual" person. But I do believe that the universe gives you certain signs, and if the tide is carrying you one way as opposed to the other, sometimes it's best to just throw up your hands and go with the flow. But what was the universe trying to tell me? I let my mind drift. Suddenly, the answer

---

[126] If you're reading this chapter on mushrooms, maybe this is a good place to stop.

came to me. I imagined God—or someone much bigger and greater than me, like Yao Ming—grabbing me by the shoulders and holding me over a pool of water. As he prepared to submerge me, He said, "I'm sorry I have to do this to you. I know this is going to be unpleasant. But you have to trust me: You *will* be okay." Then He dunked me in the water. I struggled and panicked; I was sure I was going to drown. Then, suddenly, I could breathe. I relaxed under the water and felt totally at ease. As I reached a state of calm, He brought me out of the water and smiled, as if to say, "See? I told you it would be okay."

I don't know how or why, but somehow, I had divined the answer. The water was my cancer, and even though it felt scary to be dunked right into it, I'd get through it soon enough if I just stayed calm and relaxed. Don't ask me to explain. I just . . . felt it. With every fiber of my being. You know when you have a dream and you try to explain it to someone, only it doesn't make any sense to him or her but it makes perfect sense to you? You could say, "In my dream, I was talking to this fat turtle with a mustache, only it wasn't a turtle, it was my ex-girlfriend." Your friend may look at you as if you're nuts, but you think you just made your case convincingly. That's how I feel right now as I'm writing this. As sure as I knew that I existed, I felt I had the answer. I opened my eyes and bounced out of bed.

Christie was on the couch. I stood in the door and smiled at her. "What?" she said. "Did you have a good meditation?"

I smiled. "Everything's going to be okay."

Christie raised her eyebrows. "It is?"

"Yeah. I'm going to get better, and it's going to be"—I smiled and shrugged—"okay."

"Oh. Great!"

I must have been quite a sight: half-dressed, bleary-eyed, and limping a little bit. Yet here I was, explaining to her that it was all going to be okay. Still, she humored me, and we shared a celebratory kiss.

After the Great Diamond Incident of 2009, we had two immediate tasks: get Christie's ring fixed and get thank-you gifts for everyone involved in finding it. The first part was the easiest: We visited the jewelers who had sold us our ring. The shop was run by a husband and wife team named Harry and Rita, and they had been selling jewelry to Christie's family for three generations—Christie's grandmother used to shop there when she was a young woman. This was a delicate visit to their store because they were friendly with Christie's family and had always given them a fair deal on jewelry. Yet, I was righteously pissed off that they had essentially sold us a defective product. And not just any product—*our engagement ring.*

Rita greeted us as we entered the store. We showed her the ring, and she stared at us, mouth agape, as we told her the story of what had happened. She called Harry over to examine the ring. Harry, who'd built the ring, is a proud older man, so he never really admitted any culpability for making a faulty ring. But they offered to remake it for us at no charge. As we left the store, I called back over my shoulder, "Rita, this time, I need you to make that ring indestructible. Whatever Harry did last time, I need him to do it better." Think about how many times a day you (or your wife) bang your ring against something—your desk, your steering wheel, your computer. Diamonds are *not* supposed to fall out of engagement rings. Rita assured us that, yes, our ring would be remade much stronger.

Our next task required a little more thought: what to get the staff as a thank-you for helping us find our diamond? We decided on something edible—a cake! But what kind of cake? We went to the cake shop armed with questions. I barraged the poor girl working behind the counter:

"What flavors do you have?"

"What fillings do you have?"

"How fresh are the cakes?"

"What is your most popular?"

"What do *you* like the most?"

"If I come tomorrow, will the cakes be different?"

"What are the differences between the chocolate ganache and the chocolate cream?"

"Why are some of the chocolate ganaches shiny while the others are matte?"

"Can you write on the cake?"

I eventually decided on a chocolate cake with chocolate frosting and flowers piped on top. Then the countergirl made the mistake of asking me what I wanted written on the cake. I looked at Christie. What the hell do you write on a cake in this situation?

Luckily, Christie had the answer. "Why don't you just write a simple *Thank You!* on the cake, then write something personal in a card for each person?"

Bingo. "That's what we'll do," I told the girl.

She looked at me and opened a big drawer full of at least a dozen colored frosting bags. "What color would you like the *Thank You!* to be in?" she asked. Christie just laughed and walked off to the card section.

Once I had the cake all done and wrapped nicely in a box, I met Christie at the greeting cards. We settled on four thank-you cards:

The thank-you cards and cake. *(Christie Bishop)*

one each for Len, Francine, Leila, and the receptionist. We would write heartfelt, personal messages of thanks inside the cards, describing how much it meant to us that everyone had dropped what they were doing to help us.

"Perfect, we're finally done," Christie said. We headed to the register to check out. "By the way, what color did you end up choosing for the *Thank You!*?"

"All of them."

20.

My Bachelor Party

or, I Can't Be the First Guy to Take Chemo
in a Strip Club . . . Can I?

Given our good fortune in finding Christie's engagement diamond the same day we lost it, it's appropriate that my bachelor party took me and my friends to Las Vegas just a couple of weeks later. Twelve guys were invited to my bachelor party. They ranged from family (my brother, Adam) to inherited family (Christie's brother, Chris) to my best man (JD) to a handful of other close friends.

Las Vegas had been such a common destination for bachelor parties among my friends that it had gotten a little bit clichéd. One of the reasons it was so popular was its proximity to Los Angeles. You could fly there in less than an hour, or—if you were poor and in your early-to-mid twenties—you could drive there in just four hours. Plus, Vegas can cater to any crowd—from high rollers to cheapskates. Again, when you're dealing with broke twenty-one-year-olds, this is an attractive quality. So Vegas may have been overdone for bachelor parties, but I was determined to do a Vegas bachelor party and—more important—do it *right*.

Quick backstory: From 2006 to 2009, our radio show was syndicated in a dozen or so markets across the country. One of our strongest markets was Las Vegas. We were consistently number one in the ratings and did several live shows from the Palms Hotel and Casino. So I had a handful of connections and favors to call in.

Of course, our show had been canceled just three months earlier. Had the show still been on at the time of my bachelor party, who knows what favors the local affiliate would have been offering me and my idiot friends. For example, a couple of years earlier, I went to Las Vegas for my buddy Adam's bachelor party (yes, the same Adam at whose Scottsdale wedding Christie and I met). The show was doing extremely well in Vegas, so the local affiliate hooked us up with the VIP treatment: limos everywhere, a private room at Scores, comped beer flights at the Burger Bar, and bottle service every night at a variety of clubs. We had so much free vodka shoved in our faces that by the last night, we left two virginal bottles untouched; we had reached our limit. Sometimes, when I'm hankering for a cocktail and there's no booze around, I'll think about those two lonely bottles of vodka that we abandoned and shudder.

So although I could never make my own bachelor party as awesomely sweet as my buddy Adam's, I worked my connections for some pretty cool hookups. First, we got a great price on a block of rooms at Palms Place, which was the newer residential tower at the Palms Hotel and Casino. The biggest difference between these newer residential towers—which were popping up all around the Las Vegas Strip—and the older, more traditional hotel towers? There was no casino on the ground floor of the building. So when you took the elevator down to the first floor and the doors opened, you weren't greeted with the smell of cigarette smoke combined with the *ding-ding-ding-ding!* of slot machines. It was actually kind of quiet and subdued. Maybe that's another sign that we had outgrown the typical Vegas bachelor party: We welcomed the relative peace and quiet of a normal hotel lobby.

To get to the casino—or the pool or restaurants or anything—you had to take a long hallway that connected the newer building to the casino. The hallway was so long (and traveled so frequently by drunk people, I'm guessing) that the Palms had installed a moving walkway to make the trip smoother. I'll never forget the first time we took the moving walkway. I was in the back of this group of twelve guys, standing next to my friend Frank. Frank is a man of few words. Just one month earlier, when he first learned about my diagnosis, he emailed me that same day and said that it was some of the worst news he had heard since his father passed. Only I had no idea that his dad had died. *That's* how close to the vest Frank played his cards.

So Frank and I are standing together on the moving walkway, just a couple of feet behind everyone else. We were making small talk about the bachelor party when he paused and asked me, "You're going to be okay, right?" I looked at him, half expecting a joke to follow. But he was 100 percent serious.

"Yeah," I assured him. "Of course."

He exhaled. That was all he needed to be able to enjoy the weekend. I thought about what he had said, and I realized that everyone in the bachelor party had thought more or less the same thing at some point: "Can we have permission to enjoy ourselves?"

> **Tumor Tip:** *Your friends and family are most likely full of questions about your condition. Everything from how you knew you were sick, to the prognosis, to how you feel day to day. Their questions probably include mundane ones as well: Does chemo make you as sick as they say in the movies? What's the cancer center like? Do you have any attractive nurses? Are you going to be okay? My advice is to "open the floor to questions," as they say at a press conference. To the extent that you're comfortable, invite questions from friends and family. I'll never forget how my aunt Judy, when she first had breast cancer, lost all of her hair and chose to wear a wig. She asked if I wanted to touch her bald head. Um, not really, I thought. "Well, I never really considered it," I said. "Plus, I kind of know what a bald head feels like."*
>
> *"Go ahead!" she said as she whipped off her wig. She grabbed my hand and put it to her head. It felt . . . like a bald head. She was right, it totally broke the ice between us, and I followed with about a dozen questions. And while I don't necessarily recommend that kind of personal invitation among everyone you know, the point is to make people feel welcome to ask you questions about what you're going through. All our lives, we've been raised not to stare, not to point, and not to make people who may have an ailment feel uncomfortable. A lot of that bleeds over into our adult lives, and you end up with sympa-*

thetic people who are hesitant to ask a basic question. Plus, you never know what people are holding back around you.

Just before my bachelor party, Adam Carolla hosted a fund-raising event at his house benefiting Shakespeare Festival/LA.[127] Many of Adam's friends and coworkers were at the event, including his high school buddy Ray. Fans of the podcast know all about Ray: in a word, he's . . . intense. He dives into the pool of life headfirst. With no clothes on. Most of the people I knew at the event hadn't seen me since I announced my diagnosis on the podcast, including Ray. When he saw me, Ray—who may or may not have been drinking—grabbed me in a massive bear hug and screamed, "You gotta live!" He was 100 percent genuine and on the verge of tears. "You gotta LIVE!!" he bellowed. Picture the scene: People who purchased $300-and-up tickets to a fund-raiser benefiting Shakespeare education are sipping white wine and champagne at a house in Malibu as a muscle-bound man in shorts holds me in his arms, wailing.

So a lot of uncertainty surrounded my condition; I was clearly a little bit worse off than I had been a month ago, when I was diagnosed. Yet here I was, full steam ahead on such things as my bachelor party and wedding. I even asked Dr. Rudnick beforehand how much I should drink (if at all) and if I should avoid any prolonged sun exposure. He told me, "Have one or two beers, but don't get sloshed. And if you're going to be in the sun for more than twenty minutes, wear a wide-brimmed hat and plenty of sunblock." I took this as a green light to have a normal bachelor party.

My insistence on having a "normal" bachelor party must have rubbed off because everyone had a good time. Some people had a little too good of a time. The second day of the weekend, the Palms had provided us with a free cabana at their pool. I had insisted that it was medically necessary to keep me out of the oppressive Vegas

---

[127] This is the the only time you'll ever see the words *Adam Carolla* and *Shakespeare* in the same sentence.

summer heat—which it was, technically. We drank and hung out all morning long. By the time the afternoon rolled around, my brother had adjourned to the bar, where he had stepped up from light beer (which the rest of us were drinking) to shots of Jägermeister. After an hour's worth of shots, he stumbled toward the elevator to go up to his room and pass out—err, take a nap. He got to the elevator just as my best man, JD, did. They got in the elevator and pressed the buttons for their respective floors—Adam on the thirtieth, JD on the thirty-second. As soon as the elevator doors closed—*ding!*—my brother attempted to engage JD in a serious conversation. Only he was too drunk to talk.

"JD," he said, "Bluarghum blahh. Mmblofus pragham, sssefously rawrgel." This went on for thirty floors. My brother assaulted JD with a barrage of loosely connected vowels, to which JD never responded. He just looked at Adam and nodded politely as the "words" continued to spill out.

Finally, the elevator reached the thirtieth floor. The elevator doors opened—*ding!*—and Adam staggered out. As the doors were about to close, he looked back at JD.

"Good talk," he said.

Then the elevator doors closed, leaving a dumbfounded JD to ride the rest of the way to his floor, alone and confused.

Suffice to say, Adam elected to "skip" dinner that night. Which was too bad, because JD had arranged a very cool dinner in a private room at Nove, the Italian restaurant at the Palms. Little did I know, but my friends had prepared not one but two videos for everyone to watch. The videos were 20 percent flattering, 80 percent embarrassing. Actually, they might have been worse. Good thing I was drunk *and* radiated!

Dinner concluded with a roast in which my friends told horrible stories about me, mainly involving my ex-girlfriends. At the end I was given the chance to roast all of them, but I consider it one of the great missed opportunities of my life. I was a month into radiation and was really starting to feel the effects mentally. I was having a hard time concentrating. I was overstimulated. As my friend Anderson put it a week earlier, "Everything feels like you're in Las Vegas." Only now, I actually *was* in Las Vegas, so you can imagine how difficult this was for me. I couldn't write any original jokes for the roast, so I just watched a bunch of old roasts on YouTube and ripped off their jokes. I long for the day one of my friends has a roast for *his* bachelor party. I'll be making up for lost time, if you know what I mean.

After dinner, we loaded up on a van bound for Spearmint Rhino, where they were providing us with bottle service.[128] Strangely enough, my brother felt well enough to make *that* trip. It was almost 10:00 p.m. Our visit to Spearmint Rhino would coincide with my nightly chemotherapy-taking session.

We got to Spearmint Rhino, and they showed us to a semiprivate area where they had some red velvet couches surrounding a bottle of vodka and some mixers. My friends bought themselves lap-dances.[129] A dancer sat down next to me and started chatting me up. One thing women don't realize about strip clubs is how the dancers will just sit down next to you and strike up a conversation about nothing. Do they think they're stimulating our minds? I have several smart and accomplished female friends who I can talk to for hours about everything from sports to politics to *Top Chef.* Can you guess the one place I *don't* go for engaging conversation? *The strip club!* I would just as soon ask to see my wife's friends' boobs as I would think about having an in-depth, meaningful conversation with Lexxxi, the girl on Stage 3.

So I'm sitting on one of the couches, club music is absolutely *pounding* away at my brain, we've been comped enough vodka to make Jon Lovitz seem funny,[130] there's a dancer sitting next to me who I wish

---

[128] Note for my mom: *Bottle service* is where a group of guys donates their time feeding sick babies in a maternity ward; Spearmint Rhino is the finest nonprofit children's hospital in all of Nevada.

[129] My least favorite part of any bachelor party. This is more for the guys who've already been married for years and for whom random boobies are a distant memory. For me, lap dances are kind of a pain in the ass. "Thanks for the boner. I'll just take this with me to my hotel room. If you're looking for me at the pool tomorrow, I'll be the one with the crippling case of blue balls."

[130] I really wish Tom Leykis were more famous so I could start using him for these jokes. Wait, no, I don't.

would just leave, and it's 10:00 p.m.—time to take my chemo pill. At the beginning of the night, I took the trouble to put my pills in a hard case with a rubber band around them, lest I break and spill what is essentially poison on myself and/or a stripper. (Responsible, huh?)

I reached into my pocket, pulled out the case with the pills, and poured one in my hand. The dancer sitting next to me saw this and her previously glassed-over eyes lit up.

"Oooo, whaddaya got there?" The childlike delight in her voice told me she thought (hoped) it was ecstasy or some other illegal drug.[131]

I had to break her heart. "Nothing you want, honey. Nothing good."

With that, I threw back the pill and washed it down with a Red Bull and vodka. At various points in my life, whenever I'd done something foolish, I'd make myself feel better by telling myself, "Well, I can't be the *first* person to do that." It totally alleviated any guilt I might be feeling. If I accidentally walked into a girls' restroom at a restaurant, or if I mistakenly turned down a one-way street downtown, I'd just shrug and say (probably correctly), "I can't be the first guy who's done that." Try it the next time you're in a mildly awkward social situation.[132] Well, that's what I said to myself as I took my chemotherapy pills inside the Spearmint Rhino: "I can't be the *first* guy to take chemo in a strip club." Then I paused and thought about it. "Can I?"

Who do I talk to over at *Guinness World Records* for verification on this being a first?

---

[131] Not that all strippers take drugs or anything. If you had a hundred guys groping you every night, you'd want to dull the pain, too.

[132] I said *mildly* awkward. If your boss walks in on you making love to his wife, don't shrug and say, "Hey, I can't be the *first* guy to do this!" Even though you might be correct.

21.

Lies Doctors Tell You

or, "You're Going to Feel Like a Million Bucks!"

Once I got back from my bachelor party in Las Vegas, I only had three more weeks of chemotherapy and radiation left. I was at the halfway point in my first round of treatment. Once I finished those six total weeks, I'd be done with radiation for good. Radiation was a one-shot deal, my doctors told me. Chemotherapy, on the other hand, would continue indefinitely after I got a four-week "holiday" when I didn't need to take my nightly chemo pills. My body had essentially been poisoned for six weeks with daily radiation and chemotherapy. It needed time to recover.

Luckily, the end of my first round of treatment coincided with the start of our wedding celebrations. Just a week or so after I was scheduled to have my last radiation treatment, we would drive up north to the Napa Valley—California's wine country—where we would be married, just a few miles away from where we got engaged.

My doctors were supportive of our quest to do everything as "normally" as possible for our wedding. I specifically asked a lot of the same questions that I asked about my bachelor party: Could I drink? (Yes, just not to excess.) Could I be in the midday sun? (Yes, just wear a high SPF and don't get burned.) Could I take my chemotherapy pills into a topless club and ingest them in front of a confused stripper? (Um . . .)

Our doctors assured us, on several occasions, that I'd "feel like a million bucks!" once the radiation had ended and I was off my chemo pills. "Wow," I remember thinking, "a million bucks. Sounds far-fetched, but, hey, if they say so . . ."

Despite my worsening condition, I was optimistic. The last three weeks of radiation were considerably harder than the first three, and the chemotherapy I was taking every night was only exacerbating things. My vision was getting a little worse. Due to weakening muscles in my face, lips, and tongue, my speech was getting harder to understand. I had lost about ten or twelve pounds. My slight limp had degenerated into a pronounced limp. It got so bad that I was fitted with an ankle brace that I was now wearing full-time. Only the ankle brace required a larger-size shoe on my left foot. So with my tail between my legs and my pride swallowed, I went to the discount shoe store and bought two pairs of "old-man shoes": all-black, Velcro shoes in two sizes—a normal size for my right foot, a size larger for my left. Further adding insult to injury was the fact that my parents were in town for this humiliating shopping trip; they had flown in for a weekend visit. In the saddest prewedding family outing ever, my parents, Christie, and I went shopping for cheap shoes that I could wear with my new leg brace.

I mentioned earlier how I had been trying to meditate, or at least do some "positive visualizations." Kind of like "the Secret" that Oprah's always yammering on about. If you concentrate on something enough—a positive outcome to a situation, or something you want to achieve or attain—then you supposedly increase your chances of attaining it. You always hear these (possibly apocryphal) stories: One group of basketball players physically practiced shooting their free throws, while another just visualized making free throws. When they both went to shoot free throws for real, they both made the same percentage.

When I meditated, I'd picture my last day of radiation. I'd picture my tumor, shrunken and shriveled, and I'd picture how good I'd feel. I'd picture Christie and me in a celebratory embrace, with everyone else in the waiting room applauding us for a job well done. There also may have been swelling music and singing birds. Hey, it was *my* fantasy.

Toward the end of radiation, after a particularly taxing morning, I remember seeing Christie in the waiting room. She looked tired and run-down. I'm sure I looked ten times worse—limping, slurring, skinny, probably in my pajamas, and with my usual crisscross pattern imprinted on my face from the too-tight radiation mask. We were both beat. Plus, we had the stress of an out-of-town wedding to look forward to. I held her hand as we walked out of the radiation center. "I swear," I muttered under my breath, "I'm going to *dance* out of this place." My optimism was crashing head-on into my frustration, resulting in a pool of defiance on the asphalt. I was pissed. Why was I feeling worse with each passing day? Wasn't all of this—the medicine, the radiation, the meditation—supposed to be making me better? I was happy that my time in the radiation center was almost over. I was glad to hear that soon I'd be feeling "like a million bucks." I was excited to get married. But I was also angry. This was supposed to be a glorious, celebratory time in two young people's lives. And cancer was cheating us of it. I wanted to yell at my tumor the way Lieutenant Dan yelled at Forrest Gump: "Did you hear what I said? You cheated me! I had a destiny. I was supposed to die in the field with honor! That was my destiny, and you cheated me out of it! This wasn't supposed to happen. Not to me. I had a destiny."

Unfortunately, I couldn't yell at my tumor, or else I'd look like a crazy person. So I kept calm and focused on Friday, June 12: my last day of radiation. Graduation Day.

When Graduation Day came around, I really was feeling like a million bucks—emotionally, anyway. Physically, not so much. Most of the time, Christie was now helping me walk around, usually in subtle ways such as just holding my hand. But between my worsening sense of balance and my weakening left side, I needed constant monitoring. The risk of my losing my balance and falling to the ground was very real. As a result, I never strayed far from Christie's side. I'm sure to casual observers it seemed sweet: "Oh, look at that devoted young couple. They're always by each other's side, holding hands." But to us—and especially to Christie, I'm sure—that kind of thing gets old, fast. Besides, who wants to be that kind of a burden to his fiancée? Needless to say, I was very much looking forward to a few weeks down the road, when I'd "feel like a million bucks."

Graduation Day started out like any other day of radiation: I checked in, got buzzed on my restaurant-style pager, and lay still for ten minutes of radiation. When it was over, Len, the sushi-loving tech who had helped us find our lost diamond, handed me my radiation mask. "Here. It's yours. We don't need it anymore." He paused and smiled. "Neither do you."

I held the plastic mold of my face in my hands. I stared at it for a second. Here was a memento from my life, quite possibly the most important artifact I'd ever hold in my hands, if you think about it. And all I could think was "What the hell would I want this for?" Seriously, what was I going to do with it? Hang it in our guest bedroom? Scare neighborhood children with it? Eat popcorn out of it? But I could tell Len considered this to be a solemn occasion, so I graciously accepted my "gift."

Back in the waiting room, Christie was standing, saying good-bye to some of the friends we'd made in our six weeks there. She was exchanging hugs with Herb and Faye, the older couple whose mother had lived in our very apartment years earlier. While I was inside getting treated, they had given Christie a gift: a box of See's candy. "Sweets for two sweet people," they said. They had included a card that read, *To the Happy Couple*. It was part wedding gift, part graduation gift. "You two are just the sweetest, most wonderful couple," they had told Christie earlier. "So we wanted to give this to you."

I didn't know it at the time, but another patient—a woman named Anne—approached Christie that morning while I was being radiated. Christie wrote in her blog that day:

> While [Herb, Faye, and I] were chatting, Anne came out after finishing her treatment session. Bryan and I hadn't chatted or gotten to know Anne more than the daily smile and "Hello, how are you" when we walked into the waiting room. But as she was about to

leave, Anne walked up to me and says, "I don't think I even know your name (*at which point we introduced ourselves*) but I wanted to tell you that you and your fiancé made every day here better for me, without even knowing it. Your energy and your smiles really made me feel good, and I wanted to say thank you and congratulations on your wedding."

Christie was overwhelmed. So was I, when she told me about it later.

> **Tumor Tip:** *You never know who's watching. You never know whom you're inspiring, either, just by being yourself. Just showing up every day with a smile on your face can brighten someone else's day. And most of the time, you're not even aware of the effect you're having on people just by being positive and upbeat. If everyone went through their daily life thinking, "Hm, I bet my behavior is affecting someone right now," I promise this world would be a much better place to live.*

I came out of the radiation room with my mask in hand. "Ready to go?" I asked Christie. Just then, Sinead, our other favorite tech, came running out with a piece of paper.

"Here!" she said, extending her arm. "Before you leave." I looked at the paper. It was a diploma, signed by everyone who worked there. *Certificate of Achievement*, it read.

"Oh, great," I said with a smile. "A participation trophy."

We all laughed. Sinead wished us well and went back to work.

I hugged Christie and gave her a kiss. "Do you remember what I promised you on the first day here?"

She smiled. "I do."

I took her right hand in mine and wrapped my other hand around her waist. It was time to dance.

We only got a few wobbly steps into our impromptu dance when a man came up to us whom we had never met before. He was wearing a knit cap, presumably to conceal his radiated and/or scarred head.

All the items we walked out of radiation with. *(Christie Bishop)*

He introduced himself as Amit, his voice revealing a Middle Eastern accent. It was his first day there, and his partner, Miguel, looked terrified. Amit's brother, who was also there, looked exhausted. Apparently he had just flown fifteen hours from Israel to be there to support Amit.

In a shaky voice, Amit looked at us and said, "I don't know you and I don't know what kind of brain tumor you have, but I have one, too. This is my first day of radiation. Would it be okay if we exchanged numbers if I have any questions? If I can look the way you look after six weeks of treatment, I will be a really happy man."

Christie later remarked that meeting Amit and his entourage was like looking into a mirror at us just six weeks earlier. Nervous. Scared. Uncertain. But willing to cling to any hope that might turn up, no matter what it looked like. For Amit, hope looked like a guy dancing with his fiancée on his last day of treatment. We exchanged phone numbers that day, and I told him to call me anytime, about anything. Amit never called me. I have no idea if he's even alive today. But that day, for at least a few minutes, we helped make his first day of cancer treatment a little less scary.

You really never know who's watching.

22.

Our Wedding

or, Michael Jackson, Simply Red, and Glow Sticks

I'll be honest with you: I don't remember a ton about our wedding weekend. Part of it, I'm sure, has to do with my having just finished six weeks of radiation on my brain. But an equal amount was just normal wedding-day jitters.

I *do* remember that it was just a couple of weeks after I finished radiation. And I *do* remember my doctors lying to me—err, *explaining* to me that I would "feel like a million bucks" by the time my wedding rolled around, as the effects of radiation would wear off over the prior couple of weeks.

Well, by the time we arrived in Northern California, I remember thinking, "Wow, inflation must really have taken its toll on our currency, because this isn't what I was expecting a million bucks to feel like." I felt like about eighty-eight cents' worth of loose change—a far cry from the million bucks I had been promised. My limping had gotten worse. My overall coordination was deteriorating. And things were beginning to distract me more easily—especially bright lights, loud noises, and crowds. In other words, the perfect recipe for a wedding!

Here are a few observations, impressions, recollections, and musings on our wedding weekend:

- We arrived at my parents' house (in nearby San Carlos, about an hour away from Napa Valley) on Tuesday. The plan was to pick up a few things, put together the welcome baskets for the guests, and spend the night before heading off the next morning to our wedding site. Our gift bags were especially cool: Christie had ordered some small canvas tote bags off the Internet and had them printed with a simple map of the Napa Valley. Then we would fill them with homemade cookies, fudge, and assorted sundries, as well as a cool wall map of the Napa Valley (donated by a listener who made them professionally). Christie had made some personalized *B&C* stickers to seal the cellophane bags of cookies. And of course, I was tasked with peeling the stickers and applying them to the cellophane bags. I say "of course" because, with my decaying coordination, it ended up being the hardest possible job I could have done: attempting to peel two-inch-by-two-inch stickers with my fingertips. Let's just say that the gift-bag assembly line got a little backed up around the cookies-and-sticker station. I felt like Lucy and Ethel when the chocolates wouldn't stop coming down the conveyer belt.

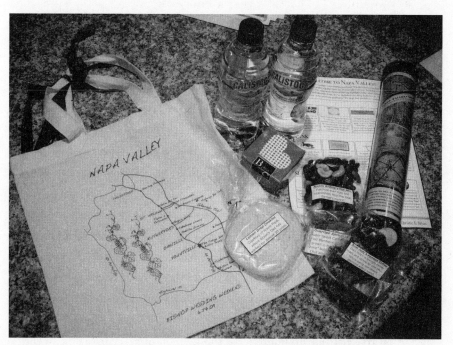

Our gift bag and all of its contents. You see all those stickers and labels?
The guy with the brain tumor applied all of those. *(Christie Bishop)*

• The next morning, we drove to our wedding location (the Vintage Estate in Yountville, California). We checked into the hotel (the wedding was taking place on the hotel grounds) and spent the rest of the day walking around the town. Yountville is a very small town with a main street that stretches about four blocks. It's incredibly quaint and completely delightful. The town is probably best known as the home of Thomas Keller's famous restaurant the French Laundry, but it has a ton to offer: a few small wineries, some great bed-and-breakfasts, and a couple of fantastic hotels. We chose one of them (The Vintage Estate) to be the location of our wedding. The Vintage Estate is actually two hotels—Villagio and the Vintage Inn—with the awesome brick Barrel Room from the 1800s in between the two properties. That's where our reception would be. The wedding ceremony itself would be just a few yards away from the Barrel Room on an outdoor pavilion. It was stunning, intimate, and picturesque—everything you could possibly want out of a wine-country wedding.

• Thursday, we arranged a wine-tasting day for all of our friends. We hired a shuttle and a driver to take us to a few wineries. Everything was going great and everyone was having a fun time; it was midday on a Thursday, so the crowds were sparse, the wineries were beautiful, and the weather was perfect. But that's not why I remember that day so well. June 25, 2009, is burned into my memory for a different reason: It's the day Michael Jackson died. Christie and I and about a dozen of our friends were sipping wine on the back patio of Paraduxx Winery when the news broke. "Oh my God," one of our friends exclaimed to the group. "Michael Jackson died!" The news spread like a virus; everyone got on his or her smartphone to check the news. Sure enough, the King of Pop had passed away. Being a group of rhythmless, drunk white people in our thirties, we decided to honor his memory in the best way we knew how: by plugging an iPod into the shuttle bus's stereo system and blasting his greatest-hits collection. We became an impromptu rolling memorial, cruising down the Silverado Trail and singing "P.Y.T." at the top of our lungs. It was a fitting tribute. Michael would have wanted it that way.

- Friday was our rehearsal dinner. It was held at Duckhorn winery, which not only makes world-class wines, but whose property is reminiscent of an old Southern plantation. About twenty-five of us were seated on the back porch, overlooking the sprawling vineyards at sunset. It was stunningly gorgeous—and this was just the rehearsal dinner! My grandpa Babe was there—my mom's dad—and he amused everyone with an off-color joke involving African Pygmies, walnuts, AIDS, and condoms. My parents and I had heard the joke before—*several* times—but this was a whole new audience of youngish people, a rarity when you're eighty-three years old. The joke killed. And why not? The joke isn't bad, per se, it's just . . . not politically correct.

- Saturday was the big day. One of the great things about the Vintage Estate—and part of the reason we chose to have our wedding there— was that they had two separate areas for the bridal party and the groomsmen to get ready. One, called the Retreat, was the hotel's old spa (before they built a bigger one). Here, Christie and her bridesmaids got all dolled up for the wedding. Ladies, imagine getting primped in your own private spa on the day of your wedding. Who *wouldn't* want that? We fellas were given the Groezinger Estate, which used to be a restaurant before they (again) built a bigger and better one. Now it was used as a place for wedding parties to hang out, get ready, and take pictures. It was awesome, like our own brick clubhouse. Wedding venues, take note: Rather than offer up a simple hotel room as a base of operations for your wedding guests, spend a few thousand bucks and develop something cool on your property. I promise you'll recoup your expenses and then some with increased business.

- The details of the actual temperature that day seem to fluctuate wildly depending on whom you talk to. Christie has told multiple people on multiple occasions that it was as high as 105 degrees. Despite my half recollections due to radiation, this seemed insanely high—especially considering the ceremony was at 6:00 p.m., well after the sun would have been at its hottest. Luckily (for me, not her) we have this thing called the Internet, which can tell you anything about any day, ever, with 100 percent accuracy. I looked up the temperature in Yountville for June 27, 2009. Sure enough, the high that day was ninety-eight degrees. And that was around one in the afternoon. By the time the ceremony started, it couldn't possibly have been hotter than ninety-five degrees. But, please, if you're ever talking to Christie about our wedding and she starts in with "Oh my God, it must have been 132 degrees," just smile and nod. Like I do.

- Because it was so hot, we decided to start the ceremony on time: 6 pm SHARP. Adam Carolla and his wife, Lynette—who had both traveled from Los Angeles to be there for the wedding—apparently took a looser interpretation of the printed "6 pm" start time on the invitation and strolled into the ceremony at about 6:20—just in time to see us walk back down the aisle as a married couple. Ironically, by being the last people to show up to the ceremony, they were the first ones to congratulate us as a married couple; everyone else was still in their seats at the ceremony site.[133]

Wedding Tip: *Hire a good photographer. And if said photographer offers a package where you get to keep all the pictures after the wedding, definitely do it. Especially if they can be sent to you digitally, which pretty much all pictures can be these days. We hired a really talented wedding photographer, who took a ton of photographs that day of us, our guests, the grounds, the food . . . everything. My memory was a little fuzzy after the wedding, so looking at the pictures now helps solidify my recollections of that day: "Oh, yeah, that happened. I almost forgot about that." Plus, if they're digital, you can do anything with them: mail them, print them, make a slide show out of them . . . Christie and I had a couple of the photos mounted on canvas and hung them in our bedroom. Only I insisted that we choose pictures where you can't see our faces.*

---

[133] Adam claims that Lynette, as the wife, should be "the time keeper" when it comes to things like making it to weddings on time. He offered this up on more than one occasion in his own defense of being late. What can I say? He's old-school.

> Number one, how narcissistic would that be? You walk into some-
> one's bedroom and boom! You're greeted with a huge photograph
> of that person. Second, why would I want to be greeted by my own
> face every day when I woke up? As I got older over the years, it
> would be a sad reminder of how young I once looked.

- Speaking of photographs and sad reminders . . . I "ruined" most of our wedding pictures. Let me explain: My tumor was resting right on my cranial nerves—the nerves that control your body functions; specifically, in my case, the nerves that control motor skills, sight, hearing, taste, and facial expression. Radiation had not been kind to these nerves, especially the ones that controlled the muscles in my face. The right side of my face was effectively paralyzed. Luckily, no one could really notice . . . until I smiled. And it turns out you do a lot of smiling at your wedding. Especially in your wedding pictures. In every picture where I'm supposed to be smiling, I'm actually giving a stupid "half smile." If you look at our pictures and use your thumb to cover up the right (paralyzed) side of my face, you'd probably think, "Oh, how wonderful, look at what a great time he's having!" But if you covered up the left side of my face—the side that was working normally—you might think, "Why does he look so surprised to be photographed each time?" It was pretty bad. Ladies, imagine taking all your wedding portraits next to your husband, only he's doing his best Popeye impression.

- As I mentioned in an earlier chapter, the music was *very* important to me. Music can make or break a wedding. I've been to more than one wedding that was perfectly fine in every other respect, but because of the lame music, I came away with a negative impression. And vice versa: I've been at weddings where *all* I can remember is the good music. So I went over the music in painstaking detail with Chad, our DJ, prior to the wedding. I didn't give him a playlist, per se—I know people who've done this, and honestly, at that point, why are you even paying a DJ? Just program an iPod and save yourself $500. But Chad and I were on the same page as to the *type* of music to play at certain times . . . or so I thought. We had music selected for our cocktail hour (big-band, Rat Pack–style swing tunes), dinner (crowd favorites that people could hum along to), and the reception (fun dance songs).

> **Wedding Tip:** *You know those songs that everyone loves but you can't dance to? Songs such as Bon Jovi's "Livin' on a Prayer"? Play those during dinner. No one wants to dance to them, but no one would mind hearing them, either. Plus it's a fun way to get everyone in a party mood. Plus, if people are drinking enough, you'll get a nice big sing-along. It takes the right kind of crowd, but you can get a hundred people to shout in unison, "OHHHHH, YOU'RE HALFWAY THERE! WHOOAA-OH! LIVING ON A PRAYER!" Your grandparents will be confused, so make sure you seat them away from any large speakers.*

Unfortunately, for some reason—and I never figured out how or why—Chad started playing the wrong music during dinner. I was admittedly a little distracted—people were coming up to our table constantly throughout the night—but at one point my ears perked up and I leaned over and said to Christie, "Why is the DJ playing Simply Red?" He was playing "Holding Back the Years," a fine enough song, but all wrong for the type of vibe I had envisioned. Christie, who has no idea who or what Simply Red is, just shrugged and went back to actually enjoying her wedding day. But I had to settle this right away. I dispatched someone—it could have been my brother—to tell Chad to play the dinner music we had talked about. I don't know if it was a creative decision on Chad's part, or if he made an audible at the line, but my message must have made it to him, because a few seconds later we were treated to some Jovi.

- Thankfully, due to the open bar, nobody gave a crap what music was playing during dinner. The bar was apparently elaborate—people still bring it up to us whenever our wedding comes up. I say "apparently" because I never actually made it to the bar. That's right—between my limited mobility, my general feeling of being overstimulated by all the bright lights and loud music, and everyone else's willingness to fetch me drinks, I never actually made it outside to see the bar setup. I hear it was nice, though.

- Speaking of being overwhelmed by bright lights . . . one of the worst decisions we made was to hire a videographer to shoot the whole thing and burn it to a DVD. This was really for our out-of-town grandparents who couldn't make it to the wedding, so I guess it was defensible. But we must have watched that DVD one time—the day we got it. That's it. Actually, we "got it" twice—one copy on which they misspelled Christie's name on the cover, and one corrected version. But the worst part was at the actual reception. It never occurred to me that I'd be the "star" of my own wedding video and have a camera pointed in my face the entire evening . . . a camera with a very bright spotlight. As someone with brain cancer who had just finished six weeks of radiation, a spotlight shining in my face was the last thing I needed that night. After about half an hour of squinting and holding my hand up to block out the light, I told our wedding planner, "I know we paid these people to videotape us. But now I'm begging you, please tell them to *stop* videotaping me. I'm going blind from the spotlight. I'm afraid I'm going to accidentally stab Christie with the spatula when it's time to cut the cake."

- And speaking of cake-cutting . . . here are a few things *not* to do at your wedding. Don't smash cake in each other's face. Don't have more than three speeches (best man, maid of honor, and father of the bride).[134] And for God's sake, never, under any circumstances, do the bouquet toss and garter toss into the crowd of single wedding guests. First of all, if you're having a party—*any* party, but especially the

---

[134] Two of those are movie titles. Come on, Tyler Perry, hurry up and make *Best Mann*, the story of Freddie Mann, the ne'er-do-well brother of Theodore Mann, an engaged Wall Street investor.

biggest party of your life—why would you abruptly stop the party to play parlor games? That's like having a cocktail party and stopping everything to play pin the tail on the donkey. Second, if you're having a wedding in your thirties (as we were) then "singling out" (so to speak) your friends who aren't married is kind of cruel. Especially when the DJ announces, "Okay, we need all the single ladies on the dance floor!"—and only three women come out. It reaches a new level of sadness when said three women actually fight over the bouquet. The only thing worse is when the bride makes an errant toss and the closest one of the three women has to trudge over to pick up the bouquet off the ground, as though she "won" the toss by default. If you're getting married in your teens or early twenties, you can get away with this stale tradition, I guess. But once you reach legal drinking age, go ahead and retire it, along with your fake ID.

- Obviously, I have a lot of strong opinions on weddings—music, bouquet tossing, etc. But I can admit when I'm wrong. Such is the case when it came to glow sticks. Early on in the planning stages of our wedding, Christie and her mom, Sheryl, came up with the idea of having glow sticks at our reception. Halfway through, they thought, we'd give them out to people to wear or wave around or whatever. I was instantly opposed. This wasn't a rave. This was going to be a classy affair, I argued. Glow sticks have no business at a Napa Valley wedding. Plus, we already had plenty of "accessories," or extras, planned for our guests: We offered parasols at the ceremony, so people wouldn't be in the direct sunlight—a good idea. We gave away glasses of wine *during* the ceremony so people could toast along with us (and so we could "kick-start" the party)—a great idea. We also provided a couple of crates of flip-flops at the reception for the ladies. That way they could kick off their uncomfortable shoes and dance the night away in comfort—a *brilliant* idea. None of these ideas were mine, by the way. Credit where it's due: Christie, Sheryl, and our wedding planner, Michelle, cooked up most of this. Plus we had a photo booth, a coffee bar, and some late-night snacks. There were plenty of *accoutrements* for our guests. Sheryl and Christie listened to my reasonable, thought-out arguments . . . and rejected them. Glow sticks were definitely happening. Looking back, I should have realized who was signing the checks and basically said, "Look, Christie can have a veil made of glow sticks if she wants." But I silently objected. And you know what? The glow sticks were a huge hit. People freaked out when they saw them. Everyone—from the youngest attendee to the oldest—fashioned the glow sticks into necklaces, bracelets, and crowns. There's a point in our wedding pictures where you can tell when the glow sticks came out because all of a sudden, *everyone* is wearing one. So congrats, Sheryl and Christie, you were right and I was wrong. The glow sticks were absolutely the right call. Luckily, that was the last time I was ever wrong about anything. *Ever.*

My frat buddies, adorned in glow sticks, singing to Christie. What can I say? They were a hit (the glow sticks, not my singing frat buddies). *(Anna Kuperberg)*

We must have done the whole thing right because everyone was spent after the reception. I actually had to be driven the hundred yards back to our room, I was so worn-out. Our wedding planner had snuck into our room during the reception and laid out a bunch of flower petals and candles to surprise us when we got back. It would have been romantic had we not been so damn tired. We barely managed to get into our pajamas before we passed out asleep. Needless to say, we did not consummate the marriage that night. I honestly wonder what percentage of newlyweds do. Anecdotally, I hear it's pretty common to be so wiped out after your wedding that you don't get around to sexy time until your honeymoon. Throw in a husband with cancer, and you can count us in that portion of the population. Still, it was a magical night. Christie looked beautiful. And now we were about to depart on a weeklong honeymoon in Hawaii—where my worsening symptoms would be exposed even more.

23.

Our Honeymoon

or, The Time My Wife Drugged Me
at a Kids Pool in Maui

My wife almost killed me on our honeymoon.

Although, to be fair, I don't think she meant to.

Life's all about simple pleasures. One thing I love to do is get an old-timey hot shave. The kind where they wrap your face in hot towels and use freshly foamed shaving cream and a straight razor and give you a happy ending (maybe they do it differently here in Los Angeles). When researching where to spend our honeymoon, one of the deciding factors was if the hotel had a swim-up bar. I'd never been to a swim-up bar, but it seemed wildly exotic, like a Burmese python or Brigitte Nielsen.

We decided on Hawaii. Traveling out of the country seemed like an added layer of stress that we didn't need at that point in our lives. So we booked a swanky hotel in Maui that, yes, had a swim-up bar. The plan was to spend a week there starting two days after our wedding. For the day immediately after our wedding, we'd spend the night at a fancy hotel in San Francisco, then fly out to Maui the next morning. You might be asking yourself, "How could you afford this when neither of you were working?" Fair question. For the one night in the fancy San Francisco hotel, I had won a charity auction a year earlier, so not only was it cheap, but we had to use that one-night's stay soon. (And the money went to charity.) For Maui, Christie's mom had worked in the hospitality (read: hotel) industry for years and had a close work friend who helped run the hotel. So she was able to offer us a "friends and family" rate for our stay. As I said earlier, Adam (my boss) often asked me how I was able to afford such an "extravagant lifestyle" (as he put it) on such a meager salary (at the time). Well, this is one example of how I did it.

These plans were all made precancer. By the time our honeymoon rolled around, my condition had declined considerably: I needed more than a little help getting around, and I couldn't be left alone for too long. Even though I was off my chemo pills for a few weeks, I was also on a twice-daily regimen of steroid pills to control the brain swelling caused by my recently completed radiation. Still, I was going to achieve my (somewhat pathetic) lifelong dream of drinking at a swim-up bar.

The flight out to Maui was eventful. Christie used her airline miles that she had accumulated through business travel to secure us two free round-trip tickets. Spending airline miles can be tricky; we had to call exactly ninety days before the day we wanted to travel—at midnight, no less—to get two seats. Since Christie called at just the right time, she booked us two seats in an exit row. If you're making the early-morning, six-hour flight to Maui two days after your wedding, you definitely want a couple of more inches of legroom. By the time the date of travel rolled around three months later, however, I was limping noticeably as we boarded the plane. As Christie put away my luggage and eased me into my seat, the flight attendant came over. "Sir," she said, "this is an exit row. Are you able to perform the necessary safety requirements to sit in this row?"

"Of course," I said.

She didn't look convinced. "Sir, that emergency-exit door weighs fifty pounds. Can you open it if you have to?"

I looked her in the eye. "Yes."

She frowned. My mouth may have said yes, but my ankle brace was telling her no. "Sir, I may have to reseat you."

Christie then became indignant. The stress and strain of caring for someone in my condition must have been building up silently, because it all came out right there in our exit row. After phrases like "How dare you," "We booked these seats three months ago," and "It's our honeymoon, for God's sake" were bandied about, the flight attendant backed down. For the record, I *could* have opened the door if I had to, so it's not as if I were endangering anyone's life. I think the flight attendant just wanted to exercise her rarely used power of being able to reseat someone whom she didn't deem fit to sit in an exit row. But come on, I was in an aisle seat, for crying out loud. Two people—Christie being one of them—were between me and the emergency door, whose dead bodies I would have to crawl over to open it if it came to that. Highly, highly unlikely.

Of course, the airline cosmically got revenge on us by promptly losing my luggage. For two days, I wore what I wore on the plane: shorts and a Hawaiian shirt. Luckily, if you're going to be stuck with nothing but shorts and a tropical, silk, button-up shirt, Hawaii is the place you want it to be. We bought a pair of boardshorts and some toiletries, and I was able to ride out the first couple of days. I will say this about getting cancer: It's great for refocusing your priorities on what to truly get upset about and what "crises" you can just laugh off. When the airline representative at the airport told me my bags were officially lost, I shrugged and said to Christie, "Eh, not the *worst* thing to happen to us this year." Two days later, I was reunited with my suitcase.

For the first two days of our honeymoon, we did nothing. It was great. The smartest thing we ever did that week was ask about the hotel's poolside cabanas. They were just $50 for a two-day rental. Not only were they reserved for us ahead of time, but they offered a shaded place to nap and escape from the midday sun—helpful for me, as I was now napping for several hours a day, due to the lingering radiation effects. They also gave you all the fruit, water, and juice you asked for. This was also welcome news, since any oncologist will tell you that you should eat and drink as healthfully as possible. We booked a cabana for four days right away.

One day, we decided to actually venture "off campus" and check out some of Maui's legendary beaches. We had rented a car, so Christie drove us down the coast to Turtle Beach, so named for all the turtles that migrated onto its shores. When we took a few steps on the beach, I realized I was in trouble: I couldn't walk on sand anymore. My ankle was just too weak. Christie grabbed my arm and attempted to help me get a little farther onto the beach, but it was futile. Every tiny hill of sand was conspiring to trip me. I simply could not navigate the terrain. I felt awful. Here we were, in one of the best beach areas on earth, and I was ruining it. Christie was a good sport, but I could tell she was disappointed. She wanted to walk hand in hand on the sand, taking pictures of our buried toes and splashing each other in the surf. We did none of it. In one of the greatest regrets of my life, I was unable to walk on the beach with my new wife on our honeymoon.

To her credit, Christie had a "go forth" attitude about the whole thing. We got back in the car and headed to a black-sand beach. Maybe, we thought, I'd have an easier time with the black sand.[135] No such luck. I had the same trouble at this beach as the last one. Dejected, we went back to the car. I was getting tired. I was jet-lagged, I hadn't taken my daily steroid pills, and the sand debacles were making me frustrated. We went to one more beach, but this time Christie went alone. "I'm just going to take some pictures," she said. I agreed to stay in the car and wait for her. It was a heartbreaking moment for me, watching her walk off to the beach alone with her little digital camera, but without me.

It wasn't all bad. Far from it. I think it was overall a good, relaxing week for both of us. One day, we decided to drive Maui's famous Honoapiilani Highway, an absurdly narrow, steep road along Maui's northwest coast. Even though it allows traffic going both ways, there were several stretches where just one car could fit. We know this be-

---

[135] Because, as the saying goes, "Black sand don't crack . . . sand."

cause on one occasion, we had to stop and slowly back down the cliff-side road when we came face-to-face with an oncoming car. Needless to say, traffic moved slowly on the Honoapiilani Highway. So slow, that at one point I had to pee. I mean, I *really* had to pee. The radiation and chemotherapy had made it so that I couldn't hold what was in my bladder for long. When the urge to go came on, it came on *strong*. And that day, I had to go *right now*. So Christie looked for a place to pull over. The only thing we saw—the only thing for miles—was a tiny church. I had no choice; there were no trees or anything else to obstruct views of my public urination. So we pulled off the road and—God help me—I peed on the church's property. Now, when this story gets repeated these days, Christie likes to say that I peed *on* a church. Not true. I technically peed on their driveway, which was just a dirt path. But to be fair, yes, I did pee on the grounds of a tiny church in northwest Maui. I initially felt bad about it—well, that's not true. My *immediate* feeling was relief . . . sweet, sweet relief. But once that faded away, I felt ashamed, as if I had committed some sacrilegious act. But I figured God knew what I was dealing with, and if ever He was going to forgive someone for peeing on a church's driveway . . . well, this would probably be the time.

The next day, we decided to go back to the pool. We were more than halfway into our honeymoon but still hadn't gone to the swim-up bar, even though I could see it from our hotel room. There it was, taunting me from five stories away. I was like a kid who could see the Matterhorn's peak from the fleabag motel his parents rented next to Disneyland. Every moment spent *looking* at it was a moment we weren't *there*. "Let's do this, already!" I yelled to Christie.

In their infinite wisdom, the hotel had put their swim-up bar in the same pool where kids lined up to get on the hotel's waterslide. I can understand the initial thinking—"Let's put the kids where their parents can keep an eye on them, no matter how many Lava Flows they drink"—but why the hell would you put your swim-up bar in what is essentially a kiddie pool?

The swim-up bar is toward the upper right. Note the line of kids on the left, waiting to go down the waterslide. *(Christie Bishop)*

No matter. It was time to get our soggy drink on. We made our way down to the pool (actually, Christie made the way for both of us . . . my condition was so bad that I pretty much leaned on her everywhere I went), kicked off our flip-flops, and jumped (fell) in. We waded up to the bar and ordered a couple of drinks. Then a couple of more. It was everything I had hoped for: good beer, relaxing atmosphere, and you never had to get up to pee (if you know what I mean).

We were at the bar longer than we anticipated, so it became time to take my afternoon dose of steroids. Luckily, Christie, being the wonderful wife she is, had brought along all my potential pills in a plastic baggie. "Steroid time!" she said, and fished out a pill. I downed it with a beer. (Look, the strip-club thing hadn't killed me, so I figured I was in the clear.)

After another forty-five minutes or so of just hanging out and enjoying the view from the bar, we decided to leave. Christie said, "I'm going to get out and grab our flip-flops from the side of the pool. I'll meet you on the other side, by the steps." She jumped out of the pool and I finished my beer. I slid off the barstool and was shocked by a sudden feeling of extreme tipsiness. Much more than I had anticipated; I felt *wasted*.

I'd only had a couple of beers, but things had been changing so frequently with my physical condition lately that I figured, "Well, this is just the next thing to go." Like when you're driving a run-down car and the air-conditioning goes out on a hot day; you don't scream, shocked, "What the hell?!" You shrug and say, "I'm surprised it held out *that* long."

So my mission became to get out of the pool without hurting myself. Christie was standing on the side of the pool with all of our dry belongings in her hands. Rather than have her put them all back down and reenter the pool just to humiliatingly help me out of it, I decided to make a go of it. But there was one problem.

The kids.

I had to negotiate a pool full of kids to make it to the other side. Sloppily, I waded through them. Keep in mind, I felt *bombed*. I was like Will Ferrell in *Old School*.[136] I was slurring my words and pushing kids out of the way. Some of the other adults were giving me "What the hell is he doing?" looks as I shoved their kids aside and lost my balance (more than once, I might add). While watching this grotesque display, Christie hissed at me from the side of the pool, "Bryan! *Bryan!* You have got to *maintain!*" I pulled myself together and waded the final ten feet to the stairs, where Christie helped me out of the pool. We went upstairs to our room and I immediately passed out for two hours.

The next day, we went to a different pool at the hotel, so as not to be recognized as "the couple who got wasted at the bar and stumbled into all those kids." When it was time for my morning dose of ste-

---

136 "I like you . . . but you're *crazy*."

roids, Christie pulled out our bag of pills and began to fish one out. With a confused look on her face, she paused.

"What's up?" I asked.

"There are still two steroid pills in here," she said.

"So? Give me one of them."

"I put two in the baggie yesterday before the pool. There should only be one left."

She did a little more digging around in the pill bag.

"But you know what? One of my Valiums is missing."

And that was the time my wife drugged me in a kids pool in Maui.

24.

Worsening Symptoms

or, "You're Not Driving a Car . . . Are You?"

Things started to get significantly worse after our honeymoon. For the next month, my symptoms worsened almost by the day. I remember being incredibly frustrated and saying to Christie more than once, "I just want to wake up one day and start feeling better." I wanted my *Vanilla Sky* moment, where I'd just wake up one day and things simply got . . . *better*. I was tired of waking up each day and feeling worse than I did the day before. Anyone who's recovering from *anything* serious can tell you that it doesn't work that way; you never wake up one morning and magically "feel better." It's incremental. Usually, your recovery is so slow and gradual that you don't even notice it day to day. Only after weeks—or sometimes months—have passed do you look at the distance you've put between yourself now and before and think, "Man, I've really come a long way."

Unfortunately, I was nowhere near even starting to recover. If you were to chart my physical progress on a graph, the arrow would be pointing precipitously down. In fact, calling it *progress* is a misnomer. Here, now, a description of my physical *regression* over the month following our wedding:

Obviously, I've discussed my weakening left side. Specifically, my left arm, shoulder, and hand were becoming totally useless. And my leg, hip, knee, and foot were rapidly declining, too. I walked with a pronounced limp. At our wedding, I couldn't even make it up and down the three (!) steps to the altar by myself. So we rearranged things so that when Christie and I walked back down the aisle in our first steps as a married couple, she would hold my hand, and JD, my best man, would walk down the steps with us and hold my other hand. To make things look symmetrical, Christie also held hands with her maid of honor, Lyndsey. I'm sure it looked oddly adorable to our wedding guests, but it was the only way to ensure that I would make it down the stairs without falling or—worse—taking Christie down with me. This became a microcosm of our lives for the next few months: modifying everything (in this case, the traditional walk down the aisle) to accommodate my worsening condition.

Lyndsey and JD helping us walk down the steps after our wedding ceremony. *(Anna Kuperberg)*

Because my left hand was essentially not working, I began to do all my typing with my right hand. This, combined with my becoming overwhelmed at even the smallest of tasks, made writing any email longer than two sentences a monumental task. If you're a friend or family member reading this, and you got even a medium-length email from me that summer, it must have been *very* important. Since I had a daily regimen of about a half dozen pills to take, I tried to turn pill-taking time into therapy: I'd recline a little on the couch, spread the pills out on my shirt, and attempt to put them in my mouth with just my left hand. Sounds simple enough, right? Wrong. Not when you've all but lost the use of said hand. It regularly took me up to forty-five minutes to get the pills into my mouth. Think about that: six pills. Forty-five minutes. First, I had to get my hand *to* the pills. Remember, everything about my left side—my fingers, hand, wrist, elbow, and shoulder—was affected. I had no strength at all. No fine motor skills either. Once I got my hand in the general vicinity of the pills, I had to pinch one between my thumb and forefinger. After several failed attempts to actually pick up a pill, if I managed to finally get one, I had to transport it to my mouth. Often, I'd drop the pill back onto my shirt, putting me back to square one. For forty-five minutes a day, I'd do this tedious dance. I remember once, when my parents came down to visit, how shocked they were at how difficult this had become for me. They later told me how painful it was for them to watch me struggle with one of the easiest tasks for a healthy person to perform. How they wanted to just come over and help me by putting the pills in my hand for me.

I also began to get overstimulated very easily. Like my friend Anderson had told me before my bachelor party, being overstimulated feels as if you were in Vegas, all the time. Only without the free booze and gambling. Every light seemed brighter and every noise seemed louder. Everything was just . . . more *intense*. I couldn't deal with complex issues for more than a couple of minutes at a time. Hooking up a printer or our AppleTV became insurmountable tasks. As a result of all the overstimulation, I started needing a lot more sleep than normal. Before long, I was sleeping eighteen hours a day.

I had some other odd neurological symptoms. Presumably because the radiation had essentially "burned" my brain, I began to regularly detect the faint odor of grilled onions and peppers. You might be thinking, "That sounds like a delicious side effect!" It was, for a short while, but after a few weeks of smelling nothing but grilled onions and peppers, it got old.[137] My hearing was also affected. My ears rang a lot, and for a short period I would often hear the sound of water "bubbling" inside them. My eyes also started blinking out of sequence. Christie first noticed this. There would be a half-second delay in my right eye's closing whenever I blinked. Our doctors chalked this up to the facial-cranial nerves that were being impacted by the tumor. I also had trouble focusing my eyes on anything moving, and especially anything in my peripheral vision. When I had a follow-up appointment with Dr. Rudnick around this time, I began to describe my worsening symptoms. After hearing about everything going on with my vision, he paused and looked at Rebecca, who said, "You're not driving, are you?" No, I assured them, I hadn't driven for weeks. In fact, my dad had flown down to Los Angeles and driven my truck back up to Northern California so we wouldn't have to worry about moving it all the time. Rudnick and Rebecca actually sighed with relief. If I was still trying to drive, they explained, they'd have to report me to the DMV and have my license revoked.

My speech was also getting worse. Psychologically, this was one of the hardest symptoms to deal with. I made my living on the radio. I had dreams of having a long career in broadcasting. Now my ability to speak was clearly deteriorating, and my career options—if I could even resume working at some point in my life—were disappearing. My speech declined rapidly, but amazingly, Adam Carolla kept inviting me to be a guest on his podcast almost every week. Part of me suspects it was out of pity, but there I was, every week, mumbling into a microphone when, honestly, I had no business being near one.[138] It actually became a way to chart my speech and how bad it was getting. Longtime listeners of the show will certainly remember the dark days of mid-2009 when I would trudge into the studio and mumble a few unintelligible words during a sixty-minute podcast. I became good at recognizing the signs of when someone wouldn't understand me but

---

[137] My greatest fear at the time was that I would never be able to enjoy another Philly cheesesteak sandwich again.

[138] Some people might suggest I *never* had any business being near a microphone.

would *pretend* to understand me. I would mumble a "joke," and then Adam (and Teresa, who was usually there with me) would look at me, pause, smile, and half laugh, as if to say, "I recognize by your cadence that you just made a joke, and you probably think it's funny, but I have no idea what you just said." Sadly, I got more laughs out of them this way than I did when I was speaking clearly over the previous three years.

It was around this time that my mobility got so bad that I needed to use a walker full-time. Good walkers are actually quite expensive, so Christie's dad, Don—ever the resourceful guy—said, "Hey, my parents have a couple of walkers they're not using! Let's go down to Orange County and get them!" So we made the forty-five-minute drive down to their house. This was a new low for me: borrowing used walkers from Christie's eightysomething-year-old grandparents. I'm sure they didn't mind—they were thrilled to help—but it was another sign that I was getting worse, not better. We arrived at their house, got ahold of the walkers, and decided to take them on a test run around the block.[139] I barely made it around the first corner. It was hot, we were all sweating, I wasn't used to the walker yet, and I was already overstimulated. Don wiped his brow. Christie exhaled deeply and put her hands on her hips. We called off the rest of the walk and headed back to the house.

My left side was a mess. I couldn't bend my leg much, and I couldn't lift my arm over my head. Both of these activities are necessary for doing basic things in your life such as walking and getting dressed. Since I could barely dress myself each day, I resorted to wearing a lot of loose-fitting clothes. Let's just say there are a lot of pictures from that summer of me wearing basketball shorts and ringer T's. You don't think about how things like buckling a belt and tying your shoes require fine motor skills. So I stopped wearing anything that would require a belt (hence the basketball shorts). And if I ever did need a belt—or jeans or socks or anything with buttons—Christie

---

[139] I'm using the word *run* VERY loosely here.

would have to dress me. It was totally emasculating. As for my shoes . . . well, remember those old-man Velcro shoes I had to buy in two different sizes? They got a lot of use that summer.

Getting dressed was hard, but just working up the energy to get dressed was even harder. I would get out of the shower but, because I couldn't lift my arm or leg very high—and because my balance was all but gone—I couldn't even dry myself off. So I would sit on the bed and air-dry.[140] I would be so wiped out from the shower—a shower!— that the idea of drying myself off and then getting myself dressed was too much to bear. Before long, Christie had to dry me off after all my showers. I would turn off the water, open the shower door, and call out to her in the other room, *"Cleeeaan!"* This shorthand signal meant that I had finished showering and needed to be dried off. She would help me out of the shower and towel me off. Every day. As this amazing woman bent over to dry my legs and feet, I would hold on to her back for balance. When she popped back up, I'd give her a smile—or a half smile, which was the best I could muster at that point—and say to her, "I promise, I'm going to get better." She'd smile back, but I honestly wondered if she believed me, if deep down she thought her cancer-stricken husband—whom she needed to dry and dress at age thirty every day—would be able to keep his promise.

I mentioned that I had to wear two different-size shoes to accommodate the ankle brace my doctors had recently fitted me with. I went through a few different leg braces. The first one—the one that necessitated the different-size shoes—was a horrible, bulky brace that held my ankle in a fixed position while a rigid, inflexible "arm" went up my leg and encircled my calf. My ankle had lost almost all mobility—I could not move it under my own power; hence walking on the sandy beaches of Hawaii was so difficult. So, when I was walking with my already-weakened left side, my ankle would buckle underneath me and cause a dangerous fall. The brace was designed to keep my ankle from buckling, thus preventing any falls. It failed.

---

[140] Ladies, I know what you're picturing right now, so calm yourselves down.

Here now is a chronological list-
ing of a few of the places I fell
during that summer:

At my parents' house. This happened soon after I was diagnosed
and was actually the first time I
fell. It was incredibly embarrassing for me and incredibly shocking for everyone else who was
there—Christie, my parents, and
my aunt Denise. I got up from the
table to do something—go to the
bathroom, perhaps—and down I
went. My dad instinctively sprang
into action and leaped to my aid,

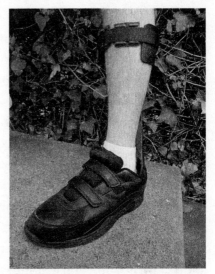

Sweet Velcro shoes, bro. *(Christie Bishop)*

inadvertently knocking Christie out of the way. It all happened so
fast that he didn't even know he had done it. But Christie felt shoved
out of the way—literally and figuratively. This precipitated a period
of stress and strain between my parents and Christie that I'll address
in a future chapter. Just know that trauma (such as cancer) and stress
(which we were all going through) is a volatile, toxic combination.
Like two strangers in a bar who are drunk, on steroids, and are both
huge mixed martial arts fans. You just *know* that some shit's getting
broken in a couple of hours.

On the plane to Hawaii. I actually had a decent excuse for this fall. It
was midflight and I was walking toward the back of the plane, back to
my seat. Some lady in an aisle seat had something sticking out into the
aisle—her purse or a jacket—and I tripped on it. Then I couldn't regain my balance with my other foot on the airplane carpeting. So I hit
the floor. I was able to get myself up, but not before a couple of pas-
sengers and a flight attendant came running to my aid. This was my
most public and thus my most embarrassing fall.

At my own house, on the way to the bathroom. This time, our friend
Catie was assigned to babysit me. That's how badly things had

deteriorated—I couldn't be left alone if Christie needed to be out of the house for more than ten minutes. Catie came over to watch me, but she needed to move her car or something—we had a lot of metered and restricted parking at our old apartment. I mentioned that I needed to go to the bathroom, so she basically said, "Hang tight, I'll go move my car and come right back in and help you." Well, Catie left, and I became empowered by a combination of my desire to prove my independence and my need to pee. So I slowly got off the couch, took a few steps around some chairs we had in the living room . . . and promptly fell to the floor. Luckily, as on most occasions when I fell, I landed on my butt, so no serious damage was done. But I couldn't get up. You know that classic commercial from the eighties? "I've fallen . . . and I can't get up!" That shit *happens*. People fall all the time who are incapable of getting up. It's just that most of them are octogenarians. Catie came back in the apartment and found me lying on the floor. "Oh, my!" she said. She came over to help me up, and with a little coaching she managed to do so.[141] Christie must have picked up a reputation as a ball-breaker somewhere along the way because the first thing Catie said to me—after asking if I was okay, obviously—was "Let's not tell your wife about this, okay?" I looked at her. "Catie," I said, "I would be in *much* more trouble than you if Christie found out about this."

At a Jet concert in Hollywood. The Australian band Jet is one of my favorites. They were playing at a small venue on Hollywood Boulevard, and I decided that Christie and I had to go. If you've ever been to Hollywood, you know that parking is extremely difficult. Luckily, a lot was right next door to the venue and still had a couple of spaces left on the roof. Hollywood—specifically Hollywood Boulevard—also has a lot of hills, and this garage had a sloping roof. After Christie and I parked in one of the last remaining spots, I got out on the passenger's side, and the parking attendant came over to collect the

---

[141] Catie isn't exactly "muscle-bound," and in her defense, most people don't have a ton of experience picking up invalids off the floor.

fee. I turned around and took one step toward him, and *boom*. Down I went. The tiny slope of this roof was too much for me. The parking attendant was more shocked than I was; I think he actually tried to catch me. As I lay there in a dried puddle of leaked motor oil, Christie ran around the car, yelling to the man, "It's okay! I've got him!" She helped me up, we paid for our parking, and we went and tried to enjoy the concert.

At Cedars-Sinai. You would think that the hospital would be the *last* place I would have a fall. Not only are there orderlies and other people to assist you everywhere, but they are quick to push you around in a wheelchair if you need it. On this occasion, Christie's dad, Don, was taking me to an appointment (I'll explain why in a later chapter). Don is a caring, attentive guy, so he was a perfect choice to take me. He pulled up right in front of the hospital entrance, helped me out on the passenger's side, and said, "Wait here, I'll give my car to the valet and come around and help you the rest of the way." Then he went to give his keys to the parking attendant. In those twelve seconds, I decided, "Hey, I got this!" and tried to walk/limp/stagger into the hospital myself. Well, I didn't "have this." I took a few steps and fell straight to the concrete sidewalk. Don couldn't believe it; not only had he (rightly) told me to stay right there, he had only taken his eyes off me for a few seconds. Regardless, I fell stealthily, and Don helped pick me up. The hospital staff saw what was going on and promptly brought me out a wheelchair to use the rest of the day. Ironically, by trying to prove to myself that I could walk on my own, I ended up getting the right to walk on my own revoked.

At my brother's bachelor party. This was at a rented house in San Diego. I was drinking beer on the front patio—we all were—all day long. After a couple of hours, I needed to pee. So I got up, took a few steps toward the front door, opened it . . . and crashed on the patio, against the wall. Of all my falls, this one was both the most and least painful: the most because I hit the cement floor *and* the stucco wall at the same time; the least because I was drunk. But I did get a nice scrape on my back to remind me of how stupid I had been to attempt a bathroom trip on my own under those circumstances—drunk, and after a history of recent falls. I think I freaked my brother and his friends out, too. Most of them hadn't seen me since well before they'd heard about my brain tumor. This was a "Holy crap" moment for them, as in "Holy crap, he's *really* not doing well." My brother and a couple of his friends decided (correctly) that it was time for me to take a nap. They helped me to bed (after helping me to the bathroom first), and I fell right asleep.

In our apartment in the middle of the night. Now my falls were about to get worse. By this point, I was using a walker full-time just to get around our apartment, let alone the outside world. And because of the chemotherapy I was now back on, I was getting up to use the bathroom several times throughout the night.[142] The combination of my being barely able to negotiate a walker under the best circumstances and having to pee five times a night is not a recipe for success. Sure enough, one night, I put the *trip* into *bathroom trip*. I crashed to the floor, walker and all. My head actually hit the walker on the way down. Because it was a metal walker, and because I had fallen on a hollow section of our hardwood floors (right next to our furnace), the crash was even louder. Christie came running. She asked if I was okay—I think I lied and said, "Of course!"—and she helped me up. I wish I could say that was my worst bathroom-related fall, but it wasn't. That would have to be . . .

Inside our bathroom. It was normal, waking hours. I was going to pee. I don't remember exactly what happened—I took a wrong step or I tripped on the bath mat or I just wasn't paying attention—but either way, as I was about to drop my shorts, I fell. To that point I had been reasonably lucky—I hadn't fallen on or around anything particularly dangerous. I could have fallen a *lot* worse places. Unfortunately, my lucky streak came to an end right there in our bathroom. I stumbled a couple of steps and went down, my left side crashing directly into

---

[142] It wasn't just the chemo, but also the lingering radiation effects, which had weakened my bladder muscles. Plus I was drinking a ton of water during the day to try to stay hydrated. A potent peeing combination.

the toilet. Think about the physical properties of toilets for a second: They're hard, they're made of porcelain, and they don't exactly have a lot of give. I bounced off the toilet and hit the ground. This time, it hurt. A lot. Christie came running from the kitchen and asked if I was okay. I couldn't answer her—I'd knocked the air out of my lungs. I signaled to her that I was okay—or at least as okay as one could be after careening off an unforgiving toilet bowl. She came over to help me up, but I waved her off. I was sure I had broken a rib. As my breath slowly came back to me, I explained that I needed a minute to catch my breath and see if anything was seriously wrong before I attempted to get up. After a minute or so of deep breathing, I determined that I hadn't broken anything, and that it was time to get up. But the damage was done, at least to our psyches. Something had to be done, we both thought. I was clearly getting worse, not better, and I was becoming a danger to myself.

25.

My Brother's Wedding

or, "Stuck in Lodi Again"

A month after my wedding, my brother, Adam, was set to get married. His fiancée, Sarah, was an elementary-school teacher who grew up in a tight-knit family just outside the Bay Area. She is the perfect counterweight to my brother and a great example of how opposites attract. Whereas Adam can at times be boisterous and crass, Sarah is sweet and even-tempered. Her years working with second-graders perfectly prepared her for dealing with my brother.

Their wedding was to be in Lodi, California, about fifteen miles north of Sarah's childhood home. The only thing I knew about Lodi was that John Fogerty once sang about being stuck there. Still, despite my worsening symptoms, Christie and I were excited to go to their wedding . . . excited, and nervous. I now needed a walker to get around full-time. On top of that, I needed Christie, or someone else, around me at all times, just in case. Christie was now—as a thirty-year-old newlywed—my full-time caregiver, my de facto round-the-clock nurse. She dressed me. She dried me off after my showers. She fed me. She helped me to the bathroom. The whole thing was incredibly unfair to both of us, but as I would later tell people, at least I had the benefit of being radiated. Poor Christie had to experience the whole thing with a clear mind.

Getting to Adam and Sarah's wedding took much more planning than a normal trip. Driving was quickly ruled out. It would have been a five-hour road trip each way under ideal circumstances, and our circumstances were certainly less than ideal. No way could I last in the car that long. Plus, we'd be stopping every forty-five minutes (at least) so I could use a restroom. And Christie was helping me to the restroom at this point; where along the highway were we going to find a public restroom that Christie could take me into? We decided to fly into Sacramento and hire a car service to take us the final forty-five miles to the wedding site in Lodi. A little more expensive, yes, but a lot less headache.[143]

We didn't realize that by choosing flying over driving, we were just trading in one set of problems for another. Just getting through security at LAX was a nightmare. Not because the lines were long; they weren't. It was a Thursday morning, and travelers were sparse. Christie and I had packed everything we needed for the weekend into one carry-on suitcase, partly because my rented tuxedo was being delivered to the wedding venue along with my brother's, and partly so Christie could tend to me better. I brought along my metal walker. It folded flat, so it could fit into an overhead bin on the plane. It also had a couple of stylish tennis balls on the front two legs, which helped the walker glide easily over smooth surfaces, such as linoleum. Unfortunately, it had the opposite effect on concrete and carpet. If you've ever been to LAX (or almost any other airport, such as, say, Sacramento International), you know there's a lot of both. My walker was constantly catching on the carpet (and on the concrete outside). So were my old-man shoes. Christie had to catch me to prevent me from falling a few times. By the time I negotiated the forty yards from the curb to the security checkpoint inside LAX, I was already pretty tired. But now my adrenaline was pumping; this was the first time I'd put myself in this public of a setting since our wedding, and we weren't exactly surrounded by family and friends and other assorted well-wishers. I was now, in my mind anyway, That Guy whose disability was holding up a line of angry business travelers who were late for their flights.

---

[143] My parents footed the bill for the car service, which was hugely helpful. With practically no income, we were on a shoestring budget.

We got to the front of the line, to the metal detectors. Christie not only got all of our liquids out of our bag and onto the conveyor belt, but also got my shoes off and my brace off my left leg. I still had the walker, which was now even more important. Without Christie by my side, and without my brace on my left ankle, my chances of falling went from about 50 percent to about 90 percent. I *really* had to concentrate now.

Christie went through the metal detector first. They waved me to come forward after her. As I wheeled my walker forward, the TSA agent stopped me. "Sir, we can't have the walker go through."

I started to sweat. "But I need it to get through," I mumbled. (Keep in mind, my speech was worse than ever.)

Christie, ever vigilant, sensed a problem immediately. "He needs it to get through," she repeated to the agent.

"The walker can't go through the metal detector," the agent reiterated. "It's metal."

Wait, I thought, *I can't be the first person to go through security here who needs a walker.* "Can I use a wheelchair?" I slurred.

"Yeah, do you guys have a wheelchair he can use?" Christie asked the agent.

"Wheelchair can't go through either, ma'am. It's metal," he explained unhelpfully.

Well, I thought, *they better figure* something *out.*

Eventually, seeing no way around this mess they had created, TSA allowed Christie to come back and hold me—sans walker—on my side of the metal detector, and I could stagger three steps through it, where the TSA agent would be waiting on the other side to catch me if need be. I know what you're thinking, and I agree: a totally practical and efficient plan.

Those three timid steps through the metal detector were harrowing. Have you ever seen people learning to surf? How wobbly and unsure they look, arms outstretched for balance, as they attempt to stand up on a surfboard for the first time? That was me, only on dry land. I made it through the metal detector and grabbed the outstretched hand of the TSA agent. Christie came around to help me back to my waiting walker, and we proceeded to our gate. National-security crisis averted.

I remember nothing about the one-hour flight to Sacramento. I probably slept. It's probably better that I don't remember anything, because the one thing Christie remembers best from the travel portion of the trip is the staring. People in both airports stared at us—at me, mostly—as we attempted to navigate the terrain with my walker. Christie wrote in her blog at the time:

> I hadn't noticed it too much until we were in the airport, because people were looking at Bryan and me as though we were aliens. As in, bright green Martians from another planet. It was crazy; hadn't people seen a walker before? Was it the fact that he was a young man with a walker? To an untrained eye, I would assume Bryan just looks like he has a pretty severe leg injury on his left side. He was strolling pretty well along, maneuvering the tile-then-carpet-then-tile-again terrain of Terminal #1.
>
> Eventually, we got to our gate, found seats and sat down. Bryan had done incredibly well and I was so proud of him for getting to the gate. But I was severely disturbed at how people just gawked at us, some even pointing and whispering. It was outrageous to me and made me really upset. The fact is that people weren't just staring, they were overtly watching us. I tried to ignore it, but every time I looked up, people were still staring. One of our friends later tried to point out that maybe people recognized Bryan from the radio show, but people were staring as though he were Brad Pitt, not Bald Bryan from *The Adam Carolla Show*. C'mon, I love my husband more than anything in the world, but you know what I mean.
>
> Anyway, I guess this staring thing is a new addition to our newly changed lives. But I really, really hate it. I was raised to be polite, to never stare, to mind my Ps and Qs. Granted, it's not always worked out that way, but I would never, ever stare at someone the way that people stared at us. It really made me want to scream at people, to

make them feel ashamed for staring at an incredible 30-year-old man who just endured a brain tumor diagnosis, six weeks of chemotherapy and radiation and now, a seemingly never-ending slew of post-radiation symptoms and fatigue. But I didn't say anything. Sometimes I stared back, lifting an eyebrow at the people who watched us the longest.

But ultimately, no matter how upset the staring made me, I realized that it's just another thing in this whole "cancer battle" about which I'm out of control. I had to remind myself in LAX, as I continually do, that the only reactions I can control are my own. I can't control whether people stare or not. Throughout this entire process, I've realized an incredible sort of self-control that I truly never knew I had. I have always been Type-A, but when it comes to cancer, especially a brain tumor, you have to realize—quickly—that you're not in the driver's seat. I literally forced myself to block out any worries or personal fears over whether people thought I was doing a good job taking care of Bryan, or taking care of myself, or taking organized and comprehensive notes at appointments, etc. It didn't matter what other people thought, because they weren't living in our shoes. And I realized that even one second spent worrying about it took away my energy to care for Bryan and for myself (I've learned those are equally important tasks). So, while I hated (and still hate) the fact that people stare at us, it's just the latest thing that I've got to let roll off my back.

It obviously had much more of an impact on Christie than it did on me. As I said before, if there was a silver lining to this admittedly dark period, it's that I simply wasn't aware of as much going on around me as I would usually be, due to the radiation.

We landed in Sacramento, where I had a much more difficult time with the carpets than I did at LAX. My feet and my walker kept catching on the floor, and Christie had to keep body-checking me like a hockey player to keep me from falling. Finally, we got outside, where a black SUV was waiting to take us to the wedding site. It would be about an hour's drive, we were told. I remember moving the backseat as far back as I could, then trying my best to lie down. I was beat. This was the most physical activity I'd attempted in a month, and it wasn't exactly happening at a time of peak physical condition for me.

I napped most of the way there. This was around the period that I was spending more time asleep than awake, so all the commotion and activity had wiped me out. We got to the hotel and checked into our room. Once we got to the room, I realized they had put us in a handicapped-accessible room—for which I was grateful. It was on the first floor, with plenty of grab bars bolted into the walls to help prevent you from falling.

The rehearsal dinner the next night went by without a hitch. My parents were able to spell Christie, freeing her up to socialize with people and actually live a seminormal life for an hour. This is another event I have little recollection of. The three things I remember well from that night: (1) Getting dressed was a pain in the ass that seemingly took forever. (2) It seemed incredibly loud in that back room of the restaurant, which it may or may not have been. Most likely, it was only moderately loud, and I was just overstimulated. (3) I remember dreading the wedding the next day. I was in the wedding party as a groomsman, but Christie was not a bridesmaid. Thus, I'd be on my own, more or less, when it came to walking up and down the aisle. My worsening condition would be on full display in front of friends, family, and strangers, which was bad enough, but it would also be taking away from Adam and Sarah's big day, which truly was my greatest fear.

If you had given me the choice before the wedding of (a) tripping and falling during the ceremony and getting right back up, or (b) tripping and falling in the privacy of our hotel bathroom and breaking my arm, I'd have chosen B every time. That's how afraid I was of ruining their wedding. That's how afraid I was of ruining *anyone's* wedding. The last thing you should want at a wedding is to be remembered for anything other than giving a great toast. You never want to be "that guy" at the end of these sentences: "Oh, remember at your cousin's wedding? There was that guy . . . [who got too drunk / fell on the bride / clearly wasn't born a man]."

The next day was the wedding. The first "official" thing I had to do that day was the thing I was dreading the most that weekend: getting into my tuxedo. Christie not only had to get herself ready, which in girl terms meant a three-hour process, but she had volunteered to help get the reception hall set up. So my choice was either to go hang out in my parents' room for a couple of hours and have my dad dress me (ugh) or to have Christie dress me at noon and to spend three hours sitting in my tux (*ugh*). I chose the lesser of two evils . . . I think.

I lounged in my parents' room watching TV with them for a few hours prior to the wedding.[144] At T minus one hour until we had to be at the ceremony site, my dad started to dress me. I remember thinking, "Well, I had a good twenty-eight-year run where I didn't need my parents to dress me. I guess that's over."

We walked to the area of the hotel where the wedding ceremony was taking place, me in my tux, using my walker, with my parents flanking me. Thankfully, the ceremony site was only a few yards from their room. I spotted Christie, who was seated in the front row with my parents. Christie and I exchanged a brief kiss, then I was shown "backstage," as it were, to join the other groomsmen.

At the rehearsal the day before, we'd had a . . . *challenging* run-through. The heat and all the standing had gotten to me pretty quickly, so Adam and Sarah's wedding planner had arranged for a chair to be on stage for the actual wedding the next day, just a few feet back, in case I needed to sit down. It was only about eighty-five degrees, and we were in the shade, but the combination of the tuxedo, the stress, and the prolonged standing was ominous.

Walking up to the stage with all of the other groomsmen was also presenting a challenge. Just as I didn't want to use the "emergency

---

[144] I'm sure that's *exactly* what they wanted to do on the day of their son's wedding: babysit and dress their other son.

chair," I did *not* want to use my walker either. I didn't want to do *any-thing* that would distract from Adam and Sarah. Honestly, if I thought I couldn't get by without the walker or the chair, I'd just as soon have bowed out of the entire ceremony. That's how much I didn't want to be a distraction.

So we made a few minor adjustments. When the groomsmen walked up to the stage together, rather than use my walker, I would grab the shoulder of the guy walking in front of me: Adam's best man, Keenan. Keenan is a firefighter, and a strong dude. He would provide a sturdy base for me to hold on to.

My brother's groomsmen. Note the chair positioned behind me, just in case. *(Christie Bishop)*

The walk back down the aisle would be a little trickier. After Adam and Sarah did their traditional walk back down the aisle, the grooms-men and bridesmaids walked down as well, in pairs. I would have preferred to have been paired with Keenan, the bulky firefighter, but I got the next best thing: Sarah's older sister, Liesl, a mother of two.

Liesl was by no means bulky, but as a mother of two kids, she had lots of experience keeping helpless people (in her case, children) out of danger.

I made it through the ceremony without needing to sit down. Once they said "man and wife" and the music kicked in, my adrenaline started pumping. I knew it was time. I grabbed Keenan's shoulder and got into position. He took off down the aisle with his bridesmaid. Liesl, who was nervously smiling, grabbed my arm. It was our turn. We took three steps down the aisle, onto the grass . . . and I stumbled. My left ankle wasn't ready for the slight change in terrain from brick to grass. I staggered and started to fall over to my left. Thankfully, whether by luck or by design, my dad was standing right there—in the front row—applauding the new couple, along with everyone else at the wedding. He grabbed my left side. Liesl grabbed my right. No way were they letting me fall. At least half the attendees— maybe more—let out an "Oooohhh . . ." as I stumbled, but we righted the ship, and Liesl and I made our way down the rest of the aisle without incident.

After the ceremony, it was picture time. Anyone who's taken wedding pictures knows that this can be a tedious, life-sucking dance. Luckily, a lot of accommodations were made for me. First of all, the hotel provided a golf cart to get me from the ceremony site to the area where we'd be taking pictures. My grandfather also needed help getting around, so the golf cart was for the both of us. At one point, we were hopping off the cart and we grabbed one another. I looked over to him and joked (in as clear a voice as possible), "Who's holding on to who?" He chuckled. They also arranged the order of the pictures so the ones with me would be taken first. I was wilting in the heat, so being spared an hour of standing around was heavenly. The pictures with me took about twelve minutes, then I was whisked away by golf cart to the air-conditioned sanctuary of the reception hall.

The reception sucked. Not for the rest of the guests. For me. Everyone else had a fantastic time. I remember thinking, "This seems like a fun wedding. Everyone looks like they're having a great time."

Adam and Sarah had arranged to have their bridesmaids and groomsmen dance into the reception hall to music while the DJ introduced
them (forgivable, as they were still in their twenties at the time).
Only I was in no condition to dance. I could barely walk. So I sat
alone at the head table, awkwardly, while all the other wedding guests
found their seats and the DJ got ready to introduce the wedding
party. It's funny, but I had no perception at all that people were staring at me at the airport and on the plane, but I was convinced that
everyone was looking at me and talking about me at their dinner tables. "Is that Adam's brother? What's wrong with him? Why is he
sitting all alone up there? Why isn't he dancing with all the other
groomsmen? Is that walker over there his?"

Everyone at the head table standing and applauding as Adam and Sarah make their
grand entrance. Everyone except me, that is. *(Christie Bishop)*

I hated every minute of it. Worst of all, I was certain that I was dis-
tracting from what should otherwise have been a joyous reception.
Christie wasn't even seated next to me—she was assigned a seat at a

table with some of our friends—so when dinner came (steak), I couldn't even cut it myself. Remember, I could barely even take pills by myself—that would take as long as forty-five minutes sometimes. I spent most of dinner trying to cut a few pieces of steak for myself. Mostly I just ate the mashed potatoes and vegetables that came on the side. A couple of times, friends and family members came up and tried to talk to me, to keep me company, but my speech was so badly slurred, and the music was so loud (to me), that I couldn't hold a conversation. I tried once to get out and dance with Christie, but that clearly wasn't happening. Plus—you guessed it—by the time the reception was half over, I was exhausted. I told Christie I needed to turn in for the night, and she agreed. She helped me to my walker and we slipped out a side door. I desperately wanted to avoid two things: having to say an extended good night to a bunch of family and friends, and having people try to convince me to stay.

The next morning, we made the long, sad trip back to LA. I was filled with regret—regret over making a scene at the ceremony (however small it may have actually been), regret over being a distraction, regret over not being able to dance at the reception . . . regret over everything. My brother's wedding was a joyous affair filled with love and happiness, but for me, it will always be the source of some of the biggest regrets of my life.

26.

Drew Brees, My Secret Admirer, and Poop

or, My Greatest Regrets

I don't have too many regrets in my life. Before cancer, I had even fewer. Still, nothing makes you more reflective on your life's short-comings than being told as a thirty-year-old that you have six months to live. Right after I finished college, in the summer of 2000, a family friend set me up with an "informational interview" with Tom Sherak, who was then the senior executive vice president of Fox movie studios. Tom would go on to become the chairman of Fox (basically the studio head) and now serves as the president of the Academy of Motion Picture Arts and Sciences, which awards the Oscars. I had no rightful business to meet with Tom, but he sat down with me for twenty minutes and answered a bunch of my dumb questions. An informational interview is basically asking people to pick their brain about their career. You hope like hell it'll lead to a job, but it never does.

The only thing I remember superclearly about my meeting with Tom was his response when I asked him, "What advice can you give me—career or otherwise?" Without hesitation Tom replied, "Don't ever look back. Ever." He was so emphatic that I really considered what he'd said. I've thought about it a lot in the decade-plus since our meeting. On the one hand, he obviously had done quite well for himself, careerwise, by following his own advice. But it flew in the face of everything I instinctively believed. I adapted his advice to fit my own life: *Do* look back, but only to evaluate your decisions and how you can improve in the future. Don't dwell on things you've done (or haven't done). You can't change those things. Instead, always be moving forward.

So keep that in mind when you read this chapter. I've done a pretty good job of not dwelling on the past in my life. Whatever mistakes I've made, I've tried to learn from them and move forward. But there are a few things that I think of every now and then that make me shake my head with, yes, regret. Here now, in true confessional style, is a list of my ten greatest regrets—some cancer-related, some pretumor. Go easy on me.

10. Not Writing My Own Wedding Vows

Before our wedding, Christie and I had every intention of writing our own vows. I was a creative-writing major in college, and she had a master's degree from Northwestern's Medill School of Journalism. Plus, using the generic vows just seemed so cliché. So we both decided to write our own vows. In fact, we planned on writing out the whole ceremony ourselves. *That's* how ambitious we were. But Christie's uncle Brian was our wedding officiant, so we knew he'd be cool with it. Brian is spiritual guy, and not in the fake-LA-I'm-not-religious-but-I'm-spiritual way—he's a Hare Krishna who lived in Singapore for a decade. So he was the perfect outside-the-box-yet-still-personal choice for our wedding.

Unfortunately, I started treatment right around the time we were supposed to be writing our vows. We kept pushing it off, and by the time we got around to it, I was too radiated and overstimulated to be any help. I couldn't concentrate long enough to write anything meaningful, and I would lose the thread if I kept at it too long. Christie tried her best, but she had her hands full with distractions of her own. I remember clearly the day we met with Brian and Christie's parents to go over the ceremony. It was a few weeks before the wedding, and Christie handed Brian the script she had drafted. He struggled through it, and when he finished, we looked around the room. The look on everyone's face said it all: *Umm, this isn't working.* "Maybe we should print out some traditional vows," Christie's mom said. I was frustrated, but she was right. To this day, I still wish I had been clearheaded enough to write something meaningful, emotional, and poignant.

9. Not Exploiting My Tumor More

Here's one of the only silver linings to having a brain tumor: You can get away with a lot. People expect very little of you. Not surprisingly, I didn't exactly get a lot of calls from friends asking me to help them move a couch once I got diagnosed. I only wish I had pushed the envelope and tried to exploit my tumor even more. I wish I had stolen more items from big-box stores like Target—magazines, candy bars, magazines about candy bars . . . I'd have just grabbed things off the rack, then hobbled out of there with my walker. If the clerk tried to say something, I'd just train Christie to pull him aside and say, "I'm so sorry, my husband has cancer, and it's affecting his mind. He's developed kleptomania. I'll pay you for the candy bar." I'm willing to bet that nine times out of ten, the clerk would have taken pity on us and just let it go.

It's not just you who should benefit, but your friends, too. When I was first diagnosed, I encouraged my friends to use my tumor to their advantage. Feel like leaving early from work? Tell your boss that your friend with cancer needs a ride to the hospital for chemotherapy treatment. If your boss protests, tell him, "It's pretty bad. I don't know if I'll have the chance to do it again . . ." Then trail off and hold the back of your fist up to your mouth as if you were fighting off tears. What boss can say no to that?

8. Not Wearing a Jersey Number in the 50s
When I Played High School Football

I'll keep this short and sweet: If I ever have a son who ends up playing offensive line for his junior varsity football team as I did (and given the genetic hand he'll surely be dealt, that's as far as he'll get), I'll force him to wear a jersey number between 50 and 59. All offensive linemen have to wear a number between 50 and 79. The

Yep. Nothing more intimidating than a doughy white kid with glasses lining up across from you.

higher you go, the less athletic you seem. I, for example, wore number 71 one year and 75 the next. Lame. *But* . . . if you opt for jersey number 55, for example, someone might mistake you for a linebacker, which is a much more athletic (and cooler) position than offensive line. If only someone had told me that in high school.

7. Never Being Properly Diagnosed with ADHD as a Child

Covered in an earlier chapter. Can you tell I'm still bitter about it?

6. Not Being Able to Travel to the USC/Ohio State Game in 2009

This one hurts. The NCAA announces football schedules several years in advance. Sometimes, for bigger matchups between marquee schools, they'll schedule the game almost a decade beforehand. As a big USC football fan, it seemed as if I knew about this game against Ohio State—in Columbus, Ohio—forever. Not only was it between two prestigious, historic teams, but it was going to be played the day before my thirty-first birthday. Plus, one of my best friends lived in Columbus, and I had a standing invitation to stay at his house. *Plus*— and this is the big one, the one that hurts the most—a different friend (also a huge USC fan) was flying out to the game in his family's private jet, and he had offered to take a handful of us with him to the game.

A quick note on flying in a private jet: Never do it. Unless you have the means to fly private for the rest of your life, don't spoil yourself by just doing it once. People say flying first class will ruin you for air travel. Forget that. Flying private will actually make you angry whenever you set foot in another airport for the rest of your life. I'm not even talking about the plush interior of the plane, or the immaculate airplane restroom, or the free drinks, or the food, or the hot flight attendant, or any of those creature comforts (although they *are* nice). No, the best part is not having to deal with airport security. You just walk straight onto the plane and go. In the time it takes you to get through the TSA security line at any airport, you could have parked your car, boarded your plane, and taken off.

Sadly, when the game finally rolled around, I was in no condition to fly, let alone attend a college football game. I watched USC win the game on TV, thinking to myself, "My friends are there right now. And I'm at home. With cancer."

5. Never Finishing My Degree from USC

It's true. I'm one general education (GE) class shy of finishing my degree at USC. Or two. It's one or the other. A couple of things triggered this chain of events. First of all, I changed majors two years into college. As I mentioned in an earlier chapter, journalism wasn't working out for me—I was frustrated by the duplicitous nature the grading in a course taught by one of its most celebrated professors. So I changed majors to creative writing. This plan had two problems: First, I had already taken a handful of journalism classes, which were now essentially wasted courses. The degree units I'd earned from them wouldn't apply toward my new major. Second, it was too late in the semester to enroll in the creative-writing classes I *did* need for my new major, so I was caught in educational limbo. I was forced to take extra electives such as art history. Fun, but not helpful in earning a degree.

I took a couple of summer-school courses at a local junior college to make up for the classes I missed out on. But there was some problem with the transferring of the coursework, and the credits never got applied to my transcripts at USC. Finally, and this was really the *fait accompli*—my parents basically said, "We're paying for four years of college, and that's it. After that, you're on your own." I couldn't afford another year of college—I needed to find a job just to pay for rent and food. So after four years, I was done with college. I went through the graduation ceremony as a "degree pending" graduate. I got to wear the cap and gown, I got to grab a diploma from a professor I had never met, and I took tons of pictures with my family. But as far as USC is concerned, I'm still "degree pending." Which is bullshit, if you'll excuse my language, because I completed all the required coursework in my major and did quite well. In fact, that's a regret within a regret, because at the end of my final semester, my favorite professor—T. C. Boyle, the famous author—was so impressed with my creative writing that he personally invited me to enroll in his prestigious Advanced Writing Workshop the next fall. The only problem? I had no money for a fifth year of school. I regretfully declined, but not before thanking him profusely for the offer.

Sadly, this isn't even some deep, dark secret. My family and most of my friends know that I never technically earned my college degree. How lame is that? This chapter is supposed to be a confession of some of my biggest regrets and this one isn't even a secret.

4. Not Recording My Interview with Drew Brees

Ugh. This one still makes me ill. In 2011, the New Orleans Saints held a week of preseason practices in nearby Oxnard, California. The Saints had won the 2010 Super Bowl and were still a good team. Since Los Angeles had no professional football team at the time, the Saints' coming to town was big news. Well, one of the Saints' assistant coaches, Carter, was a big fan of *The Adam Carolla Show*. Carter contacted me and arranged for me to be a guest on the sidelines at practice.

While at practice, I thought it would be fun to play a game we call Jockwalking on the podcast. The title is a play on Jay Leno's *Tonight Show* bit called Jaywalking, where he asks unsuspecting people general trivia questions. In our version, we ask athletes about stuff that most athletes (jocks) wouldn't know, such as questions about *Star Wars* and *The Lord of the Rings*.

Carter got me an interview with Drew Brees, the quarterback of the

Saints. This was a big deal—he was easily one of the five or six most famous players in the league at this point. I asked him all of my Jock-walking questions, and he did great. Much better than I expected. It turns out that Drew Brees is a closet nerd. He rattled off one correct answer after another and was funny and engaging the whole time. It couldn't have gone better.

If you're a regular listener of the show, you might be thinking, "Hm, I don't remember hearing the episode where they played Jock-walking with Drew Brees." That's because the digital recorder the show provided didn't work. It may somehow have been my fault—I'm not ruling it out. But I'm pretty sure I did everything right, and the thing still didn't record our interview. When I discovered the nonrecording a few days later, I was devastated. I mean, the interview happened, and I'll always have my memory of it, but what good does that do when I'm trying to do a segment for the podcast?

3. Not Being a Better Brother to Adam

I touched on this briefly in an earlier chapter. Our strained relationship—at least during my teen years—was the result of a "perfect storm" of circumstances. He was popular. I was not. We were forced to share a room for nine years—as well as a bathroom. I also felt that he had too many things handed to him, whereas I had to work harder. I had an after-school job for two years. He never had to. I had to drive my parents' fifteen-year-old 1981 Toyota Corona[145] station wagon when I was in high school. He got to drive a five-year-old Jeep Cherokee Sport (a *much* cooler car) *with personalized license plates.*

Not that I'm still bitter or anything. Okay, I am. But that's no excuse for not being a better brother. I wasn't friendly to him, frankly, until around the time he started college. I'd like to think that I'm doing a better job of being a big brother now, but for a few years I didn't do a very good job of it.

---

[145] Not *Corolla. Corona.* Look up a picture of it sometime. There's a reason why they don't make that model anymore.

Halloween 1986. The first (but not last) documented instance of my wanting to kill Adam. *(Bishop Family)*

2. Pooping My Pants as an Adult. Twice

You read that right. If there's a silver lining to my poop-brown cloud, it's that both occasions were the result of chemotherapy. I'll explain.

Both instances happened in our old apartment, within a month of each other. Both times, we were coming back from some small outing—a walk or errands or something. As I mentioned in my constipation chapter, chemo stops you up. As a result, you have to take some pretty serious laxatives to make everything normal again. Unfortunately, it takes time to regulate exactly how much laxative you need to get everything back on track. So it's a constant game of trial and error. Too little laxative, and you're crying for mercy on the toilet. Too much, and . . . well, read on.

Compounding the problem were three things: First, the laxative I was taking was combined with a potent stool softener. Second, I was eating a lot of milk shakes at the time—both to correct my rapid weight loss and also because they required no chewing (remember, half of my face was numb, so solid foods were a choking risk). Finally—and this was the main culprit—radiation and chemotherapy had left my muscles extremely weak. Specifically, the muscles in my midsection and butt that I use to hold back poop.

Well, you can imagine what this toxic combination resulted in: ruined underwear. The first time it happened, Christie was able to salvage my boxer briefs. She took the shellacked undies and hosed them off in the shower—then she hosed *me* off in the shower. The second time, my underwear was ruined. It was like Hurricane Katrina in there; just mud everywhere. Christie helped undress me and she walked my soiled boxers right outside to the Dumpster. Then she threw my jeans (which had also suffered significant collateral damage) into the washing machine before helping me shower. As she hosed down my naked body, I looked up at her and said again—weakly, with as much of a wet smile as I could muster—"I'm gonna get better."

The only good thing to come out of this? I would never doubt how much Christie loved me. This is a woman who stood by me not only through cancer, but also when *I couldn't even get myself to the bathroom in time*. This is a pretty big regret and might be number one on most people's list. But I do have one bigger regret in my life.

1. Not Dancing with My Secret Admirer at Camp Mather

When I was about thirteen years old, my family took a weeklong summer vacation to Camp Mather, which is near Yosemite, in Northern California. It's just a woodsy campsite where they have all sorts of activities for kids—swimming, badminton, softball, and an end-of-summer dance where the kids all stand around awkwardly while an adult plays an MC Hammer cassette.

Camp Mather is situated on a big lake. A couple of days into camp, I was sitting on the dock, getting ready to take a swim test.[146] All of a sudden a girl about my age came up behind me and tapped me on the shoulder. "Excuse me, what's your name?" I told her my name, and she smiled and said, "Okay, thanks!," and ran away. I didn't think anything of it, and I went back to mentally preparing for my swim test. When I finished, I went back to the beach where my mom and dad were sitting on a beach blanket.

"Someone has a crush on you," my mom said to me teasingly.

"Huh?"

"That girl who came up to you?"

"Yeah, she asked my name," I told her.

"I think she was asking for her friend."

"Really?" I looked around, but the girl from the dock was nowhere in sight. For the rest of the week, I wondered who this mystery woman was—or if there even *was* a mystery woman. My mom was probably mistaken, I thought, or she was just pulling my leg. Remember, I wasn't exactly used to female attention at this point in my life.[147]

Not until the final night of camp, at the big end-of-summer dance, did I discover who my secret admirer was. The dance had just started. The boys were all standing along one wall, and the girls were all standing against the opposite wall. It was like the world's most uncomfortable game of red rover. Finally, one of the girls broke ranks: a redheaded tomboy with freckles dotting her chubby cheeks. She was probably adorable, but she didn't look like the popular girls at *my* school, thus, like a dick, I deemed her to be unattractive.

She courageously walked over to the boys' side of the room. Some of the guys snickered in that horribly snarky thirteen-year-old way. As she got closer, I thought to myself, "Holy crap, she's coming right at me." Sure enough, she walked right up to me and said, in a quiet, almost apologetic way, "Do you want to dance?" *This was my secret admirer.*

---

[146] All the kids who wanted to swim in the lake had to pass a swim test first for the lifeguards. In front of all the other campers. Talk about a rite of passage.

[147] *This point* being from birth to the present day.

Suddenly, like the last scene of *The Usual Suspects*, it all came together. Her friend had asked me my name on the dock *for her*. I remembered seeing her a handful of times during the week. At a nearby table at lunch. Playing softball. Swimming in the lake. I had thought it was just a coincidence that this girl kept popping up around me, but no— she had a crush on me.

What I should have done was said, "Hell yes, I'd like to dance." But I didn't. "No, that's okay," I cowardly told her. Her shoulders slumped. Then, in the saddest, most defeated voice I've ever heard before or since, she looked at the ground and said softly, "Come on, man."

I choked. "No. I don't really want to dance." *I was at a dance!*

She slunk back to the girls' side of the room with her tail between her legs.

I don't remember anything that happened after that; I never saw her again, and I never danced with anyone that night. But I've thought about that moment at least a hundred times since. I was a colossal asshole—which would be one thing if I had done it out of spite, or cruelty. But I did it out of fear. The chances of ever finding that girl have to be at least one in a million. But if I was ever somehow able to, I'd ask her to forgive me for being so stupid.

Then I'd ask her to dance.

27.

Physical Therapy

or, Koosh Balls, Crutches, and Brightly Colored Shirts

Soon after my brother's wedding, I had my first postradiation MRI. Our doctors warned us that it would look like "scrambled eggs." They said that the first MRI so close after radiation rarely tells them anything of any significance.[148] Still, we were hopeful that this scan would show something—*anything*—that might indicate that my treatment had worked and my tumor was shrinking.

Well, the MRI didn't show us anything. It indeed looked like scrambled eggs, or—more appropriately—a huge cloud of smoke after you dropped a bomb somewhere. My tumor hadn't shrunk at all. It looked exactly the same as it had before. If anything, it was worse: The MRI showed increased "enhancement" of my tumor. I could spend the rest of the chapter trying to explain exactly what enhancement is, or you can just take my word that it isn't good.

My tumor wasn't shrinking. I couldn't walk, talk, or do hardly anything for myself. We talked to our doctors about starting me on physical therapy. They wholeheartedly agreed and recommended a triple-therapy approach: physical, occupational, and speech therapy. Physical therapy for obvious reasons; this would mainly address the deficiencies in my lower body and help get me walking again. Occupational therapy would help me with my upper body: my arm and

---

[148] "Then why do it?" would be my response. But apparently they have to, to track any changes over time.

hand, specifically. They call it occupational therapy because it gets you "back to the job of living your life." Speech therapy was a no-brainer.

Our doctors told us Cedars-Sinai had a great therapy team. We made an appointment with them right away. It turned out to be one-stop shopping; they had physical therapists, occupational therapists, and speech therapists all under the same roof. This was especially helpful for insurance, which (in our case) only covered something like forty therapy appointments a year, the front-desk administrator explained to us. When you need three different types of intensive therapy, those forty visits can get used up pretty quickly. But if we made the appointments back-to-back-to-back—PT at 8:00 a.m., OT at 9:00 a.m., and speech therapy at 10:00 a.m.—they would only count as one visit. Very, very helpful.

I was set up with three different therapists who could not have been more different from one another. The physical therapist, Jodi, was a younger woman, about our age, who also went to USC. All she wanted to talk about was USC football. She was a bigger fan than me. She was *definitely* going to the Ohio State game in September, she told us. Well, then.

My occupational therapist was a hippie named Sunshine or Moon-beam (or something similar; I can't exactly remember). She was going to rehabilitate me with the power of good vibes. Whereas Jodi would use crutches, ankle braces, and walking staffs during our sessions, Moonbeam loved using toys: plush toys, plastic toys, Velcro toys, you name it. She was very much into tactile things. If it was squishy, squeezable, or if it made a sound, she used it for therapy. She once had me play "baseball" in her office with a foam bat and a Koosh ball.

My speech therapist, a quiet, gentle woman named Jill, reminded me of every first-grade teacher I'd ever met. She was patient, thank goodness, because she had her hands full with me. My speech was a mess. Jill believed in two things: mouth exercises and tape-recording our sessions. The mouth exercises basically involved stretching out your lips and tongue. You made exaggerated movements when you said

"Ooohhhh" and "Aaahhh" for ten seconds at a time. Then you stuck your tongue out in all different directions. It was all very dignified.

I enjoyed all of my therapists personally, but I wasn't satisfied with the therapy I was getting. I kept stumbling and falling whenever Jodi would try to get me to walk. Her solution was to order me crutches. Unfortunately, my left side was too weak for me to use a crutch correctly, so I kept falling. Her solution to this? More crutches. I went from the traditional under-the-armpit crutches to the more permanent clasp-around-the-forearm crutches. But again, my left side was so weak, I couldn't even use these effectively. Now I had a small collection of crutches, yet I was no closer to walking on my own again.

As for Moonbeam . . . well, what can I say for Moonbeam. She was a lovely person, full of good intentions and positive energy. But I don't think she was much of a therapist. When we weren't playing games, she was lecturing me on spirituality and other life tips. In my first session, she told me she disapproved of my earth-toned shirts. "I want you to start wearing brighter-colored shirts," she told me, because apparently everyone knows brain tumors *hate* bright colors.

She also gave me a shopping list of things to pick up at the medical-supply store, such as a tub of green putty that she wanted me to play with, using my left hand. I also had to get one of those grip-strengtheners that you see douche bags squeezing inside a tollbooth. I also was told to pick up a variety of elastic resistance bands. It was the world's saddest shopping spree.

Later, in what might have been our last session (not coincidentally), she asked if I was the kind of person who showered in the morning to help wake myself up. "You mean like every other person on earth?" I replied rhetorically. "Yes, I do that."

"I see." She nodded. "I want you to start showering at night. In the morning, let yourself wake up slowly; naturally."

"Right," I replied. "Will do. Now can we get back to the part where I try to tie my shoe?"

So therapy at Cedars was a bust. We would eventually get referred to an ex-Cedars therapist named Chris Tolos, who came highly recommended. Since I was becoming more and more immobile, Christie called Chris one day and asked him if he made house calls—in-home therapy sessions, basically. Not really, Chris told her.

"Where is your apartment?" Chris asked. Christie told him. He paused and thought about it, then said, "You're right around the corner!" We checked, and sure enough, Chris's office was around the corner, just five hundred yards away. Had I been in any kind of shape, we could have walked there quite easily. As it was, driving there was no chore at all. We made the soonest appointment we could.

Chris turned out to be everything I had hoped for in a therapist. He had a ton of experience with people in my situation (brain injuries and/or trauma). He was a tall, strong dude, so I never feared falling when I was working with him. He was just funny enough to get my jokes, but not so funny that he'd outshine me.[149] He was patient, adaptable, and knowledgeable.

> **Tumor Tip:** As with doctors, you need to shop around when it comes to physical therapists. You need to shop around more sometimes because, for the most part, medical treatment is fairly straightforward. PT, however, can be as good or as bad as the person administering it. So if you don't love your therapist, find one you do.

Chris also shared an office with a chiropractor, which worked out nicely, as Christie made a few appointments with him while I was working with Chris. Christie had never been to a chiropractor in the past—she'd never needed to—but the stress, both physical and emotional, was taking its toll on her. She was headed for a breakdown.

---

[149] I only said that because I know that Chris will read this book.

2 8.

"Sleepless Nights" and "Pain"

or, Christie's Story

"So, are you looking for work, or are you still enjoying relaxing?"

That's what one of Christie's stupid friends asked her one day while I was going through the worst of my postradiation period. The pooping-my-pants, unable-to-walk, can't-even-take-my-own-pills period. I'm going to give this dimwit the benefit of the doubt and say that she *herself* wasn't stupid, she just said a stupid thing. *Enjoying relaxing.* I don't think Christie was able to relax for one minute that summer.

I mentioned how Christie had to help shower me after I lost control of my bowels . . . twice. The irony of the situation is that showering was one of the only things I could still do for myself at that point. It was a couple of months after I had finished radiation. I was back on chemotherapy, which exhausted me. I ended up sleeping *a lot*. My personal record during that time was eighteen hours a day. When I was awake, I was all but helpless. I could do very, very little on my own. Here's just one example: If I was sitting on the toilet and I noticed that we were out of toilet paper, I couldn't reach over to the cupboard next to me to get a new roll, even though it was just one foot away. Those twelve inches were too far for me to extend my left arm and open the door beneath the sink. So I had to call out to Christie. Only I could no longer speak in a clear voice, so "Christie, can you give me a hand?" became "Christie, caauuyahhh guumma haaannn!" She'd come running from the kitchen as she always did, fearing I'd fallen or otherwise hurt myself. But no, I just needed her to hand me a new roll of toilet paper.

Christie came running from the kitchen to help me so many times that she probably burned a path into our wooden floors. Imagine that scenario, repeating daily. For months, Christie lived her life completely on edge, constantly afraid that I'd take one false step or that I'd try to grab hold of something to steady myself and miss. It's almost unfathomable to people in a "normal" relationship, but every moment I was awake was a moment when I could potentially hurt myself.

As I said, my speech had become a completely unintelligible slur. If I wanted anyone to have a chance at understanding me, I'd have to slow my speech down to a ridiculous level: "Where . . . is . . . your . . . bath-room?" And even that didn't always work. Christie ended up doing 90 percent of the talking for both of us. Add that to her pile of stress: not only is she physically *doing* everything for me, but now she's my interpreter as well. She was the only person who could even remotely understand me, but, ironically, I was so tired and frustrated with my inability to articulate that I simply stopped talking. So here she was, trapped in this daily hell of constantly watching over me so I wouldn't hurt myself, and the one person she *could* talk to—me— was shutting down. She *literally* had no one to talk to.

One day, my friend Anderson took me out to see *District 9* at the movie theater. Anderson and I had together hosted a radio show about movies called *The Film Vault*. My "friendly" persona played well against his "gruff" exterior. Only Anderson's actually a sweet guy. He volunteers at a camp for kids with cancer, so he felt well suited to take me out for an afternoon at the movies. He's also a strong, burly guy, which also suited him well for taking care of me. Plus it had the ancillary benefit of giving Christie a much-needed day off from watching me like a hawk.

The movie was fine, but I was too radiated to really appreciate it. Plus, I hadn't been outside in public for weeks. I was on my walker full-time now. At one point, Anderson and I used the public restroom at the same time. Only when I was done, I was having trouble buttoning up my shorts. I tried and tried, but my left hand was just too weak. Remember, I couldn't even take a pill with my left hand, let alone button up a pair of shorts. Anderson saw me struggling and actually came over and buttoned up my shorts for me. As he faced me, just inches away, with the back of his hand grazing my groin, I said to him, "Well, I guess this is rock bottom."

Christie also enjoyed a day at the movies. She went to a different theater and saw *Julie & Julia*, starring Amy Adams and Meryl Streep. It's the true story of a modern-day girl named Julie (played by Adams) who reads one of Julia Child's cookbooks and is inspired to start a blog documenting her attempt to cook every one of Child's recipes over one year. Christie felt a weird sense of déjà vu as she watched the movie: the main character was stuck in a corporate job she hated, so as a form of self-therapy, she turned to cooking. Christie felt a kinship with the main character; she *loved* to cook. Specifically, she found something incredibly therapeutic about the act of chopping. She would cut vegetables for hours if she could.

Christie also picked up on some parallels between the Amy Adams character's starting her blog and Christie's starting hers. Here's what she blogged about after seeing the movie:

> When Julie decided to start her blog, she had no idea what she was doing. She didn't have a clue why anyone in the world would want to hear anything she had to say, much less her opinions about food. I felt the same way about Bryan's and my story, but starting the blog originally helped us keep all our friends and family in the loop in regards to Bryan's medical condition.
>
> In the movie, Julie's husband helped her start her blog, just as Bryan helped me start mine. Bryan surprised me one morning by announcing that he had bought the rights to www.aninconvenienttumor.com and that I was all set to start blogging. It was so incredibly thoughtful of him to do that for me, because I had mentioned that I'd like to start blogging but never proactively took any steps towards actually doing it. Because like Julie, I had no idea what to say. I was

used to writing for work, not for pleasure. Granted, there's not always a ton of pleasure in blogging about a personal cancer story, but there is a lot of stress relief. Sometimes when my brain experiences information overload, blogging helps me get it all out. Then I can move on to the next activity or appointment with a renewed attention to detail.

Christie also found some commonalities with another online blogger: A woman in Texas named Tyra had a blog about her husband of fifteen years, Steve, who had been diagnosed less than two years earlier with a GBM (glioblastoma multiforme), one of the deadliest types of brain tumors. Remember earlier that Dr. Black told me, "No one wants to have a brain tumor. But if you have to have one, [yours] is the one to have. It's bad, but I've seen much, much worse." Well, GBMs are the "much, much worse" ones he was talking about. And unfortunately, Tyra's husband, Steve, had one.

Christie and Tyra began corresponding via email shortly after Christie started *An Inconvenient Tumor.* Christie talked about her correspondence with Tyra in a deeply personal and revealing blog entry called "Sleepless Nights":

> This wonderful, wonderful woman (stronger than I'll ever be) started a blog detailing her journey with her husband's tumor. Yesterday afternoon, I made the mistake of reading every single word. It's brilliant. She's brilliant. But now I'm scared shitless because it is literally our exact same story. The only difference being that we're at the beginning and we still don't know our outcome. Bryan's outcome. But after reading, the thoughts that I control every single day and push WAY WAY WAY down—you know, the mortality thoughts—came screaming up to the surface because after 1 year and 8 months, her husband is not doing well. Not at all. In one of her emails to me, she said that the thing she regrets the most is not traveling with her husband during the 12 months after his diagnosis, when he was primarily mobile on his own. Now it's too late and they'll most likely

never get to realize their dreams of going to places like Australia or Italy. He's now wheelchair-bound and has a hard time speaking and eating. He's on various types of "big gun" chemotherapies, which make him very sick. He's lost all his hair. He has a hard time breathing and has constant chest X-rays to check for pneumonia. He was just in the hospital for several days and truly makes Bryan's few doctors' appointments and 12 pills per day regime look like "An Idiot's Guide to Cancer."

Here's where I start to cry.

I'm 29 years old. Bryan is undoubtedly the love of my life. Not a lot of people ever get to say that they met theirs, but we did. We knew it within two weeks of meeting each other. And this is the time of our lives where we are supposed to START the rest of our lives. To create our home, our family, our future. All of our closest friends are married and most are starting to have adorable little babies. Just the cutest, happy families. I saw a picture on Facebook earlier today of some of our friends at a lake over the weekend, and they had taken a group shot of each couple with their (give or take) six-month-old babies. It literally brought tears to my eyes because I don't know if we'll ever get to have that. It's what Bryan and I want more than anything in life; to have a wonderful family and live until we're 85 years old. To raise our kids and create amazing memories with our incredible parents, siblings and friends. To come home every night to each other, after a long (or even not-so-long) day of work, open a bottle of wine and just enjoy each other's company and inevitable laughter. To take trips with our friends, have dinner parties and relish in the comfort and joy that is being with our closest friends on a random Saturday night. To not only have children, but to watch our babies' first steps, first words, first Christmas, first day of school, first break-up. To watch the wrinkles start to appear on each other's face over the years and still love each and every new line.

I can't let myself imagine Bryan getting sick. Like really sick. He's the most joyous, balanced, full-of-life person I've ever known. Just seeing him go through these "symptoms" is really hard, because there is nothing I can do. Bryan makes me a better person by just being around him. He's my best friend in all the world and we literally read each other's minds; we've got a connection where we don't have to say anything at all. We know what the other person is thinking 100% of the time. It's pretty crazy, actually. To imagine my life, or our families' or friends' lives without Bryan, is unacceptable to me. But the reality of this situation is that the risk is there. We're so aware of our time together now because, just as it is in anyone's life, you never know how much time you've got.

Steve's time ran out on September 7, 2009. I remember that day well because Christie took the news hard. She had never met Steve or Tyra, but she felt a connection with them. Partly because she was able to forge a relationship with Tyra, who reached out to Christie at her lowest point. And partly because Steve's story so closely paralleled mine. A lot of the things I was going through—physical decline, exhaustion, my face puffing up from chemotherapy—Steve had already experienced. So when Steve finally succumbed to his cancer, Christie naturally took it particularly rough. "Will it be Bryan's time soon?" she thought. As she sat there on the couch, crying next to me, I did my best to put Christie at ease: I looked her in the eye, and in as clear a voice as I could muster, I repeated, "I'm *gonna* get better."

All of the daily (hourly?) stress eventually got to be too much for Christie to handle. Her body began to break down physically. She was admitted to the hospital herself for acute colitis, which was (in her case) a stress-induced inflammation of the large intestine. Read that again. She didn't *go to the doctor* because of colitis. *She was admitted to the hospital.* For four days, which was a veritable lifetime for us. Her parents came and essentially babysat me for a couple of days, thank goodness, because leaving me home alone was like leaving a toddler home alone, only the toddler isn't tall enough to reach the knives.

I remember going to visit Christie in her hospital bed, and we must have made a pathetic pair: me in a wheelchair (I couldn't make it all the way through a hospital's hallways anymore), her in her hospital bed, gown on, tubes sticking out of her. We just sat and held hands for a while. There was nothing I could do for her. There was nothing she could do for me. We were helpless.

Here's how she described it in a blog post titled simply "Pain," written that night from her hospital bed:

> I'm trying to hold back the tears, but it is useless because I'm finally alone. No phone calls from frantic parents, no emails to answer, no husband to hold and love. Just me, my hospital bed, the "whir" of the A/C and the occasional click from my IV machine.
>
> Seeing Bryan in such a weakened state kills me. Seeing our entire lives flash before my eyes kills me. Trying to see the forest for the trees—or some happy ending to this current nightmare—wears on me every moment. Being the mediator and messenger for everything wears me out. Being forced to explain why I value Bryan's wants and needs above those of anyone else angers and exhausts me. And it's stress from those types of situations that kills me the most, because at the end of the day, if anything happens to Bryan everyone else will still have their spouse to go home to, to love and laugh with, to have and raise children with, to grow old with. And for me, the thought of being without my soul mate and best friend by my side throughout the rest of my life makes my pain scale soar right to about 200.
>
> Ouch.
>
> People often ask questions like, "Do you ever let yourself go to a dark place?" or "Do you ever think the worst?"
>
> The answer to that is obviously "yes." But you have to shoo away the bad thoughts like you would a threatening bee. Because there is always hope, there is always love, and there is always the optimism of our doctors.

Speaking of our doctors, I had a doctor's appointment the next day, a checkup with Dr. Rudnick and Rebecca. Christie would still be in the hospital. Not only had Christie never missed one of my doctor's appointments to that point, she was the designated note-taker and question-asker at said appointments. I wasn't exactly "clearheaded" those days, so having someone there who could actually comprehend what the doctor was saying was obviously important.

Don and Sheryl took me to my appointment, and we got Christie on speakerphone so she could be in on the discussion. I was again in a wheelchair. My physical condition was at its worst. I was a mess: slumped over in my chair, barely able to talk.

Rudnick looked me over. "How do you think you're doing?"

"Eh, I'm okay. Just trying to get better."

Rudnick frowned. He raised his voice so Christie could hear. "Christie, how do *you* think Bryan is doing?"

She didn't hesitate. "He is definitely *not* doing okay. He's getting worse."

"I agree," Rudnick said. The steroids that I was taking every day were supposed to be helping reduce the swelling in my brain, but they weren't working. He had seen patients respond (or not respond) to radiation like this before, but the degree to which I was getting worse was, in his words, "tremendous." If we didn't do something soon, some of my symptoms could become permanent or, worse, life-threatening.

He likened the whole situation to a funnel that wasn't draining; my swollen brain was choking off my brain-stem (the funnel in his example), which was causing problems for the rest of my body—the weakness, the speech problems, everything. If it got any worse, it could start to affect even more essential functions such as awareness and breathing. If that happened, the next stage . . . well, there was no next stage after that. If you know what I mean.

Rudnick looked at Rebecca and then looked me over once more.

He exhaled a deep breath. "I think it's time for the big gun."

29.

Avastin

or, The Big Gun

The "big gun" my doctor was referring to was Avastin, an "angio-genesis inhibitor," whose technical name was bevacizumab.[150] I know, it looks like the devil's name.[151] It was first approved by the Food and Drug Administration (FDA) in 2004 to treat colorectal cancer. Soon after, the FDA approved it to treat lung cancer as well. Doctors started using it in combination with traditional chemotherapies and found that it worked. Really well. I could bore you with a ton of technical details, but you can find those online if you're supercurious. For the purposes of this story, here's what you need to know about Avastin, as explained to me by Dr. Rudnick:

> It ostensibly works by stopping the growth of new blood vessels, which tumors co-opt to promote their own growth. A tumor wants to grow; it wants to supply itself with nutrients and oxygen—basically, all the things that anything needs to grow. Imagine the way a tree grows roots. That's what a tumor does with blood vessels. And it does that with the secretion of a substance called VEGF—vascular endothelial growth factor. Avastin is an antibody that binds to VEGF and soaks it up like a sponge so that it's not released. And

---

[150] I've looked at that word a hundred times and I still have no idea how to pronounce it. It would be easier if it were spelled backward: *bamuzicaveb*. Hell, maybe it *is* spelled backward and we don't know it.

[151] If Avastin didn't work, our only choice was an off-label drug: Mephistopheles-umab.

sometimes, if you shut that down, for some tumors it shuts down the tumor.

I mentioned earlier in the book that you either believe in the "universe" presenting you with "signs," or you don't. You just chalk them up to coincidence. Well, in a wonderful coincidence, the FDA approved Avastin for use in brain tumors in May 2009—the same month I began treatment for my own brain tumor. It ended up working so well that some doctors started using it as a frontline defense against brain tumors—that is, they didn't wait for a patient's brain tumor to start growing out of control to start using Avastin. As soon as a patient of theirs was diagnosed, *boom*, they put him or her on a steady dose of it.

In another weird "sign," the drug's manufacturer, Genentech, was located just a few miles from where I grew up, in South San Francisco. Yes, the same South San Francisco where my mom grew up and my grandfather still lives. The same South San Francisco where my grandfather spent decades saving people's lives as a fire captain. Now Genentech was going to try to save mine.

Avastin wasn't without risks, which were made very clear to me. Here are some of the possible side effects, as listed on the Web site for the National Institutes of Health.

This medicine may increase your risk of bleeding problems. Stop using this medicine and tell your doctor right away if you start to notice any signs of bleeding, such as a nosebleed, coughing up blood, or black, tarry stools.

This medicine may increase your risk of blood clots or damage to your nervous system. Stop this medicine and tell your doctor right away if you develop chest pain, sudden and severe headache, seizure, unusual drowsiness, confusion, or problems with vision, speech, or walking.

Tell your doctor right away if you have severe stomach pain with constipation, fever, nausea, and vomiting. Tell your doctor right away if you have trouble swallowing, cough or choking, trouble breathing, or chest pain or discomfort. These could be symptoms of a hole in your digestive system.

This medicine may affect the way your body heals. Make sure any doctor who treats you knows that you are using this medicine. You may need to stop this medicine several weeks before and after surgery.

This medicine lowers the number of some types of blood cells in your body.

Because of this, you may bleed or get infections more easily. To help with these problems, avoid being near people who are sick or have infections. Wash your hands often. Stay away from rough sports or other situations where you could be bruised, cut, or injured. Brush and floss your teeth gently. Be careful when using sharp objects, including razors and fingernail clippers.

Tell your doctor or nurse right away if you have a fever, chills, trouble breathing, lightheadedness, fainting, or chest pain within a few hours after you receive this medicine. You might be having an infusion reaction.

Your doctor will need to check your urine and blood pressure at regular visits while you are receiving this medicine. Be sure to keep all appointments.

Call your doctor right away if you notice any of these side effects:

Allergic reaction: itching or hives, swelling in your face or hands, swelling or tingling in your mouth or throat, chest tightness, trouble breathing

Bleeding from your rectum, or black, tarry stools

Chest pain or coughing up blood

Cloudy urine

Constipation, stomach pain, nausea, or vomiting

Fever, chills, cough, sore throat, and body aches

Menstrual periods stop[152]

Nosebleeds

Numbness or weakness in your arm or leg, or on one side of your body

Numbness, tingling, or burning pain in your hands, arms, legs, or feet

Pain in your lower leg (calf)

Seizures, confusion, or unusual drowsiness

Slow healing

Sudden or severe headaches, or problems with vision, speech, or walking

Swollen hands, ankles, or feet

Trouble breathing, cold sweats, and bluish-colored skin

Trouble swallowing, or coughing or choking while eating

Unusual bleeding, bruising, or weakness

Vomiting blood or material that looks like coffee grounds

Earlier, I detailed my anxiety on my first day of chemotherapy. The potential side effects then were nothing compared to this. Whatever nervousness I felt now was exacerbated because I was basically told that Avastin was more or less a "last resort" drug for me. Whatever the doctors could try next if this didn't work had a much lower probability of success. Plus, given the way my tumor was progressing, time wasn't exactly on our side.

I got my first Avastin infusion on August 28, 2009—barely four

---

[152] Jesus! I've got to call my doctor!

months after I was diagnosed with brain cancer and told I had between six months and a year left. The infusion center was just down the hall from the radiation center, but spiritually it was a million miles away. The hospital had recently completed a multimillion-dollar renovation of the infusion center, and it showed. The place looked gorgeous. Cancer treatments aside, you might actually consider hanging out there. That's how nice it was. Every patient got his or her own "room," an eight-by-eight foot cubicle. Inside each cube was a comfy leather recliner, a flat-screen television on an articulated arm, and all the power outlets you could ever need. The idea was, if you're going to be sitting here for hours, getting chemotherapy injections, you might as well be comfortable.

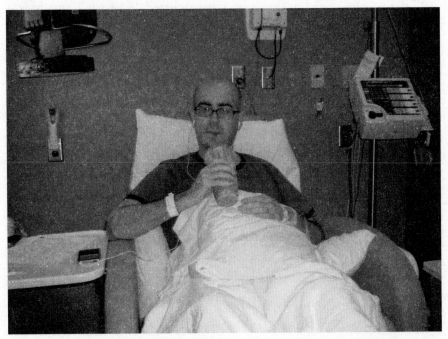

My first Avastin infusion. Because I was losing so much weight, I was actually encouraged to drink a lot of milk shakes. *(Christie Bishop)*

Unfortunately, I was a little *too* comfortable. I reclined in the leather chair immediately, and Cindy, my nurse, brought me a warm blanket and an extra pillow. I planned on resting and meditating as much as I could to alleviate any stress and to ensure (as much as I could) that the infusion went well. I must have rested a little too much because the nurse kept taking my blood pressure and frowning. "What's wrong?" Christie and I asked.

"Blood pressure too low," Cindy replied in her heavy Asian accent. They couldn't start my infusion until my blood pressure reached a normal level. Considering this was already going to be a three-hour-plus ordeal, I was eager to get started. She took it again, but no luck. She called over another nurse, and they huddled outside my cube like a small football team, discussing strategy. Finally, they broke their huddle and came back to us.

"Sit up, please?" Cindy said. I unreclined. She took my blood pressure. Still too low. "Lean forward?" I did. She took it again. *Finally*, it read a normal number. Cindy actually clasped her fists together and pumped them over her head as she looked up, thanking God or Buddha or whomever she prayed to. It was time to start Avastin.

The actual infusion was underwhelming, just like the experience when I'd whipped myself into a frenzy prior to taking my chemo pills the first time. I meditated for a good portion of the treatment, and when I came to, I ordered some crappy hospital food—an egg-salad sandwich, I think.[153] When the infusion was finally over, we packed up my walker and went home. I wondered how long it would take for me to feel something—*anything*—good or bad.

The effects were almost instantaneous. Within a few days, I started to notice a change, whereas I hadn't noticed anything when I first started chemo and radiation—and what I *did* notice wasn't for a few weeks. Right away, I had an increase in energy with the Avastin. It was almost like the world's best vitamin B_{12} shot. After just a few days, I resumed a near-normal sleep schedule. I wasn't sleeping in un-

---

[153] A multimillion-dollar renovation, yet none of that money apparently went into the menu.

til noon (or later). I bounced (relatively speaking) out of bed at a normal hour. One day, just after my first infusion, I woke up before Christie, which hadn't happened in months. I just rolled over in bed one morning and gently woke her up with a kiss. She probably thought she was still dreaming.

My energy continued to improve over the next two weeks, which had a positive impact on my physical therapy. It turns out you can do a lot more in your PT sessions when you have near-normal energy. More significant, I had renewed motivation for things that once seemed insurmountable—simple things such as getting dressed in the morning or going to the grocery store. I was still incapable of doing these things by myself—Christie was still my full-time caregiver—but at least I wanted to do them.

For example, I mentioned the grocery store. For over two months, Christie did all the shopping. Not only did I have no interest, but the idea of going to the grocery store—of going out into the world, and everything involved—was just too overwhelming to even consider. So I didn't. And remember, I'm the guy who taught Christie how to shop. Under normal circumstances, I'd actually look forward to buying groceries.

Well, Avastin helped turn me back toward normal. I shocked Christie by declaring that I wanted to go with her to the grocery store. And because I still needed the walker full-time, I would push the cart, which would act as a walker while we were in the store. We made a mini-PT session out of our grocery-store trip. It was still a little overwhelming—you forget how people at Whole Foods want to move fast and get out of there to get on with their day—but nowhere near as bad as it had been for the last few months.

We started gradually reintegrating me into society. Usually it was short walks around our neighborhood. And I mean short. Sometimes it was just to the end of the block and back. But at least I *wanted* to do it. That was the biggest difference I noticed right away: Along with my energy, my ambition was coming back as well.

> **Tumor Tip:** *For anyone who's recovering from treatment: You gotta start somewhere. Yes, it's frustrating to only be able to walk a hundred feet to the end of the block. But you know what? You just walked a hundred feet. Tomorrow, you may walk a hundred and ten feet. And ten more feet the next day. And ten more the next. What I'm trying to say is, recovery is gradual. It's incremental. It sometimes moves so slowly, you don't even notice that you're improving. You wake up and you think to yourself, "Man, I feel the same as I did yesterday: crappy." Not until two or three months down the road do you look back and think, "Wow, I've come a long way." Don't get frustrated (as I did). I know—easier said than done.*

I started measuring my progress in tiny milestones. I still remember the first time—shortly after starting Avastin—that I was able to stand up and hug Christie while she was dressing me. With both arms. Pretty much all my hugs over the previous couple of months had been of the one-handed variety. My left arm was too weak to even hug my new wife. I held her as tightly as I could (probably not very tightly, to be honest) and whispered my familiar promise into her ear: "I'm going to get better."

I was suddenly able to do some of the little things again. Such as take my own pills, or even just open the pill bottle myself. I could take my socks off again (getting them on was still a tall order that required Christie's help). I would do these things and then proudly exclaim to her, "I'm helping *you!*" Even my speech started to improve. I started making phone calls without needing Christie to act as my interpreter.

We started venturing out into the world more. A week or so after my first infusion, Christie took me for one of my favorite outings: to get a hot shave. This particular barbershop was on Melrose Avenue, a busy and popular street near Hollywood. Not only was it a busy street, but it was . . . "colorful." Lots of bright neon signs and hipsters wearing chains connecting their nose to their eyebrow. In other words, a lot of potential distractions. Luckily, I handled it quite well.

Just a few weeks earlier, the notion of my traversing Melrose Avenue was unfathomable. Now, it was just another challenge to tackle.

Our little, daily neighborhood walks must have attracted the attention of our neighbors, because one day, while Christie was out front alone, a little old man in his eighties came out of the apartment building next door and asked Christie, "How's your husband doing?" Apparently people tend to notice a young woman who's helping her husband down the sidewalk with his walker.

"He's good," Christie told him.

"Good, good." He smiled. "That's good." Over the next few weeks, Christie would run into him from time to time, and each time he asked how I was doing. Christie always told him I was doing well, and he seemed happy about the news. One day, he presented her with a bouquet of rosemary from a plant he had been growing. Maybe he saw her bringing in groceries and figured she loved to cook, or maybe he was trying to get in good with her in case I didn't make it. Hey, who can blame him? Christie's quite a catch.

30.

Inpatient Therapy

or, The Closest I Ever Got to a Threesome

September 13, 2009. My thirty-first birthday.

It had been nearly five months since my diagnosis. The night before, Christie had thrown me a big birthday party at her parents' house, just a few miles away from our apartment. All of our friends—the ones who weren't in Columbus, Ohio, watching the USC/Ohio State game in person—came over to watch the game and help celebrate my birthday. Two of my closest high school friends even drove down from Northern California. I hadn't seen either of them in a couple of years, so it was a nice surprise.

Here's all I remember from my birthday party: USC beat the Buckeyes in a comeback thriller, 18–15. Christie went way over the top and bought me a huge Optimus Prime/Transformers–themed cake. It may have not been age appropriate; when Christie picked it up that afternoon, the cake decorator asked her, "How old is the birthday boy?" To which Christie replied, "Thirty-one." My only other impression from that night: I looked terrible in all the pictures. Not in the way drunk girls look at a picture and say, "Oh, God, I look *awful*!" But I legitimately looked bad. My face was swollen and puffy on account of the steroids I was still on. It was still warm in Los Angeles, so I was wearing shorts; thus you could see my rigid, black brace on my calf and ankle, as well as my huge, black old-man Velcro shoes. My arms and legs were skinny due to muscle atrophy, but my gut was growing due to inactivity. It wasn't hard to see why, later, when I asked Christie why she got me such an elaborate cake, she said, voice cracking, "I was afraid it might be your last birthday."

A few notes about this picture: First, that's my high school buddy Jon on the left. Second, that's the sweet Transformers cake that Christie got me. You can also see how skinny my left arm had gotten from muscle atrophy, as well as my rigid, black leg brace. You can also see my lopsided smile and how much the steroids were puffing up my face. Just an overall bleak portrait. *(Author's Collection)*

The next morning, on my actual birthday, I woke up with a hankering—several hankerings. Christie asked if I wanted anything special to eat for my birthday. "Mmmm," I said. "Sushi." Then I paused. "And cheesecake." I paused again. "And guacamole."

Christie's eyes widened. "You really want *all* of that? Today?"

Yeah, I told her, I really did. Besides, it was a celebration: my first of many birthdays with cancer!

Christie smiled. In that case, she said, she'd be happy to oblige my bizarre tastes. She went out shopping for my Frankensteinian grocery list. We had some celebrating to do. Not only for my birthday, but for another reason: The next morning, I was checking into the hospital for a week's worth of inpatient therapy.

The therapy I had been doing—physical, occupational, and

speech—had all been *out*patient therapy; that is, when my sessions were over, I'd go home and go about my day. For the next week, I'd be living in the hospital, getting near round-the-clock therapy. And it wouldn't be an hour of each therapy; I was scheduled to get several sessions each day of each kind of therapy, with an ever-rotating cast of nurses and therapists. Christie and I—along with our doctors and therapists—had batted around for a few weeks the idea of admitting me to Cedars' inpatient unit. I was nervous—I hadn't spent more than a day in a hospital to that point in my life—and the thought of being without Christie, especially at night, wasn't exactly comforting. I had come to rely on her for almost everything, and although I had improved a tiny bit over the previous couple of weeks, to do almost anything I still needed her around.

That was the main reason I agreed to go to inpatient therapy. Although I was still a little nervous—a week in a nice hospital was still a week in a hospital—I was eager to kick-start my physical recovery. Plus, with my increased energy due to Avastin, I felt that a window of opportunity had been cracked open. I didn't know how long the window would stay open; all I knew was the iron was hot—I was starting to feel a little bit better—and I was going to strike.

So on Monday morning, we got the call that it all was clear to check in. Of course, insurance had been making things difficult, so we didn't know for sure if I could be admitted until the last minute. I got a call at nine thirty Monday morning saying I could check in at eleven thirty. So for an hour, we packed for a week. Which wasn't difficult; it's not as if I had any fancy dinners planned that required a three-piece suit. Just a few T-shirts, underwear, and some pairs of athletic shorts. We also packed everything related to my therapy: my ankle brace, my walker, and all of the equipment we'd picked up at the medical-supply store.

Christie also packed an overnight bag for one night's stay in the hospital. The previous night, I broke down and admitted to Christie that part of the reason I was nervous about signing up for inpatient therapy was because I was afraid to be away from her at night. I must have sold her on it because she agreed to come spend the first night with me in my hospital room. When we checked in, that was the first thing I asked my nurse: if they had a rollaway bed for Christie. The nurse smiled and said they could probably rustle one up.

The first thing I noticed when I checked in: I was the youngest patient on the floor by about fifty years (at least as far as I could see). As we walked in, a pretty young nurse came up to us and said, "You must be the Bishops." I doubt very much she recognized me from the radio show. I guess we stood out among the octogenarians. It quickly began to dawn on me what inpatient therapy was really for: people recovering from traumatic brain injuries, specifically (but not exclusively) strokes, aneurysms, and brain surgeries. Thus, most of my fellow inpatients were senior citizens who had to be coached on how to walk again, or how to lift their arms over their head, or how to say their names. Patients in this ward were in pretty bad shape, but at least they were going to start getting better. Until recently, I was headed in the opposite direction.

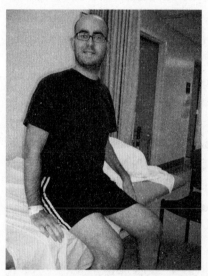

My first day of inpatient therapy. One of the most unflattering pictures anyone will ever take. Look how incredibly skinny my left arm had become. My left leg, too. Yet my face kept getting fatter from the steroids. Ugh. *(Christie Bishop)*

I didn't do a ton of actual therapy on that first day. Instead, I had several evaluation sessions. I was visited by a half dozen therapists and nurses, each of whom asked me a batch of questions and put me through a myriad of physical tests. They were establishing a baseline of what I could do—both so they could customize a program for me, and so they could track my progress. They determined, right away, that I was a fall risk; that is, I was not to walk on my own under any circumstances. They underscored this by giving me a bright yellow bracelet with the words **FALL RISK** in big black letters. The humiliating yellow bracelet should have said, *Don't sue us if you fall, we tried to warn you.* This was to be worn the entire week I was in inpatient therapy. If anyone—a therapist, nurse, or orderly—saw me attempting to walk on my own, he or she would drop everything and come assist me.

Luckily, I was not much of a "risk" to walk anywhere. I needed Christie and/or a walker to get even just a few feet. I had entered the therapy unit in a wheelchair. The hospital hallways were simply too long for me to walk without risking a fall. And even if I did make it down the hallway without incident, the effort it took would have wiped me out. So an orderly wheeled me onto the unit, where I was assigned a room and a nurse.

Here was the wonderful (yet semi-uncomfortable) part: All of my therapists and nurses—at least the ones I met on the first day—were gorgeous, nubile women in their twenties. The kind that, if you saw them in a movie, you'd say, "Oh, come on!" The hallways looked like a casting call for an eighties hair band's video about strippers dressed as nurses. On that first day, a couple of male ultrasound techs came up to my room to check me for blood clots, one of the side effects of Avastin. As they were scanning me, one of them said to me in a low voice, "Your nurses are hot, bro."

"Yes, I suppose they are." What was I supposed to say? "You're damn right they are!" Then give him a high five?

Things reached an uncomfortable apex right away. On the first morning of therapy, one of the hot therapists[154] came in for my first session. She introduced herself as Katie, an occupational therapist. An OT session essentially meant "life skills and games." Whereas physical therapy (PT) would be focusing on getting me walking again, OT would be engaging my upper body to deal with everyday life. Katie was going to incorporate my everyday activities into my therapy.

---

[154] From now on, I'm just going to say *therapists*. You can do the hot math.

"Okay," she said, "time to shower!"

I looked at Christie—who, like me, was still waking up—and then back at Katie. "Um, it's nine o'clock." I pointed at the daily schedule they'd given me. "I'm supposed to have an hour of OT."

"That *is* your OT," Katie replied with a smile. "Come on, we're headed across the hall!"

She seemed way too excited. Or maybe she was just a cheerful person. Either way, I was already embarrassed. And I hadn't even gotten out of bed for the day.

"I have a question," Christie said. *Thank God*, I thought, *she's going to ask if this is totally necessary, or if we can just do this ourselves.*

"Can I come?" Christie asked.

"Of course!" Katie said. "Actually, it's better if you do. That way, you can see the proper way to help Bryan in the shower when he needs it."

Katie helped me to the shower, where the hospital had towels, soap, and shampoo. I tried to break the ice by making a bald joke about the shampoo. "What is this?" I feigned as I examined the label. "Sham . . . *poo? And what do people use this for?" She laughed at my joke, but it didn't work. I felt even more tense. *Damnit, now Christie's going to think I'm flirting with this girl.* I looked over at Christie and my fears were instantly alleviated. She looked more amused than anything else. As if to say, "Enjoy it now, pal, because this is as close as you're ever getting to a threesome."

Then we showered together. It was actually incredibly unerotic. Katie kept talking to Christie as if she were a football coach explaining a defensive scheme: "Now, you're gonna want to hold his hand like this and help him reach around here." It was borderline emasculating. I was showered by two different OTs that week—Katie and Megan (or, as they later became known among the other therapists, "Poor Katie" and "Poor Megan")—which, sadly, increased my list of Women Who Have Seen My Adult Penis by about 20 percent. I'd better move on, or else I'm going to have to go back and add to my "Regrets" chapter.

All told, I had two sessions each of physical, occupational, and speech therapy that first full day. I felt confident enough that I told Christie I didn't need her to stay with me that night. She asked if I was sure, but I told her I'd be fine. I was in a therapy unit; what's the worst that could happen? Besides, they provided me with a bedside urinal that I could pee into in the middle of the night so I didn't have to get out of bed and try to walk to the bathroom.

I don't remember everything about my inpatient hospital stay. But what I do remember is shockingly vivid. Kind of like when you were a kid and you'd watch scrambled porn on Cinemax because every once in a while a clear shot of a boob would peek through the mess. That was my hospital stay: mostly scrambled memories, with a few images leaving an impression.

One of those clear images was a bright yellow sign, hung directly in my line of sight across from my hospital bed, taunting me: STOP! DO NOT ATTEMPT TO STAND UP ON YOUR OWN! PLEASE CALL FOR A NURSE. It was one of the first things I noticed upon checking into rehab, and one of the few things I remember clearly today. I also remember the moment I decided to defy it.

When you're on chemotherapy and steroids, the urge to pee comes on pretty quickly. The time elapsed between "Hmm, I think I might need to pee soon" and "If I don't pee *now*, we're going to have a mess on our hands" is not long. Especially in the middle of the night. So when the thought hit me around midnight, I began weighing my options: call a nurse (as the yellow sign demanded) or attempt to navigate the eight feet of hospital floor between my bed and my bathroom without aid.

Here's what I was up against: My bedside urinal was full. It was midnight. I was barefoot. I had been having enough trouble getting around with the help of a walker and an ankle brace during daylight hours; now I was groggy and essentially wheelchairbound when alone. The wheelchair now sat a few feet from me. Not that it would do any good; radiation had rendered my left arm useless, so had I even gotten myself into the wheelchair, I would only have been able to push myself in circles with my right arm.

And while the therapy unit is a beehive of hot-nurse activity when the sun shines, it's understaffed in the middle of the night. It would undoubtedly take a nurse a couple of minutes to get to my room, and I had to pee *now*.

I made the executive decision to defy the sign. I decided to walk to the bathroom.

In my groggy state, I remembered a couple of things from my physical therapy: Do not lean too much on anything, and go slowly. Forgetting (or ignoring) either of these rules would probably result in a nasty spill, along with the ensuing mess from my intractable bathroom urges.

The main thing I remember from this: fear. I was afraid I'd fall; afraid I'd embarrass myself; afraid I'd get yelled at by Christie and the therapists the next morning. Still, I soldiered on, step by extremely cautious step. I made it around the bed. I *really* had to pee. I made it to the bathroom-door handle, which provided me a semi-sturdy surface to grab on to and steady myself with. The urge to pee crested (thank God) at the exact moment I wobbled over the toilet.

Getting back into bed was 75 percent easier because (A) I no longer had to pee, and (B) collapsing into a bed is considerably easier than getting out of one. Obviously, I didn't tell Christie about this. This was one of those little victories one keeps to oneself. But coincidentally, here's what Christie wrote in her blog just two days later:

> I was pretty freaked out to leave him two nights ago because it was the first night we've spent apart in God knows how long, but he did great. My main concern was that Bryan doesn't like to "bother" people, so I was really worried that he would try to get up and go to the bathroom himself instead of calling for a nurse.

Ha ha! Good thing *that* never happened!

The rest of my week at inpatient therapy went mostly smoothly. I continued to make progress with both my physical abilities and my speech. The PTs even switched out my rigid, black brace for a much more comfortable (and subtle) athletic ankle brace. I was nowhere near normal, but I was much, much better than I had been just a few weeks before. Halfway through the week, Dr. Rudnick and Rebecca came to visit me in my room. They were thrilled at the improvements I'd made since they last saw me. They scheduled another Avastin infusion for the next day, and they scheduled another MRI for October 7—less than a month away. This, they told me, would be the Big One, the test that told us if everything—the radiation, the chemo, and the Avastin—had worked. It would be our first clear look at my tumor since before I started treatment. We wrote the date on our calendar in big red letters.

A number of my friends came to visit me while I was in the hospital, which was sweet. Unfortunately, visiting hours were at the end of the day, after eight solid hours of therapy, when I was most tired. And unfortunately (as it were), my friends were all really good guys (and gals) who wanted to stay and visit for hours. At one point, when some of my friends had been in my hospital room for close to an hour, I motioned for Christie to come over. She bent over and I whispered into her ear, "I love these guys, but I need to rest. Badly. Can you get them to leave?" She got what I meant. Christie tactfully thanked them for visiting but explained that I was worn-out from a full day of therapy and I needed some rest.

Tumor Tip: For anyone visiting a friend in the hospital: Know when to leave. Your ailing friend is no doubt happy to see you, but he or she is in the hospital for a reason: to rest and recover. There's a sweet spot you should aim for when you're visiting someone in the hospital: twenty-one minutes. Anything more and you're wearing out your welcome. Anything less and you'll seem as if you've got better things to do.

So my friends said their good-byes and left. Before they all left, one of them—Frank, the same guy who had asked me in Vegas if I was going to be okay—leaned over and whispered, "You've got a *lot* of hot nurses on your floor."

31.

Family Stress

or, Save the Drama for Your Mama

Cancer takes its toll on you physically, in obvious ways. It also takes its toll on you mentally, again obviously. But it takes an emotional toll, too, in sometimes not-so-obvious ways. People sometimes ask me if I'm mad at my cancer, and I tell them no. Cancer helped me appreciate things around me more, and it gave me a new perspective on life. But I am mad at it for one thing: Cancer turned the most important people in my life—Christie and my parents—against each other.

I'll be honest with you: I dreaded writing this chapter. I put it off until I was almost done with the book altogether. I actually considered leaving it out of the book entirely. For one thing, I knew it would be painful to write. Secondly, it didn't fit in the timeline. Where do you put a series of events that took place over the entire first five months of treatment? Finally, no one comes out of this situation looking great, and I include myself in that. It's sort of like that old biography of Jim Morrison of the Doors, *No One Here Gets Out Alive*. In this case, no one here got out unscathed.

But I had to write it. For better or worse, this book is my legacy. It's my truth of what happened and how I felt about it. And since this part of the story is easily the most traumatic for me, I wouldn't be being true to myself if I left it out.

I also feel a sense of responsibility to include it. I recently spoke at a cancer conference for young adults, and the survivors I talked to—specifically the men—almost universally brought up "family stress" as a huge problem in their lives. It was eye-opening to see how common this issue was for young men with cancer. I was also shocked to see how many of these young men's parents were actually making their lives more difficult, thereby hindering their recovery. If stress brought on by your family is such a universal theme in the recovery of cancer patients, then what good am I doing by leaving my own story out of this book? If, as I hope, this book inspires people affected by cancer, aren't I doing them a disservice by not including what I consider to be one of the biggest issues in my own recovery? Am I not doing the same disservice to myself?

I believe that to beat something as big and bad as cancer you need all elements of your life firing on all cylinders: physical, mental, and emotional. When I started my cancer journey back in April, I was good physically. I was going to the gym every day as a thirty-year-old and was as ready for the physical repercussions of cancer treatment as I'd ever be. Mentally, I was getting there, hence the meditation and related "mind maintenance." But things were never quite right emotionally; specifically, between my parents, Christie, and me. The problems mirrored my symptoms at the time: At first, they were easily ignored. Then, they demanded attention. Finally, things got so bad that they required some sort of emergency intervention, or else the damage might have been permanent.

I flew up to my parents' home in Northern California to interview them for this book. To say I wasn't looking forward to it is an understatement; I was dreading it the way Punxsutawney Phil probably dreads Groundhog Day. For the record, if you're ever proposing an interview session with your parents, don't do it the exceptionally honest way: "Hey, Mom and Dad, want to relive some extremely painful memories for a couple of hours?" It actually ended up being cathartic and therapeutic. We talked for almost two hours. We laughed. We cried. And we ultimately ended up in a much better place than where we started.

Speaking of which, that's where it all started: at my parents' house, the day after I was diagnosed. We had flown up that day—a

Friday—for Christie's bridal shower. But it became sort of a "medical update" weekend. I filled them in on what we knew and what our plan was; they offered to help in any way they could. Later in the weekend, Ryan—the childhood friend who now worked in medical-device sales—helped get us an appointment with Dr. Black on extremely short notice. We were obviously all elated. My mom asked, "What flight should we get on?"

"Huh?" I asked her.

"To go to your appointment with Dr. Black. What flight should we book?"

"Oh, you're not coming," I told her matter-of-factly.

"Oh," she said. They were both clearly dejected. They later told me that this was the first of many times they felt as if they were being kept away during my treatments. But this was husband-and-wife stuff, as far as I was concerned. And though my parents would be the first people I called after the appointment, I didn't feel it was appropriate for them to fly to LA to come to my doctor's appointments with me. Plus, they were already scheduled to fly down for Christie's LA shower in just five days. So it wasn't as if we weren't ever going to see each other again.

Five days later, we did see each other again. My parents arrived in the middle of the day, and Christie and I took them to lunch at one of our favorite restaurants, C&O Cucina. The conversation at lunch started with Christie's shower the next day, then turned to my treatment, which I was scheduled to start the following week. I had just met with Dr. Rudnick for the first time a couple of days earlier, and I was eager to tell them all about it.

Suddenly, my dad announces he's written a letter that he'd like to read. *Okay* . . ., I thought. Two things to know about my dad: He's very sensitive and he's very introspective. Put those things together, and when he's got something weighing on him emotionally, he's going to put it into writing.

This letter was several handwritten pages. My dad struggled through it, his voice cracking occasionally. Honestly, I don't remember much about the specifics of the letter. My impressions were, one, it must have been difficult for him to write and even more difficult for him to read it aloud to us. Two, the themes were "We're always going to be his mom and dad" and "We're always going to be there" and an overall feeling of being excluded. I reached out and grabbed his hand when he was done and said, "It's okay, Pops. I love you."

I looked over at Christie, who was sitting next to me with an "*Oh, HELL no*" look on her face. "No," she said, "that is *not* okay." And a huge fight ensued. In the restaurant. A fight that dragged on for what seemed like twenty minutes. Actually, it may have been more than twenty minutes because the server kept coming over to our table, only to find three out of the four of us crying and/or yelling at any given moment. Eventually she stopped coming to our table.[155] If there was a silver lining to this awful mess, it's that the restaurant was otherwise empty. So we could have our (very public) family melt-down in the "privacy" of an open restaurant.

My dad got so mad at one point that he left the restaurant to go stand in the parking lot by himself. I went out to calm him down and left my mom and Christie to keep hashing things out inside the restaurant. I found him pacing next to the parking lot. "Well, that sucked," I said to him.

He shook his head. "Bry, I just want you to get better."

"Well, this isn't the way it's going to happen!" I snapped back. We eventually made our way back into the restaurant, where Christie and my mom had reached a more civil tone. I don't remember how we left it at the restaurant, but I do know my parents discussed turning around and heading back to Northern California right then and there. Thank God they didn't. Can you imagine the mess that would have created at the shower the next day? "Hey, Christie, where's Bryan's mom? I thought she was going to be here." "Oh, we got into a huge public fight yesterday and she hopped the next flight back to SFO." [Awkward pause.] "Oh. Um . . . please enjoy the toaster oven I got you . . . ?"

---

[155] I can only imagine the conversation she was having back at the hostess stand.

Things only got worse from there. My parents genuinely felt they were being kept away, as if we were telling them not to come down to LA to visit us. In a sense, they were right. I had no problem with their planning a trip to see us. But that was the thing—these proposed trips were rarely "planned." I would often get a call from my (crying) mom or (concerned) dad saying something to the effect of "We haven't seen you in a few weeks, we miss you, we're worried about you, can we come down to see you this weekend?" Unfortunately, these calls would often come on a Tuesday or a Wednesday. My life already felt out of control enough. I had cancer in my brain that wouldn't stop growing. I had physical symptoms that were worsening. Christie and I didn't have jobs or an income, yet we had normal-person bills to pay. Medical paperwork was piling up. Our apartment was too small. *I couldn't dress myself.* My life needed *order*, yet it was in chaos. And having your doting/loving/bordering-on-overbearing parents spontaneously pop in for an out-of-town visit was *not* helping with putting things in order.

So I kept them away. I felt guilty about it then and I feel guilty about it now. I once told them that part of the reason I did what I did was to protect them. I didn't want them seeing what my life had become. I didn't want them to see their oldest son reduced to being dressed or fed or having his butt wiped when he crapped his pants. And for the record, my parents would have loved nothing more than to be there to help me with all this and more. But I wanted to be the one to dole out the information to them. If something good happened—a good test scan, or some physical improvement—I wanted to brag about it to them. If something bad occurred—a fall, or a negative doctor's appointment—I wanted to filter the information to them in a gentle way, if at all. I needed to feel some small measure of control in my life, which was spiraling decidedly *out* of control. Unfortunately, my parents bore the brunt of it.

When it came to emotional pain, there was plenty to go around. It was a symbiotic relationship, unfortunately. Whereas my parents took on a fair amount of my emotional neglect, Christie took on the lion's share of the stress caused by the whole situation. This became a big factor in what eventually landed her in the hospital for colitis. As my symptoms worsened over the months, and as it became increasingly difficult for me to even speak, Christie became the one to relay information to all parties, including my parents. She would often call them with updates from the car—she would speak to them on the Bluetooth speaker so I could hear everything and occasionally chime in if I needed to. She'd give them a rundown of what we'd done that day: doctors' appointments, rehab sessions, etc. They'd listen patiently, then say at the end, "Okay. Thanks. Is there anything you're not telling us?" They were feeling so kept-away from our situation that they had started to suspect that we were now keeping information from them. When I interviewed them, they both denied ever saying that. But it's seared into my memory as an example of how helpless they were feeling, sequestered in Northern California.

My mom and my dad both mentioned how envious they were of Don and Sheryl for living so close to us. That part made perfect sense to me, especially because Adam and Sarah live just three blocks from my parents. They know how nice it is to have the luxury of seeing your son and his wife whenever you want, to say nothing of a son who's battling cancer. One weekend, my mom came down to visit us with her best friend, Theresa. I had known Theresa my entire life, so she was like family. I know her better than I know some (most?) of my actual aunts.

One night when they were down visiting, they took me to Cafe 50's, a 1950s-themed diner in West Los Angeles. I was still under orders to eat high-calorie foods to try to keep from losing more weight. So we all ordered milk shakes. I got my favorite: the Elvis Shake. Ice cream, banana, and peanut butter. Lots of calories, lots of fun! We're halfway through our shakes when my mom whips out a stack of papers she'd printed out at home. "Bryan," she says, "I've been doing some research, and I think I'm going to rent a place down here."

My eyes must have widened as big as the milk-shake glass. I looked over at Theresa, who had a look that said, "Hoo, boy, *this* is not going to go well."

"You want to rent an apartment here?" I asked her. "In LA?"

"Well, actually, these are just rooms that I'd be renting from people," she clarified. "Look, these are close by. . . ." She handed me some of the pages.

"No," I said. "*No!* Are you nuts?" I asked (rhetorically; clearly I already knew the answer).

She protested mildly. "Well, I was just thinking—"

"No!" I reiterated. "Just . . . no." I handed the pages back to her without even looking at them.

She must have realized beforehand that this was a long shot at best because she barely put up a fight. Later, when I interviewed her for the book, we had this exchange:

BRYAN: You were going to live with a stranger?

NANCY: (Incredulous) Yeah! I was only going to come down like every other weekend.

(Hysterical laughter from me and my dad)

BRYAN: That quote's going in the book. I'm so glad you restrained yourself. You'd 'only' come down every fourteen days.

This is the type of chaos my life didn't need. My mom wanted to rent a room in someone's house just to be nearby? What kind of a monster had I created?

Things came to a head at the end of my week in inpatient therapy. Which brings us to the current point in the story. When I scheduled my week in the hospital, I encouraged my parents to come down and visit me. Being in the hospital for a week sounds scary, but they hadn't seen me since before I started Avastin. They hadn't seen the improvements I'd made in the ensuing weeks, and the strides I was sure to make with almost round-the-clock therapy.

They arrived on Friday and came straight to the hospital. Unfortunately, tensions between them and Christie had reached a boiling point. She was there when they arrived, and they exchanged terse pleasantries. The strain in the room when they were together was palpable. The next day, USC was scheduled to play Washington in a day game, and being USC football fans, we were all going to watch the game together. The hospital even arranged for us to use their communal activity room, where we could watch the game on a big screen as opposed to the little bedside TV in my hospital room. Christie never showed up. She texted me that morning after visiting me and basically said, "I can't be around your parents right now. I'm so sorry." So we watched the game without her. And, of course, as fate would have it, USC lost that day in painful fashion.

My parents were scheduled to leave the next day, on Sunday morning. Saturday night, they brought me dinner in my hospital bed from the deli across the street. I knew I had to talk to them about Christie. The situation had become untenable. I could never get better with the three most important people in my life fighting like this. Something had to give. Something had to be done.

I had been putting it off all weekend, just as I put off writing this chapter. And just as I didn't want to call them with the news that their son had a brain tumor while they were on vacation in Tahoe, I didn't want to have this conversation with them now. But I had to.

"Guys," I warbled, "we need to talk. About this situation with you and Christie."

They nodded and acknowledged that things were out of control.

"I understand things are not great with you and Christie right now. I also understand that things have been said and done on both sides. No one's innocent, and no one's guilty. Whatever happened, happened. To get better—to physically recover—I need you guys to get along."

My dad initially protested, "Bryan, there's so much more to it. You haven't heard what we have to say—"

"I don't care," I cut him off, saying it as clearly as I could articulate at the time. "And I don't want to know. I just need you guys to be nice to her. Even if you have to fake it. Starting now, I just want to move forward."

To their immense credit, my parents were basically like, "Okay, that's fair, we understand." They later said that they felt terrible that I was even in the position to have to be a mediator while I was sick and fighting for my life.

My parents left the next day as scheduled, and I was discharged from inpatient therapy a day later. Unbeknownst to me, shortly thereafter Christie and my mom had a long heart-to-heart talk on the phone. They cleared the air and got on the same page emotionally—or at least the same chapter. The whole episode was traumatic, unnerving, and damaging, but we ultimately all ended up in a better place. I honestly think I turned an emotional corner in my recovery the night I had that uncomfortable talk with my parents in my hospital bed. And I needed it. Mentally, I had begun my recovery a long time ago. My physical recovery had started a few weeks prior, with my first infusion of Avastin. Now my emotional recovery had begun.

32.

The Exam of a Lifetime

or, My Next MRI

Upon seeing my improvement when he visited me during inpatient therapy, Dr. Rudnick scheduled my next MRI for October 7, a Wednesday. I would meet with him in his office two days later, on Friday morning, to review the the results. *That* was an excruciating two days. People ask all the time about the time between my first MRI (all the way back in April) and my diagnosis a couple of days later. "Wasn't that awful," they ask, "having to wait to find out what was wrong with you?" Not really, I'd tell them, because I didn't *know* what was wrong with me. There was nothing to fear but fear itself, you know what I mean?

This time, the fear was much more real: If the scan went well, it meant the Avastin was working, and our Hail Mary pass had paid off. If the scan didn't show any improvement . . . well, we were pretty much out of safety nets at that point.

My mom drove down with her friend Theresa for the appointment. My dad had to work, so we'd have to call him right away with the results. I had no idea what to expect. I certainly *felt* better than I did a few months or even a few weeks ago. I was cautiously optimistic. I projected the details of the appointment in my imagination over and over. I pictured a good MRI; I honestly couldn't let myself imagine the alternative.

The morning of the appointment, I was more nervous than I'd ever been. More nervous than when I proposed to Christie, more nervous than I was on our wedding day, and more nervous than when they announced in 2002 that USC's Carson Palmer had won the Heisman Trophy. Theresa offered to stay in the waiting room while we met with Rudnick. This was a family-only affair.

We checked in and were shown to an exam room, where we waited for what seemed like ten agonizing minutes. I remember thinking like a person awaiting a jury to return a verdict in a murder trial. Would Rudnick be smiling? Would he get right to it? Would Rebecca be with him? Would *she* be smiling? She never smiled, so maybe it wouldn't be that bad if she didn't smile. . . .

All of these scenarios ran through my head as we waited. My mom and Christie were silent, too. We were all one big tightly wound bundle of nerves. Suddenly, the door opened: It was Rebecca, alone. "Oh, no," I thought. "This can't be good. She's taking us to Rudnick's office. Nothing good happens in Rudnick's office. That's where he gives you the bad news."

Rebecca glanced at the three of us. "Hey, guys." We must have looked like tortured POWs because she then simply said, "The MRI looks good. Wanna see it?"

The MRI looks good.

It took me a full second and a half to process what she said. I let out a deep, long exhale. The kind of exhale that has built up over almost six months of holding your breath. "Yeah, we want to see it," I told her.

She led the three of us across the narrow hallway to a viewing room where Dr. Rudnick had two computer screens in front of him, each with an MRI.

"Hey, how's it going?" he asked me with a smile.

"You tell me."

He pointed to the screen on the right. "This is the MRI from two days ago." Then he pointed to the screen on the left. "And this is the last one, from two months ago. And you can see right away," he said, pointing back to the new MRI, "that your tumor has shrunk significantly."

I looked; he was obviously right. My tumor was about half the size that it was before. The change was dramatic.

I was overjoyed. I slumped in my chair and, for the first time in months, I actually relaxed a little. I looked over at my mom and Christie. They were locked in a long, tearful embrace. A lot of the emotions, fear and anger they'd been holding on to so tightly for months washed away in that moment. Seeing them hugging in a moment of pure joy made me happier than seeing the actual MRI.

I turned back around to the screen, and Rudnick continued describing the new MRI. "When we get these type of scans," he explained, "we want to see two things: that the swelling goes down, and the amount of contrast goes down. And you had both of those things."

Christie and my mom both grabbed my shoulders from behind. They were both just so happy. Rudnick explained a few more things before my mom excused herself to go to the waiting room, where poor Theresa had been sitting on pins and needles for upward of fifteen torturous minutes. Mom left Christie and me with Rudnick, who wrapped up his explanation by basically saying, "I'm really, really happy with these results."

We still had a full day ahead of us: I was scheduled for another Avastin infusion in an hour, plus we had to email, call, and text everyone we knew with the good news. On our way from the MRI viewing room to the waiting room, Christie and I had a brief, private moment together to quietly celebrate before rejoining my mom and Theresa. I hugged Christie tightly in the hallway. I pulled her as close as I could. Then I leaned in and whispered in her ear . . .

"I told you I'd get better."

33.

"Laughs for Bald Bryan"

or, *"Baby,* *How?!"*

I'd had a good MRI. My tumor had shrunk significantly. Going back to the rock analogy from earlier, that was like finding a huge stone for a foothold to get out of that pit. But I wasn't out quite yet. There was still a lot of work to do.

Thanks to my week of inpatient therapy and my continuing work with Chris Tolos, I was almost ready to stop using my walker to get around. I was gaining strength and confidence. My speech was starting to clear up as well. Listeners of *The Adam Carolla Show* will remember that late in 2009 I started becoming easier to understand when I'd make my semiregular appearances on the podcast.

Speaking of Adam, I really owe that guy a major debt of gratitude. Not only for essentially giving me my start in show business, but for showing me tremendous loyalty when I was at my lowest point: cancer-stricken, mostly immobile, and barely able to talk. Despite the fact that I was probably doing his show more harm than good during my treatment,[156] he kept inviting me back. I remember wheeling my walker and myself into his studio, where he and Teresa would already be sitting and announcing as I shuffled in, "Grandpa's here!"

From the moment I announced my diagnosis on his show in early May, Adam was determined to throw a big fund-raiser for me. He even announced it on the podcast: "Let's have a big ol' fund-raiser,

---

[156] You could really make that same claim now, as a matter of fact.

what do you say?" What did I say? Hell yes, let's definitely do that! The idea was to get a bunch of comedians and bands—"friends of the show"—to perform, and we'd sell tickets. When the idea for an event first got mentioned on the podcast, a listener even emailed me offering to help organize it. I put a little star next to her email, just in case. We'd need all the help we could get.

Christie and I were both laid off. I was incapable of working and she was my full-time caregiver and thus couldn't go back to work. We had medical bills that insurance wouldn't cover: deductibles, copays, and out-of-pocket costs. Plus, insurance itself. We were on COBRA from CBS radio. COBRA (continued health coverage for out-of-work employees) is helpful—in our case, a godsend—but expensive. You still have to pay the premiums, which for us were over $1,000 a month. Pricey, but worth it. Especially when that $1,000 a month pays for insurance that covers $50,000 twice-monthly Avastin infusions.

Then there was simply our cost of living. Plenty of our expenses—rent, car payments, insurance, student loans—were incurred long before either of us were ever laid off. For example, Christie was leasing a car for $400 a month before she got laid off, when she could easily afford it. But once we both ended up jobless, she still had two years left on her lease. What were we going to do? Those kinds of "fixed" monthly expenses we could do nothing about except to continue to pay them. Add in food, water, electricity, and gas, and the bills started to pile up fast.

It didn't take long for our savings to dwindle dangerously low. So we started thinking about a fund-raiser for the fall. Adam suggested that Christie and I talk to Lynette, his wife, to brainstorm some ideas for what we could do. Unfortunately, this was pre-Avastin, so I was not much help. I was still way too overstimulated and felt overwhelmed. I started to feel depressed over the whole idea; if getting dressed every morning posed a huge problem for me, what chance did I have of helping to plan a fund-raiser?

We decided to get Mike August involved in the initial planning.

Mike had been the talent booker for the radio show. He had extensive experience booking live events similar to this. Unfortunately, Mike's approach to the event was much less can-do and much more "Here's what we *can't* do and why." He shot down pretty much every idea we had. We couldn't do a large venue, he said, because we wouldn't sell enough tickets. We couldn't do a small venue because some of the bands wouldn't play there. We couldn't sell audio recordings afterward to raise even more money because the comics wouldn't allow it. We couldn't do it at certain comedy clubs because these would demand too big a cut of the profits. The economy was so bad, he claimed—this was mid-2009—that people weren't going to pay a lot for tickets anyway. Our best bet, he guessed, would be to "four-wall" it; that is, rent out a hotel ballroom somewhere and hope to sell enough tickets to make some money. If I was depressed about the event before, I was down-right despondent about it now.

We relayed the information to Adam, thinking he'd step in and say, "*No*, we're definitely having a big event, no matter what." Instead, he said, "Eh, let's just do a telethon here in the studio." He wanted to es-sentially do an extended podcast where listeners called in and pledged money. I broke out in a cold sweat. What had started out as a grand plan was now being reduced to a "very special episode" of the pod-cast. A sweet gesture, but it wasn't going to help us that much. Some-thing needed to be done. Fast.

Suddenly, I remembered the fan who'd emailed me months earlier. The woman who offered to help organize the event. I went back and searched for her email. Here's part of what she emailed to Christie in June:

> I am a Carolla fan which is where I heard your story and have been following your blog loyally. In 1999 I became the caregiver to my best friend who had brain cancer, hers was a stage 4 glioblastoma/PNET in the front left lobe. At diagnosis she was given 2 weeks to live and made it 2 ½ years. I read your blog and have relived so much of our experience, the mask, the radiation, the friends in the

waiting room, it all comes back. I cannot imagine your experience
with your husband going through this.

I was listening to the recent podcast and heard the second reference to the telethon and my ears perked. See, I am a professional
fundraiser, raising millions of dollars for charities including cancer
research. I am a contractor and LOVE my job, which is so rewarding. Like you, going through my ordeal made me rethink my life
and I left the corporate world to do this job 10 years ago. And nothing would please me more than to see your telethon as successful as
possible. Having lived through this ordeal, setting up a research
endowment in my friend's name, and knowing how to fundraise like
I do, I know this is possible.

I would love to share some concepts that would help the success
of the telethon. This is my world of expertise and it would give me
such joy to help you. Please please let me help. I want nothing from
this but to know I have helped you both.

This woman, Deb Barge, was a huge fan of the show, was a professional fund-raiser—a good one, apparently—and wanted nothing
more than to make our event a success and work for free while doing
it. They say if something seems too good to be true, it probably is.
Well, this is the one time in my life where something seemed totally
and absolutely too good to be true . . . and it wasn't.

Deb wasn't everything she made herself out to be . . . she was more.
In addition to everything she'd bragged about in her email, here's what
she failed to mention: She's a tireless worker. She's never satisfied. She
gets involved personally in every aspect of her events. She will find a
solution to any problem. She is a brilliant negotiator. She knows how
to handle a wide variety of egos and personalities. On top of all that,
she is incredibly empathetic. If someone is ever looking for the World's
Greatest Event Planner for a charity, I could not recommend Deb
Barge highly enough.

We contacted Deb, batted around some ideas, and got to work.
This would not be a telethon—oh, no. Deb had grand plans for this

event. Forget comedy clubs and hotel ballrooms, she said. We were going to book a theater. We needed at least a thousand seats, possibly more. We'd also need to get a charitable organization on board to act as a "pass-through," meaning we would be able to use their 501(c)(3) status to make the event legally tax-exempt. And we were going to sell the tickets for a lot of money, she said. Why not? For one thing, they're tax-deductible. And, she added, people want to give. "You don't realize it," she told me when I balked on the ticket prices, "but you touch people. You inspire them. Your story, this podcast . . . people *will* turn out for this event." She was like the voice in *Field of Dreams*— "If you build it, they will come." The whole thing reminded me of my experience with Dr. Harold Kumar and Dr. Rudnick when I was first diagnosed. August had been like Kumar—grim and foreboding, essentially saying, "This is what you're up against, and why it probably won't work." Deb, on the other hand, was like Rudnick—"We can do this, here's how we're gonna do it, now let's get to work!"

So we put our faith in Deb Barge. She picked out a venue for us to visit as a possible place for the event: the Wilshire Ebell Theatre in LA's Miracle Mile district. The Ebell, as it's known, was built in the 1920s, and it is a grand sight to behold. Christie and I toured it and were blown away by how elegantly beautiful it is. Not surprisingly, it was declared a Cultural Historic Monument in 1982. It had a huge courtyard where we could hold a "backstage" VIP party for people who bought upgraded tickets. It also boasted 1,270 seats, which made me nervous.

"Are you sure it isn't too big?" I asked Deb.

"No way," she said. "No *way*. You mark my words: We will sell this place out."

If nothing else, I admired her confidence. Adam was on board, too. He likes and appreciates anyone who's a go-getter, so he really liked Deb. He mentioned the plan to his agent, James "Baby Doll" Dixon, the superagent I mentioned earlier in the book. He acquired the nickname partly because he affectionately called people "baby" all the time, as in "Baby, how's it going?" or "I spent an hour and a half

on my hair today, baby, you like?" Adam mentioned that we were going to hold the fund-raiser at the Wilshire Ebell Theatre and that
he'd be headlining. He also mentioned that he'd like his pal (and another of Dixon's clients) Jimmy Kimmel to make an appearance to
hopefully drive up ticket sales.

"How many seats are in this theater, baby?" Dixon asked.

"I don't know, maybe twelve hundred?" Adam said.

"What?" Dixon asked incredulously. "And how much are you
charging for tickets?"

"A hundred. Three hundred for VIP tickets."

"Baby, what are you doing?" Dixon pleaded. "You'll never sell that
place out."

"I don't know. People seem motivated to help."

"Baby, baby, the economy," Dixon continued. "Nobody's spending
that kind of money. Jon Stewart [another of Dixon's clients] can't
even sell out a twelve-hundred-seat venue right now."

"I appreciate that vote of confidence, Dixon, but I really think we
can do this."

"Baby, I'm not going to send Jimmy out onstage to a half-full theater," Dixon insisted. "I'm not going to allow him to *humiliate* himself like that."

Adam persisted. "We'll just get some great comics, a band or two,
and I think the fans will come through." His mind was made up.

We decided to call the event "Laughs for Bald Bryan," based on our
intention to fill the performance roster with some of our favorite comedians. I compiled a short list of comics who were not only "friends
of the show," but ones with whom I'd connected over the years. A
couple were already booked for out-of-town gigs and couldn't make
it, but everyone who was available that night said yes. Each one was a
fantastic comic who I greatly admired: Larry Miller, Dana Gould,
Greg Fitzsimmons, and Joel McHale. The Dan Band—the hilarious
(and very good) "wedding band" from *Old School* and *The Hangover*—
also signed on to play a few songs.

Tickets started selling at a brisk pace. Adam publicized the event whenever he could: on his own show, on local radio, and even on E!'s *Chelsea Lately*. The tickets were selling well enough, then a big thing happened: Bad Religion was interested in playing the event. Bad Religion, for those who don't know, is a *band*. They're Southern California legends thanks to constant airplay on KROQ, the biggest rock station in town. We had sold about half the venue's seats when we announced that they'd be joining the lineup.

That was the final push we needed to get the proverbial boulder over the top of the hill. Everything got easier after that. Sponsors lined up to provide food and drinks for the VIP lounge. People donated dozens of items for a silent auction to raise even more money. Listeners volunteered to work the event as ticket-takers, ushers, and other support staff. It was a heart-melting outpouring of support. On a macro level, it's an example of what I said earlier: People just want to help. To this point, there hadn't been a big opportunity for fans of the show to step up to the plate and swing for the fences to try to help me and Christie. Now they were gaining momentum.

Five days before the event, we had sold all but twenty-six tickets. The event was sure to be a sellout well before the curtain went up. Adam was talking to Dixon in one of their regular phone calls.

"We're all sold-out," Adam boasted.

"What?" Dixon asked, shocked.

"We've only got twentysomething tickets left. The event's going to go clean." Meaning it would sell out completely.

Dixon was dumbfounded. "Baby, *how*?!" He couldn't get his mind around how, using not much more than a podcast, we were able to sell over twelve hundred tickets—pricey tickets, I might add—to a charity event.

The night of the event was amazing. I try not to use the word *amazing* too much. We all know the annoying girl who overuses it. But in this case, I was truly amazed. Sure enough, the place was packed with 1,270 friends, family members, and fans. I must have taken five-hundred pictures that night. If I could have taken more, I would have. I was literally amazed at the number of friends and family members who came to the event, especially the ones who flew in from Northern California. My mom had advised me that a large contingent would be traveling from up north, but I wasn't prepared to see them all there, mingling with fans and the performers. Aside from somehow attending my own funeral someday, it's as close as I'll ever get to an actual episode of *This Is Your Life*!

The event was perfect. The comics were hilarious. The bands rocked. I'll never forget the image of my best man, JD, running up and down the aisles as Bad Religion—his favorite band—played. The Dan Band serenaded my mother with an inappropriate love song. Joel McHale mixed stories about me into his set. Jimmy Kimmel even made a couple of appearances onstage to lead the crowd in drunken sing-alongs. The live auction went great. The silent auction went better. The whole night could not have gone any more perfectly.

In a stroke of genius, Deb arranged for the audio recording of the event to be sold on *The Adam Carolla Show*'s Web site. That way, people all around the world could buy it and essentially donate to our cause, thereby opening up an LA-only event to a worldwide fundraiser.

All told, donations from the event brought in six figures. It was a staggering amount of money; money that would get Christie and me through the next phase of our lives and recovery. I was still at least a year away from being able to hold down a job, and Christie was equally far away from being able to leave me alone all day so *she* could resume work. In addition to Avastin infusions and other medications, I also needed more intensive physical therapy. And since our COBRA health coverage would soon run out, this money came just at the right time. But there was something else I knew we had to do.

34.

Get Busy Living or Get Busy Dying

or, Italy

Our personal savings had almost been completely depleted by the combination of my cancer treatments and our dual unemployment. The money from "Laughs for Bald Bryan" helped lift a tremendous financial weight off our shoulders. The first thing we did with the money was to enroll me in a weeklong one-on-one therapy "boot camp" with a world-renowned physical therapist named Waleed. Waleed ran a clinic in San Diego using an approach called Neuro-IFRAH, and he came highly recommended by several people, including Chris Tolos, my current therapist in Los Angeles. Waleed, it turns out, had trained Chris. So when I unknowingly asked Chris if he'd ever heard of this Waleed character, Chris endorsed him without hesitation. "He's expensive," Chris warned, "but worth it. He really is a guru when it comes to PT."

We looked into Waleed. He was indeed expensive, and like everyone else in the medical field who's really, really good, he didn't take insurance. And you had to sign up for a full week; no two-day sessions. And you had to travel to his facilities just outside San Diego. Luckily, we could now afford it. So we packed up the car and moved to San Diego for a week. We rented a room at the Courtyard by Marriott nearby, which was helpful because they offered a free breakfast. And neither of us wanted to cook in the hotel room's minikitchen that week.

The week with Waleed was extremely beneficial. It made inpatient therapy look like kindergarten playtime. It was *hard*. The physical exertion often had me sweating through my clothes. Yet by the end of the week, I was pretty much free of my dependence on the walker. Waleed even had me fitted for a new brace that was more of a walking boot. It corrected my ankle weakness and almost had me walking "normally" again. Of course, normality comes at a steep price sometimes, and the brace itself cost well over $1,000. The whole week of therapy cost several times that. But thanks to our fund-raiser, we didn't have to worry about affording this medical necessity.

This is what I mean when I say Waleed made you work hard. This is just one of the bizarre exercises he put me through that week. *(Christie Bishop)*

While we were working with Waleed, another couple was there, usually working with another therapist on the other side of the room. This older couple, from Texas, made me think of the couple that Christie had come across online, Tyra and Steve, the ones who lost their battle with a brain tumor. The ones who never got the chance to do the one thing they so desperately wanted to do together if he ever got better: travel.

Coincidentally, Waleed himself was something of a world traveler, both for work and for pleasure. Along with being a world-class therapist, he was also a world-class storyteller. All week long he regaled us with tales of his international travels. If we showed even the slightest interest in a story, he could run into his office and produce a handful of snapshots taken from that country. We even saw Chris Tolos in one of the pictures. Waleed had no shortage of things to say about all the exotic destinations he'd visited, but he saved his true reverence for Italy. Oh, the yarns he'd spin about Italy. By the time he'd finish, you were ready to hop the next flight to Rome.

I considered this the universe giving me another series of signs. For years—as long as we'd known each other—Christie and I had dreamed about traveling to Italy. When we both got laid off, we had even entertained the notion of moving there for a month or so. We had enough savings, we thought, so why not? Well, obviously cancer derailed that plan, but I'd always kept it in the back of my mind as this magical place that I might be lucky enough to someday get to, if I could only get healthy enough.

Well, once I was healthy enough—even just barely—I said to Christie, "Book a ticket for Italy. We're going."

She was excited but nervous. "Really? Are you sure? It's a lot of walking. A *lot*. And a couple of very long plane flights."

"I don't care," I told her. "I feel better. I don't know how long this is going to last. We're going to Italy."

Financially, it wouldn't ruin us. Before the fund-raiser, we still had a tiny bit of our personal savings left. We'd use it for our trip. We'd use the money from the benefit to pay for the next year of our lives.

Initially, neither of us was sure it was the right thing to do. How would it look, traveling to Italy just six months after throwing a giant fund-raiser? I thought hard about it. I thought about how it would look: crying poor, and then flying to Europe. But I also thought about Tyra and Steve. I thought about how easily that could be us: always wishing, but never getting the chance. Here was a woman with two children whose husband was *dead*. And her biggest regret? Not getting to travel more with him, the love of her life.

I wasn't going to let Christie have the same regret.

I looked back at my list of regrets in my life and noticed a common thread: They were almost all things I had *not* done. Not writing my own wedding vows. Not being a better brother to Adam. Not finishing my degree at USC. Not dancing with my thirteen-year-old secret admirer. There were very few things in my life that I regretted doing, yet my list of actual regrets was peppered with missed opportunities. I had learned my lesson. This would not be something I would add to the list.

I felt the same way as I felt when I first started Avastin. This was another occasion when the universe had opened a window of opportunity. It was cracked open only just enough to squeeze through. I had no idea how long the window would be open, or if it was going to slam shut in a month, and I wasn't going to wait around to find out.

We booked the cheapest midweek flights we could find. We stayed in bed-and-breakfasts when we could, to save money on lodging and to grab a few free meals. When we needed to stay in hotels in big cities such as Rome, we used Christie's hotel points that she'd accumulated from all her business travel. We walked everywhere we could. It was a perfect two-week trip: fun, romantic, exhilarating, unforgettable, and, best of all, underbudget. Everything had worked out perfectly. It was time to come home.

Then a volcano erupted.

You may remember it from the news in early 2010. An Icelandic volcano erupted and brought all of Europe's air travel to a halt. Literally. Airports were ghost towns. Planes were grounded. People were sleeping in terminals. When the volcano first blew, we were still in the first week of our trip. "Looks like it'll be done by the time we're ready to leave," we thought.

Well, the volcano kept spewing ash, and the flight authority kept canceling flights. Day by day, more and more flights kept getting canceled. Eventually, they reached the day we were scheduled to fly back to the United States. And, of course, they canceled our flight, too. I remember sitting in the nicest hotel in Rome—booked with Christie's points,—and saying to her, "Where the hell are we going to sleep tomorrow night?"

Luckily, Christie had a high school friend named Marta who was actually an Italian citizen and lived nearby on the outskirts of Rome. She let us crash at her flat (or "apartment," for us Yankees) for a couple of days. As they kept canceling flights, Christie and I had a decision to make. We couldn't keep crashing on Marta's floor, although I'm sure she would have let us. There was no end in sight to this volcano situation. Plus, we had spent all the money we had planned on spending.

We decided to rent a car and drive to Positano, a tiny town on the Amalfi Coast. My parents had highly recommended it to us, but it just hadn't worked into our plans. Well, now it was about to work into our plans. Whereas Rome (like, say, New York) is an expensive city, Positano is a quiet, little coastal town where not too much happens. It was the perfect place to ride out this volcano storm.

As soon as we arrived in Positano, we saw why my parents had insisted we go there. When you think of beautiful coastal Italy, Positano is what you picture. The town was stunningly gorgeous in its old-world

Christie and me inside the church. (Christie Bishop)

simplicity. Had I known what we would have missed, we would never have skipped it. But the universe, again working in weird ways, made sure we were there.

There's an old church in Positano where my parents had renewed their wedding vows just a few years earlier. It's nestled right on the Mediterranean Sea, and to call it picturesque would not be doing justice to pictures. It's breathtaking. We went to see the church on our second day in Positano. It was April 23, 2010.

We went inside. People were all over, some looking around, some praying, some lighting candles for loved ones. Christie and I held hands and walked all around the church. When we had seen most of it, I took her by the hand and led her to a quiet corner.

"What's up?" she said.

"Do you know what today is?" I asked.

"No, what is today?"

"It's April 23," I answered. "One year."

It was a year to the day since I had been diagnosed. A year to the day that I had been told I had six months to a year to live. We were supposed to be back in LA, celebrating with a glass of champagne at some fancy restaurant, but the universe saw fit to put us here, in Italy, in this church that was so special to my family.

Our eyes welled up. We hugged and kissed and cried. We cried a year's worth of tears. I wasn't dead. I wasn't going to die tomorrow, or the next day. We were now officially in year two.

We held each other for what seemed like forever. Then, through my own watery eyes and runny nose, I held Christie's tear-streamed face and smiled.

"I told you I'd get better."

25.

Razor Blades

or, How a Trip to Costco Became My Most
Life-Affirming Moment

Well, as you can probably guess, I'm still alive. I've accomplished a lot since that day in the church in Italy. Christie and I bought a house in West LA. We adopted a puppy and named him Charlie. I was named the chairman of the National Brain Tumor Society's first-ever Los Angeles Walk, in which we raised over a quarter million dollars for the organization. I got the chance to speak at a summit in Las Vegas for a great organization called Stupid Cancer, which benefits young adults affected by cancer. I've been invited to speak at the corporate headquarters of Genentech, the company that produced Avastin. But more important than all of those accomplishments is this: I bought razor blades.

I'll explain.

Remember that trip to Costco that Christie and I took on my first day of treatment? That was when I felt the overwhelming need to get *organized*. When we got to the Personal Care aisle, we split up. She needed her girlie things, and I needed my manly things.

I stopped in front of the Gillette Mach3 razor-blade refills. I needed new cartridges for my razor, but they were expensive, and neither Christie or I were working. Besides, cancer treatment was sure to eat away at our savings. As I looked at the massive twenty-pack of blades on the shelf, I considered buying a smaller (and cheaper) pack at the local drugstore. At the rate I used razor blades, it would take me over a year to go through all of these. I held the twenty-pack in my hand

and thought to myself, "Hell, I'll be dead before I can use all of these." I paused. This was the first time—the *only* time, really—that I allowed in my mind the possibility that I might not make it a full year. Then, almost as quickly, I said, "Screw it," and threw the twenty-pack of razor blades in the cart. Somehow, in my mind, buying a smaller pack of blades would essentially have been admitting defeat; that, yes, I probably *will* be dead in a year, and, no, I don't want to waste my money on razor blades I won't use. I decided to buy the larger pack and take my chances. In a way, my recovery started that day, in the Personal Care aisle of Costco.

So, months later, when I finally used the last of the twenty blades I had bought that day, I went back to Costco, bought the same ridiculously large pack of razor blades, and got to work on using those. Who knew razor-blade shopping could be so life-affirming?

26.

Epilogue

or, Postscript, Afterword, Coda, Dénouement, Etc.

I spoke earlier about Herb and Faye, the older couple we met in the radiation center. How it was a crazy coincidence that Herb's mother had lived in the exact same apartment that we lived in, and how it couldn't have been a coincidence that the universe had brought us together in that waiting room. They were the first friends that we made on this incredible journey, and over the next couple of years Christie and I would sometimes ask each other, "I wonder how Herb and Faye are doing?" Then, as quickly as the thought came to us, it was gone.

Well, just as I was finishing this book, I found out that Faye had passed away. I was in the cancer center by myself, getting my monthly infusion of Avastin. Normally Christie is with me—she hardly ever misses a doctor's appointment or an infusion—but this day she couldn't make it. So I'm sitting in my recliner, tubes poking out of me, and I'm reading an article in the hospital's monthly newsletter about Jerry and the fantastic support staff at Cedars. They quoted Herb, and then mentioned that his wife, Faye, had recently passed away after her battle with cancer.

I sobbed and sobbed. I was a mess. Worse than that, I was inconsolable. I covered my face with the newsletter and cried into it, which was crazy. I hardly knew Faye. She wasn't what you would consider a close friend; we never called or texted each other. We never even saw each other outside the hospital. But for a brief, intense period in my life, she was a very meaningful person to me. I began to think about her, and all the family and "friends" I had made since the start of my journey who, because of their own battles with cancer, were no longer with us. Brian, the friend of Christie's dad in Culver City who just wanted to drink beer and go fishing. My aunts Pam and Judy, whom I loved dearly my entire life. Jim, our neighbor, who told his doctors all about "Bryan who lived next door" who was beating a brain tumor. Jane, a fan of the show who had walked with my team at the NBTS walk. Tyra in Texas whose husband died before they could achieve their one wish of traveling more. The girl whose best friend, Stacie, asked me to write her a letter of encouragement. I thought about them and a half dozen other people whose fate I didn't know and probably never would. I've learned a lot since my diagnosis, and I'm still learning more every day. Most of all, I've learned this: Cancer is relentless. Cancer will never quit. And that is why we must be relentless, and why we must never quit.

Never, ever quit.

Acknowledgments

or, Thanks, Shout-Outs, Etc.

This book would never have happened had it not been for . . .

Mom and Dad for letting me interview them and helping find old pictures. And for raising me, I guess. You know, that whole thing.

Anthony Mattero, my terrific book agent, who said to me one day, "Why don't you write a book?" So he's to credit/blame for the book you just read.

Rob Kirkpatrick, my editor. I'd heard a lot of stories about writers fighting with their editor. Thankfully, my experience with Rob was exactly the opposite.

The entire Thomas Dunne team for turning this book from an idea into a reality.

T. C. Boyle, who inspired a young college student who thought he had lost his way as a writer.

Everyone who wrote a blurb for the book. I'm humbled by your generosity.

Jay Mohr, whose book *Gasping for Airtime* was one of the most shockingly honest books I've ever read and a direct inspiration for this book.

David Wild, Teresa Strasser, and Nick Santora, who read early, rough versions of this book. Yes, believe it or not, it was even worse at one point.

Giovanni Peluso for his valuable research.

Anna Kuperberg, our wedding photographer, for letting us use her stunning pictures.

My doctors. Especially Dr. Jeremy Rudnick. People sometimes say, "I couldn't have done it without you," but in this case, it's literally true.

My physical therapists. Especially Chris Tolos, Megan Laib, and Waleed Al-Oboudi. Before I started working with them, I couldn't even type with my left hand. So this book would have taken at least twice as long without their help.

Don and Sheryl, my in-laws, for always being willing to help at a moment's notice. And for raising such an amazing daughter. Speaking of which . . .

Christie, my wife. What can I say about the greatest partner anyone could ever ask for? If I were to actually list everything I had to thank her for, it would require writing a second book. Hey, that gives me an idea for a sequel . . .